Children *of the* River

Children *of the* River

Growing up
with 18 brothers and sisters
along the Susquehanna

Rose Stoltzfus Huyard

Children of the River

Growing up with 18 brothers and sisters along the Susquehanna

© 2017 Rose Stoltzfus Huyard

Author: Rose Stoltzfus Huyard
Editor: Heidi King
Designer: Roslyn Nelson

ISBN: 978-0-9968071-3-5
Library of Congress Control Number: 2016958125
To contact the author: 19ChildrenoftheRiver@gmail.com

Publisher: Little Big Bay LLC
littlebigbay.com

Dedication

To Mom and Dad
for giving to us in so many ways

And to my brothers and sisters
for your invigorating spirits

I am eternally grateful.

Table of Contents

Acknowledgments

Writing this book has been like running a marathon. What I'd hoped would be a 5K turned out to be more like a long-distance race across country. At times I sprinted, sometimes jogged leisurely, and other times struggled uphill, stopping to rest, out of breath. But always along the course were those cheering on the sidelines and offering refreshment, keeping me going for the duration.

I have many to thank for this.

Thank you to my English professor Dr. Robert Gross at Bucknell University in Lewisburg, Pennsylvania, who gave me the confidence so many years ago to even consider walking up to the starting line.

My deepest heartfelt thanks to my parents, Mast and Mabel Stoltzfus, who gave me a reason to write my story—our story. You loved us from the depths of your hearts and raised us out of your most authentic selves. The stories you shared from your lives spurred me onward, that I might share them with future generations.

My many brothers and sisters, to you I am forever indebted. Your different personalities, adventuresome spirits, off-the-wall humor, and undying support have filled my lungs with life-giving breath. When I stood hesitantly at the start wondering if I really had what it took to begin this race, your stories, pouring in like a stream, carried me forward in spite of myself. Then you patiently stood by and waited while your stories lay still for a season. But when I began writing, you were there with your hearty cheering and honest feedback.

Thanks, Al, my loving husband, for envisioning that a portable laptop, instead of the desktop I started out with, might speed up my stride—and then seeing to it that I got one. Your patience as I went into hiding in my writing lair and your eager willingness to read what I wrote when I emerged provided exactly the emotional space I needed to continue.

John and Marilyn, I am deeply grateful to you for the arrangements you made for me to come to Colorado for two weeks, laptop in hand, to actually cross the starting line. The inspiring snow-covered Sangre de Cristo mountain range, from the vantage point of your friend's mountaintop cabin, fueled my energy to type all the handwritten notes from my siblings along with taped interviews into a semblance of an outline.

Thanks, Mary Jo Bowman, my spiritual director, for pointing me in the direction of Michael King of Cascadia Publishing House LLC, as a resource for moving the outline along, who then directed me to his sister, Starla J. King—OutWrite Living editor, writing and creativity coach—who became my writing coach.

Starla, you were just what I needed as you held me accountable for writing on a regular basis and helped me create a training plan specific to my pace and needs. Thank you.

Sonal Nalkur, my editor as I actually started out, you conditioned me for the race with your expectations and teaching about how to finish well. For this I thank you.

Heidi King, you became my "running buddy" when you became my second editor. I can't thank you enough for your companionship on the trail, helpful suggestions, encouragement, and assurance you would be in the race for the duration.

Thanks, Ros Nelson, my publisher at Little Big Bay, waiting at the finish line to hand me the reward—my book, complete with its cover design you created.

Thanks, all my friends, for your words, "Come on, keep going, you're getting close," like music to my ears, stirring life in my soul.

Thanks, Pandora, for keeping me company on my laptop with your relaxing background music as I fashioned the words, sentences, paragraphs, pages, and chapters of this book.

And finally, I would be remiss if my thanks went unexpressed to the Susquehanna River, whose flowing waters filled me with inspiration.

Most of all, thank you to the One who gave me strength to finish to the end.

Introduction

"As you walk, you cut open and create that riverbed into which
the stream of your descendants shall enter and flow."
Nikos Kazantzakis

I grew up along the banks of the Susquehanna River in a sturdy, red brick house together with eighteen brothers and sisters. The movement of our life together formed me, defined me, much of it happening in the river itself. The river held

us together as children and continues to flood our memories as adults. As blood flows through the heart, so the river flowed through our lives, giving us refuge from summer heat, rewarding us for completing our chores, immersing us in recreation, entertaining our friends on Sunday afternoons, and forcing us to reckon with it when it overflowed its banks. We were, and will always be, *children of the river.*

As the river flowed through us children, so the essence of our parents flowed through each of us. The current was both strong and easy as we laughed and cried together, struggled and grew together. Life was simple then. Growing up in a conservative Mennonite family with clear expectations for dress and behavior brought a flow of sustainability to our lives. And the rather predictable rhythm of work and play created continuity in our days. We

Above: Rose in her Sunday best
Below: Rose waiting for a boat ride
while her siblings swim in the river

hoed in the garden before we went swimming; played in an imaginary world along the banks of the river; and shared experiences that were predictable yet surprising, demanding yet fun-loving, peaceful yet not without conflict. In our togetherness we experienced controlled chaos, hardship, joy, fun, doing without, appreciating what is, and living fully within our financial constraints. Experiencing our share of struggles and relationship difficulties, we weren't always model citizens with each other; we hurt each other, and we had to find and give forgiveness. But within the current was always a deep love that carried us along.

The current also carried with it the spirits and influences of many people outside our family—the tomato foreman striding through our field to talk to Dad on the tractor; the large, gentle bishop who baptized us and gave us communion; the neighbor lady who stopped by to talk to Mom on the front steps. Our worlds expanded, rose, and fell with the comings and goings of these people, shaping our very lives.

As I've grown older, I've come to understand the power of the influence of people and the effects of various experiences—good and bad—in my life. And I have determined to open channels that allow the positive influences and learnings to flow from me into the generations after me who will join our family's river.

Family: My Connection, My Belonging

I grew up in the comfort and security of belonging to my family; they were my first community. Of the nineteen children in our family, three of us were adopted and sixteen of us came from the same parents. Nurtured in the same environment by the same parents, yet treated as individuals, we are similar in many ways—same smiles, mannerisms, sense of humor, voice inflections—and unique in other ways, such as our manner of teasing, our response to criticism, and what we find inspiring.

As child number nine, right smack dab in the middle, I thought my place was enviable over all the others. Not only did I benefit from my older siblings caring for me, I also had the opportunity to care for my younger siblings, even learning on my own at the age of five how to change a safety-pinned cloth diaper. On the downside of being middle child, I sometimes wondered who I really was. In our Mennonite community, everyone knew me just as much for being one of Mast and Mabel's daughters as they knew me for being Rose.

In sharing the story of my family with others and hearing their responses, I've learned that all human beings long for deep and meaningful connection, for community. My foundational need for comfort and security from belonging to my family and my family belonging to me was like anyone else's; I wanted to know I had a place in the world where I could grow in a family of people who valued me.

From Conception to Birth

The idea for this book came as a surprise. As a senior in college, I took a class that I just wanted to get out of the way—a composition course comprised mostly of freshmen and required for graduation. One day, I read the following comment by my professor at the end of my graded paper: "You really need to write a book about this." He was referring to what lay within the pages of my paper: *My Experience of Growing Up in a Communal Family.* The moment I read his encouraging words was the moment the idea for this book was conceived. It hadn't occurred to me that others might be interested in hearing the story of my family and my own life in it. But if my professor thought my story—our story—was unique and worth sharing, maybe it actually was.

The original class assignment was to write about a real-life experience. I could think of nothing more real than growing up in my family and the life we had shared. Together we'd dug in the earth, harvested its yield, and eaten its fruits. Together we'd made music and joined our spirits. We had absorbed into our beings the beautiful colors of a sunset, and we had sniffed the soul-satisfying smell of bread baking in the oven. And together we'd murmured, "Mmmmm" as we let the warm, buttered bread linger on our taste buds.·

So when the idea of writing a book appeared, my first instinct was to do what I'd always done—check with my family. Practically pouring their encouragement my way, they went to great lengths to respond to a list of questions I gave them. From their responses, I realized just how much the experience of growing up in our family had formed and sustained all of us. But how, I wondered, could I ever do justice to everyone's experiences? Should I write the book as a historical account? If so, where would I begin? And where would I end? After several start-and-stop attempts to write during the years following my composition class, the reality that the book wasn't happening plagued me. My desire to write about our family remained strong, but with other life demands vying for my time and attention, I realized I needed some way to channel the book's movement forward. When family members asked me, "So how's the book coming along?" the nudge to write compelled me onward. I owed it to them—to us. But how was I to do it? I was dammed up, stymied.

After sharing my "stuckness" with a friend, I followed through on her suggestion that I work with a writing coach. That was a turning point. My writing coach held me accountable for writing on a regular basis, and with her helpful direction

I eventually decided to write this book as a memoir, from my point of view. This way, I could do justice both to my own experiences and the collective experiences of my siblings.

In reading through the pile of stories from my brothers and sisters, I kept seeing a common thread—the strong connection we had with Mom and Dad. Over the years, we saw firsthand how human they were as they made mistakes yet aspired to reach beyond themselves. In the midst of this, we observed well their genuine desire to be good parents, and this created a bond between us all.

We were quite fortunate in this regard—it was a gift, really—considering Mom and Dad's contrasting spirits and strong personalities that often created strong tension between them and surges of electric charge through our home atmosphere. My siblings and I each responded to their arguments and heated discussions differently. I, for one, absorbed the tension in the air, not knowing what else to do with it. I knew that Mom and Dad were both good people, that they both loved us, and that they each had a strong spiritual connection. So why did they have such difficulty resolving conflicts, I wondered. Wanting to better understand human nature, I began reading psychology books as a young teen and took it upon myself to place books in obvious places about how to improve one's marriage, hoping Mom and Dad would want to read them.

On the positive side of things, because of their differences, Mom and Dad connected in their own unique ways with each of us as individuals. Somehow, together they were an even balance, a united front in making clear their support for us as well as their expectations of us.

Our family stories emerged from the intense, confusing, wonderful, multifaceted human beings our parents were. Now when my siblings and I gather together in little groups at family get-togethers and begin telling stories, we relive our lives with Mom and Dad. In each retelling, the stories imprint themselves more deeply into our hearts, strengthening our connection to each of them. With every "remember when … ," it is as if the past becomes the present, forming a pool of reality from which our lives now flow. Though we siblings have gone our separate ways, we still come back to our common source—the confluence of Mom and Dad, the merging of generations past.

The stories my siblings gave me also celebrate the unique spirit within each of us—something our parents cultivated well. Keeping our individual personalities in mind, they showed us how to take responsibility, how to be innovative, how to sing and play together, how to care for pets and animals, and how to appreciate nature. They instilled in us the value of traditions, the importance of celebrating holidays and special occasions together, and the benefit of having a strong base of spirituality.

My family gave me two of my most treasured possessions—a deep understanding of the value of other human beings and the reality of love. Our individual worth and security came from the special places we each filled within the family. Our togetherness was a way of living, organized and coordinated according to a hierarchy of chronological ages and related experiences. We learned community by being it: by sharing a double bed with a sister, feeding the chickens, keeping confidences about gifts at Christmas, and so much more.

The greater the number of people living together, the greater the need to cooperate and plan strategically in order to coexist peacefully. When our arms broke and nails pierced our bare feet, we learned to give first aid and tender loving care. We learned to "button one another up" and tie each other's belts when we could not do it by ourselves.

Family picture of the children standing oldest to youngest. L-r: Parke (holding Pete), Elam, Barb, Leona, Fred, Ada, Esther, Sue, Rose, Edith, and John. Eventually, the family grew to include seven more children.

Though in the eyes of many people raising a large family is not economically feasible today, I will be forever grateful for the lessons I learned from my family about how to live simply, "making do" with what we had. We treasured the colors of a monarch butterfly, the beauty of a jar of big, yellow, canned peaches, and the joy of finding a downy nest of baby rabbits in a field. Our creative imaginations entertained us and made us wealthy.

My parents also taught us the importance of respecting and loving God and living by his guidelines day to day. Spiritual nourishment provided the basis for our togetherness and love. Daily Bible reading and praying as a family were given the same importance as eating our meals together around the same table.

In this writing venture, I have come to realize that I want to share more than just a collection of anecdotes; I want to share the spirit and the life flowing through my family. My perspective on life changed during the initial start-and-stop attempts at writing, most especially with the deaths of both of my parents. I now see them and the world in which they raised me with new eyes. And I see my siblings raising their families and passing on to their children many of the same things we received from Mom and Dad—support, nurturing, and responsibility in the midst of the twists and turns of what it means to be human.

Your Story

Though I always had a strong sense of belonging within my family, I sometimes felt a bit lost in the current. In my search to know my place in my family and in this world, I faced the questions "Who am I?" and "How did I become who I am?" As I wrote this book, I discovered some of the answers to these questions.

Your life is also a story all its own. As you read mine, I hope you will in some way be able to make connections with the stories I tell—with your own place in life, with how you were formed as a person, with your need to be loved and to love, and with how, in your own struggle, you triumphed.

At the time of this writing, my family has grown to a community of three hundred and thirty living members, of which seventy-three (roughly one-quarter) are part of the family through adoption—either directly, or indirectly through marriage. Though we are rarely all together at one time, I know I belong to you, whether present in person with you or not.

My hope for you—my brothers and sisters, your children, your children's children, and all readers—is that you will find yourself in these stories and entertain the questions of who you are and where you have come from. May you see with new eyes the experiences, events, and people that have challenged you, supported you, given you energy, and encouraged your spirit along the way.

We flow from others before us, and we merge with others after us. We are each one valuable, each one significant. We are all *children of the river.*

PART I

Our Ancestors

Mom's side of the family: **Mabel Kurtz Petersheim**

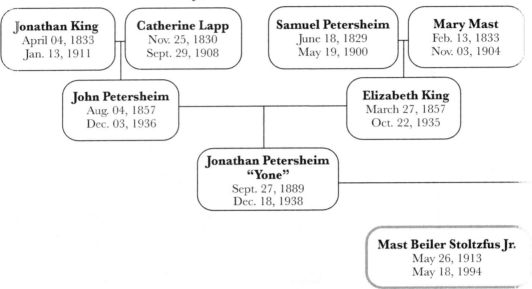

Jonathan King
April 04, 1833
Jan. 13, 1911

Catherine Lapp
Nov. 25, 1830
Sept. 29, 1908

Samuel Petersheim
June 18, 1829
May 19, 1900

Mary Mast
Feb. 13, 1833
Nov. 03, 1904

John Petersheim
Aug. 04, 1857
Dec. 03, 1936

Elizabeth King
March 27, 1857
Oct. 22, 1935

**Jonathan Petersheim
"Yone"**
Sept. 27, 1889
Dec. 18, 1938

Mast Beiler Stoltzfus Jr.
May 26, 1913
May 18, 1994

Dad's side of the family: **Mast Beiler Stoltzfus Jr.**

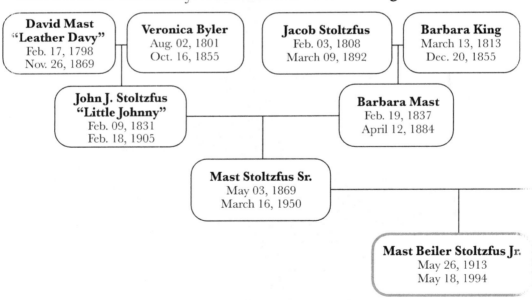

**David Mast
"Leather Davy"**
Feb. 17, 1798
Nov. 26, 1869

Veronica Byler
Aug. 02, 1801
Oct. 16, 1855

Jacob Stoltzfus
Feb. 03, 1808
March 09, 1892

Barbara King
March 13, 1813
Dec. 20, 1855

**John J. Stoltzfus
"Little Johnny"**
Feb. 09, 1831
Feb. 18, 1905

Barbara Mast
Feb. 19, 1837
April 12, 1884

Mast Stoltzfus Sr.
May 03, 1869
March 16, 1950

Mast Beiler Stoltzfus Jr.
May 26, 1913
May 18, 1994

Children of **Mast and Mabel Stoltzfus**

[Joseph] Parke
March 22, 1938

Elam Ray
Dec. 26, 1939

**Barbara Lois
(Barb)**
June 27, 1942

Leona Mae
Oct. 8, 1943

Fred Floyd
May 21, 1945
Oct. 31, 2015

Paul David (Pete)
April 18, 1956

Timothy Leroy (Tim)
June 9, 1957

Elvin Eugene
Oct. 30, 1958

Dale James
June 25, 1960

FAMILY TREE

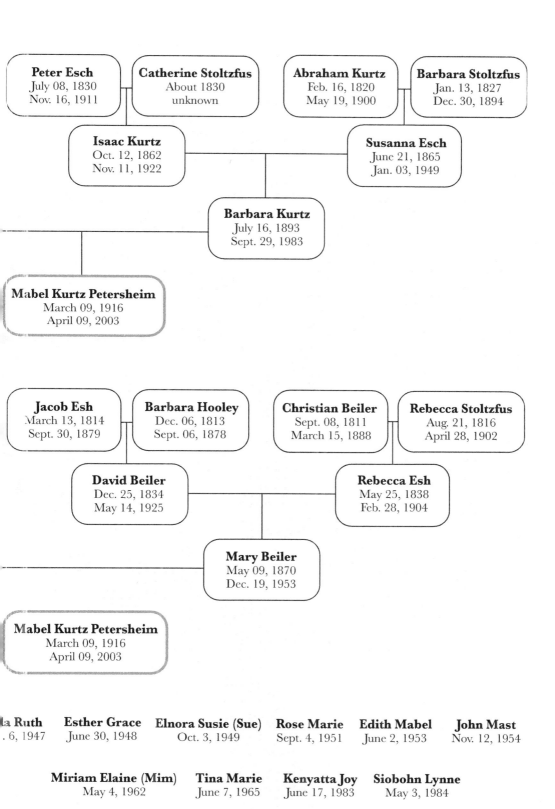

Peter Esch
July 08, 1830
Nov. 16, 1911

Catherine Stoltzfus
About 1830
unknown

Abraham Kurtz
Feb. 16, 1820
May 19, 1900

Barbara Stoltzfus
Jan. 13, 1827
Dec. 30, 1894

Isaac Kurtz
Oct. 12, 1862
Nov. 11, 1922

Susanna Esch
June 21, 1865
Jan. 03, 1949

Barbara Kurtz
July 16, 1893
Sept. 29, 1983

Mabel Kurtz Petersheim
March 09, 1916
April 09, 2003

Jacob Esh
March 13, 1814
Sept. 30, 1879

Barbara Hooley
Dec. 06, 1813
Sept. 06, 1878

Christian Beiler
Sept. 08, 1811
March 15, 1888

Rebecca Stoltzfus
Aug. 21, 1816
April 28, 1902

David Beiler
Dec. 25, 1834
May 14, 1925

Rebecca Esh
May 25, 1838
Feb. 28, 1904

Mary Beiler
May 09, 1870
Dec. 19, 1953

Mabel Kurtz Petersheim
March 09, 1916
April 09, 2003

la Ruth
. 6, 1947

Esther Grace
June 30, 1948

Elnora Susie (Sue)
Oct. 3, 1949

Rose Marie
Sept. 4, 1951

Edith Mabel
June 2, 1953

John Mast
Nov. 12, 1954

Miriam Elaine (Mim)
May 4, 1962

Tina Marie
June 7, 1965

Kenyatta Joy
June 17, 1983

Siobohn Lynne
May 3, 1984

1. The River's Source

"If ye don't know the past, then ye will not have a future. If ye don't know where your people have been, then ye won't know where your people are going."

Asa Earl Carter, The Education of Little Tree

The source of a river is its beginning. As children of the river, my siblings and I were keenly aware of the ongoing stream of life. We knew that a river begins as little trickles on mountaintops, feeds itself from small springs along the way, and eventually becomes a tributary joining other tributaries to form a river system. And we knew we were part of a system just like this created by our ancestors, the spirit that ran through our lives.

Connecting through Story

Mom and Dad conjured up that family spirit by sharing ancestral stories of tenacity, perseverance, and overcoming hardship, connecting us all the way back to our source in Switzerland in the early 1500s. Those Swiss ancestors, we learned, left their homeland in the later 1500s to escape several generations of persecution for their religious beliefs. Life was hard, but they determinedly persevered. Wanting a better life for their children, some sailed down the Rhine River to settle in the Palatinate area in southwestern Germany. Others settled in the Alsace Lorraine area of France, then left the country in the mid-1800s for America in anticipation of a more advantageous economy there.

When living conditions for those in the Palatinate became too difficult to bear in the mid-1700s, they sailed nine months across raging seas to reach the promised land of America, leaving behind extremely high taxes, constant threat of their young men being drafted into the army, and the German government's refusal to grant permission to build meetinghouses. Their decision to make this move was largely prompted by a visit from William Penn, a Quaker from England, who came to the lower Rhine country and invited them to move to "Penn's Woods" (now Pennsylvania). There, he told them, they could own land and have religious freedom.

Penn's descriptions evoked images of a paradise filled with large trees, wide open spaces, and an abundant supply of water to grow crops.

Soon after our ancestors arrived in America and settled in the Northkill area of Pennsylvania, they discovered the promised paradise would be hard-earned. Living an average of just eight years in their new homeland, many of them did not survive long enough to see their children flourish. The years were filled with hard labor—working up the stubborn sod to sow seeds (that others now reap abundantly) and felling trees to build houses. It was also a time of unrest among settlers and various Native American tribes.

Jacob Morgan, a captain in the Providential Army during the French and Indian war, encouraged our industrious, peace-loving ancestors to relocate to the head-waters of the Conestoga River after the French hired Native Americans to assault the English settlement in which our ancestors lived. Later, when General Washington rallied his troops to fight the British army, our ancestors narrowly missed being executed by the revolutionists for their pacifist beliefs and refusal to fight in the war. As Civil War gun smoke filled the air, they hauled hay to Gettysburg in the face of the approaching Confederate Army in order to feed the battle horses of the Northern forces. After hearing a rumor that the Confederate Army was advancing northward to Pennsylvania to capture their rich farmland for use as an army base, they hurriedly buried their silverware and other valuable possessions on their properties and hid their cattle on the Welsh Mountain.[1]

Along with these accounts of general history, Mom and Dad shared stories of specific individuals in our ancestral line who had met hardship and setbacks with staunch determination. Georg and Christina Petersheim, for example, left Lippenrod, Germany, in 1790 to go to the Netherlands where they expected to board a ship to sail to America. Although they persisted in waiting for three weeks at Emden, they were not able to connect with a ship. Disappointed, they returned to Germany. Twenty years later, in 1810, their stubborn tenacity paid off as they excitedly boarded a ship with their six children—three boys and three girls—and successfully emigrated to North America. Though the whereabouts of the graves of Christina and Georg Petersheim are unknown today, likely marked with no more than a field stone, their courage and perseverance mark our lives.

Then there was Peter Esch, Grandmom Petersheim's grandfather. In 1854, Peter left France for America, crossing the ocean with his family. It took them forty

[1] J. Leman Mast and Lois Ann Mast, *As Long as Wood Grows and Water Flows: A History of the Conestoga Mennonite Church* (Morgantown, PA: Conestoga Mennonite Historical Committee, 1982).

Great-great-grandparents Peter Esch (1830–1911) and Catherine Stoltzfus Esch (about 1830– ? [unknown])

days as the sailing ship repeatedly advanced only to be blown back again and again by the wind. Grandmom lamented in her later years that she had not listened to Peter's stories more: "I was just a girl, and it didn't bother me," she said.

For these individuals and others, hard work and perseverance was a way of living. They milked by hand; planted, cut, and husked corn by hand; cut grain with a cradle and threshed it with a flail; preserved food by canning or drying; baked weekly in an oven built of stone and fire bricks; cured meat by salting or smoking it; and walked to church and to their places of employment morning and evening. They lived in communities where people came together to do the threshing, silo filling, and haymaking. These times of gathering became social events as a whole neighborhood turned out to help a neighbor gather in their harvest, or whatever task needed to be done. Connecting with their community was an integral part of the hard work; our ancestors never did such work alone. In this same spirit, my family also worked hard together, individuals connected to one another for the good of all of us.

Connecting through Song

Not only did our parents share great ancestral stories, they also brought the ancestral spirit into our daily lives through music. On both good and bad days we sang while we worked, as we played, as we traveled, and as we sat around the table before meals, harmonizing our voices into a whole. As far back as we could hear, our ancestors were a singing people. And as their stories flowed throughout our home, so too did the music, helping us discover that strength takes many different shapes, sizes, and forms.

Mom's parents and ancestors, for example, persevered in the face of sickness, death, and financial difficulty. A kidney disease in Mom's family took her father at a young age, leaving her mother to raise eleven children, the youngest of which was three years old. This same kidney disease later claimed the lives of four of Mom's sisters and one brother when they were adults.

Dad's parents and ancestors influenced us in the way they overcame material and physical setbacks. They adjusted, thrived, and got on with life in hard times when the Great Depression caused the economy to dip and take unexpected twists. And they gritted their teeth in the face of the impossibly painful as their arms and toes were removed.

Mom and Dad shone the light on these stories of perseverance and overcoming as examples of how it was done and how we could do it too.

2. Dad's Family

DAVID BEILER: Dad's maternal grandfather

December 25, 1834–May 14, 1925

As a little boy, my father was inspired by his hardworking maternal grandfather, David Beiler. He would watch in amazement as Grandpa Beiler chopped wood. With his grandpa's strength in mind, Dad would run outside to milk cows and husk corn with his bare hands; he could see what hard work looked like by observing his grandfather, but he could only experience what it felt like with his own hands.

At left: Great-grandfather David Beiler (1834–1925)

Years later he would describe Grandpa Beiler with admiration saying, "He was no ordinary woodcutter."

For though Grandpa Beiler was blind and had only one arm, he chopped wood better than Dad himself could; he would set a piece of wood on the chopping block, hold his axe in his one hand, and with one swift blow from the swing of his arm, send pieces of firewood flying in two directions. My young father wished the firewood would split like that when the axe was in his own hand. Grandpa Beiler's lower arm had been amputated on the kitchen table from the elbow down due to an infection in his hand that his doctor thought might become cancerous.

Oddly enough, it seemed that the amputation only made Grandpa Beiler stronger, for he continued to swing that axe one-handedly for the last thirty years of his life. Dad would tell us this story of Grandpa Beiler with a look of transfixed admiration.

9

Grandpa Beiler is the only grandparent Dad remembers. His other three grandparents died before he was born. Thankfully, Grandpa Beiler lived to be ninety years old, giving Dad the opportunity to know him well. From early on, Dad longed to be close to Grandpa Beiler, a wish that came true with unexpected literality as a consequence of grandpa being very hard of hearing—Dad had to sit close to him and shout in his ear. Grandpa Beiler would flash Dad a friendly smile and ask him how he was doing in school. This must have been before Dad's ninth-grade year of school, because Dad told us, "When I was in ninth grade and I couldn't get the hang of Algebra, the teacher told me to stay after class. I left immediately after school and never went back. But don't tell my grandsons," he added with a grin. "I don't want them to think that's okay."

Dad knew his other grandparents only through stories. The retelling of these stories, however, made it apparent that his deceased grandparents inspired him just as much as his only living grandparent.

DAVID MAST (Leather Davy): Dad's paternal great-grandfather
February 17, 1798–November 26, 1869

One fateful morning in the mid-1840s, fifty-five-year-old Leather Davy marched resolutely over to a large wooden stump outside the house, took off his shoe, placed a chisel on his left big toe, and chopped it off with one hard blow of the hammer—his solution to a potentially gangrenous toe. I winced each time my father told me the story, while feeling proud at the same time to be related to someone so gutsy and determined. Did Leather Davy—Dad's paternal great-grandfather, David Mast—earn his nickname from the fact that he was tough as leather, or perhaps from the leather breeches he wore riding horse between his three farms to tend to matters? We don't know for sure, but in either case he lived up to his name. With a rugged toughness, his solution to any problem was to deal with it head on. Davy didn't mess around.

Leather Davy inherited almost virgin land, first tilled by the generation that preceded him, on which he very successfully raised corn, grain, and hay—a payoff from being one of the first farmers to use bone fertilizer. With the help of this new fertilizer and a complete stranger in whom he put his faith, he was able to turn that landscape into a productive farm.

The stranger was Moses Hartz, a young orphan boy who wandered up Leather Davy's lane one day asking for work. Davy at first turned him away because he had no work for him. But as he watched Moses walk back down the lane, something made him call out to the boy. Leather Davy and his family ended up giving Moses a home and treating him as one of their own.

Moses helped Leather Davy farm in the summer and drive a massive Conestoga wagon in the winter. He hauled grain to the docks of Philadelphia, Pittsburgh, and Ohio, returning with salt and other provisions each time. In those days, it was not unusual for the trips west to take several months or even an entire season. One winter, when one of Moses' trips took him to Ohio, Leather Davy became quite concerned when Moses was gone for an exceptionally long time. Not able to wait any longer, Leather Davy saddled up his horse and headed west in search of Moses. When he finally found him at the scheduled destination—the community in Ohio—Moses proudly held up several big bags of money he had earned during the winter from selling grain, then promptly handed the earnings over to Davy. Leather Davy had been correct in his initial assessment of Moses Hartz; the risk he had taken in trusting a stranger had paid off. Perhaps it was because of Davy's stoic strength that he was able to risk this kind of trust. Or perhaps we just don't trust strangers these days as much as they needed to back then.

David Mast seemed to adapt creatively to whatever life brought him. When the economy plummeted during the Civil War, the nearly broke, but ever-enterprising Leather Davy went to work loading up his three Conestoga wagons—used to haul corn grown on his farm—with hay, having realized that passing soldiers were conscripting hundreds of horses and those horses would need to be fed. With the help of his three teams of horses, he took the hay to the war horses in Gettysburg so they could survive. While so many around him suffered, the man who was tougher than cowhide came through.

Davy and his wife, Veronica, were not exempt from personal tragedy, however. Only three of their ten children lived past the age of twenty-three, the others leaving deep holes in the family as they failed to survive illnesses. But Leather Davy did not allow those holes to get filled up with resentment or sadness; instead, he poured them full with hard work and connection to other people. Davy understood that farm life was not meant for the individual. People on his farm became family for each other, the seeds of deep kinship lying beneath the soil for those who tilled it. The strangers who worked the land became family, modeling the way that others often have of filling in the gaps of our lives.

David Mast looked out for his three surviving children, holding back nothing from them. Why else would he have willed his three farms to them? But he was cautiously generous with his daughter Barbara's husband, John J. Stoltzfus, nicknamed "Little Johnny" because of his short stature. Davy, with the same scrutiny he had used to size up Moses Hartz, eyed Little Johnny. Questioning the way Little Johnny handled his finances, Davy included only Barbara's name, not John J. Stoltzfus', on the deed to the farm he gave Barbara and Little Johnny; Davy wanted to make sure that Barbara always had a place to live.

Barbara, in turn, adored her father, so she named one of her sons David. David, however, was one of her children who died. Wanting a namesake for her father, Barbara gave the name Mast to a son born later. He was my Grandpa Stoltzfus. My father was also given the name Mast—he became Mast Stoltzfus Jr.—as was one of my nephews. And one of my grandsons was given Mast for his middle name.

JOHN J. STOLTZFUS (Little Johnny): Dad's paternal grandfather
February 9, 1831–February 18, 1905

John J. Stoltzfus' poor management of personal finances could not always be written off as a character flaw. As was the practice in Civil War days, Little Johnny hired a man, Samuel (Sam) Deichley, to take his place in the war, paying him the "soldiers for hire" rate of $300. But he didn't have peace about his decision, so he was relieved to hear that Samuel was on his way home. Unbeknownst to Little Johnny, however, Sam was coming home minus one leg that had been blown off on the battlefield. Upon seeing this tragic loss, Little Johnny put his compassion to work and generously invited Sam to move in with his family, where Sam lived until he got married much later in life.

As Little Johnny got to know Sam, he became impressed with his excellent penmanship and artistic ability, so much so that he went out and bought a composition book for Sam, who copied his own poems into it, including his colored-ink creations of decorative feathers and heart illustrations.

Barbara found an emotional outlet in this same composition book, expressing both her deep grief about the losses of her children and her hope to someday meet them in heaven. Also in the book is a poem written by my grandfather Mast Stoltzfus. As a young boy, Mast admired Sam's composition book, and Sam, upon seeing this, honored my young grandfather by encouraging him to write his own poem in the book. My mother, as a young girl, also had a composition book where she recorded poems and ballads and decorated the pages with hand-drawn colorful designs. I always wondered where she found this idea.

JACOB ESH: Dad's maternal great-grandfather
March 13, 1814–September 30, 1879

Toe issues seemed to run rampant in our family. Dad's great-aunt Mattie Miller would tell a horrendous toe story about his maternal great-grandfather, Jacob Esh, and Jacob's wife, Barbara. It went like this: One day, when Mattie was a little girl, her father was cutting wood and miscalculated the swing of the axe, chopping off most of his big toe. Mattie saw her father come riding up to the house on his horse. She watched as he awkwardly dismounted, sat down on the porch and beckoned her mother to come see, then gave instructions to get needle and thread. Mattie looked on as her mother went into the house, came back out with the needle and thread in hand, and bent down before Mattie's father, determinedly setting her jaw and sewing his toe back on. Amazingly, the toe healed, though in a somewhat stiff, upright position. After this, Jacob always had to cut a hole in any new pair of shoes he bought in order to get a nice, smooth fit for his misshapen toe.

MAST STOLTZFUS SR.: Dad's father
May 3, 1869–March 16, 1950

Dad's father, Mast Stoltzfus, was a no-nonsense kind of man. Though he died long before I was born, I learned to know him through the stories Dad told about him. What stood out about Grandpa Stoltzfus was his strong sense of duty and that he loved deeply in spite of enduring a complex experience of love in his life.

From the fond, resolute way Dad talked about his father, I knew he felt special pride in being his father's namesake. He described his father as a short, muscular man who liked to wrestle; who was reluctant to express himself and never liked speaking in public; and who was compassionate yet impatient, unable to sympathize with people who were lazy. He noticed that when his father gave orders, he expected those orders to be obeyed. He also noticed, at the same time, that his father worked with the men he hired even while he supervised them.

Mast Stoltzfus Sr. was well known as a discrete and responsible farmer. He had an affinity for mules, horses, and cows and was in his element while driving his six-mule team. He was also considered to be progressive in his community, being the first to own registered Holsteins.

Above: Haymaking with Grandpa Stoltzfus and his sons. Left: Father (l.) Mast Stoltzfus Sr. (1869–1950) and son (r.) Mast Stoltzfus Jr. (1913–1994). Below left: Grandparents Mary Beiler Stoltzfus (1870–1953) and Mast Stoltzfus Sr. (1869–1950) in front of their house.

Dad always reminded us how strong Grandpa Stoltzfus' work ethic was. When Grandpa was in his teens, his mother, Barbara, died. His father, "Little Johnny," remarried and moved away, leaving Mast to take care of the farm at eighteen years of age. Mast quickly demonstrated his management savvy as he took over the family farm, rolling up his shirt sleeves to work long hours in the hot sun. After a while, he realized he would be better off financially and socially if someone lived in the big house with him, so he invited another family to move in, much as his Grandpa Leather Davy had invited Moses Hartz to move in. Farm life in Mast Senior's day still often meant keeping your home open to others and sharing your life with virtual strangers.

Mast enjoyed the company of the family who lived in his house, though it meant making adjustments and having unexpected things happen. For example, while it was convenient for Mast to eat home-cooked meals with this family at their table, the mother was not known for her cooking and she stuck with just a few dishes she knew how to fix—ones with tomato sauce. Mast grew weary of the frequent servings of tomato sauce. Unfortunately for him, tomatoes were plentiful in their garden.

One of the grown daughters from this family who sat across the table from Mast at mealtime couldn't keep her eyes off Mast's muscular fitness. One evening after dinner, she called him to come into her bedroom, saying she needed help with something. But as she closed the door behind them and motioned toward the bed, it did not take Mast long to realize she had ulterior motives. Part of him wanted to stay with her, but like the biblical Joseph, realizing he could not stay and be the kind of man he wanted to be, he quickly left the room.

Mast's moral compass also guided him when he had financial difficulties during the Depression in the late 1800s. At eighteen years of age, he found himself flailing at the wrong end of the economy and barely surviving financially. As the story goes, rather than declare bankruptcy, he chose what he thought was a more honorable option for getting his finances in order; he solicited direction (twice) from the trustees of his Amish church—a committee of three people commonly sought out for financial advice. These trustees oversaw farming operations and personal finances of those seeking help. They provided accountability by overseeing a person's checkbook, signing checks for them, and giving advice. They also placed restrictions on how large the farming operation could grow since the church had to cover for a farmer if he went under financially. The Amish still practice this alternative to filing bankruptcy.

Mast was able to get back on his feet financially as a young father after he bought another farm. This second farm was cheap because the well water was contaminated by cow manure seepage after the well was damaged by dynamite blasting at a local lime kiln. The original owners had become sick from the water. Several family members died, including the parents, and one child suffered permanent brain damage.

When Mast fell in love with Mary Zook, his troubles only became compounded, requiring him to sort through another complicated situation. One day after Mast had become engaged to Mary, she came to him crying. He beckoned to her to ease her pain, and she sat on his lap for comfort. What she told him between sobs while resting her head against his chest pierced his heart like a dagger. She eventually got out the words, "I'm pregnant," and Mast knew it was not by him. The only thing he knew to do was push her off his lap, stand up, and walk out, abruptly ending their relationship. But Mast didn't get over Mary quickly. He walked along the fence line for many days, crying as he grappled with his deep disappointment and heartache.

The man by whom Mast's fiancée became pregnant was Isaac Huyard. Isaac was a dapper young man, a school teacher who had graduated from Millersville (PA) State Teachers College (now Millersville University) with a teaching degree. Mary and Ike were neighbors and over time had become close friends. Too close. But Mast never held anything against Isaac. Instead, he said, "Ike is always so friendly." Ike and Mary got married after Ike joined the Amish church, as was required of him in order to marry Mary since she was a member of the Amish church.[2] (As fate would have it, Isaac Huyard became the grandfather of Al Huyard, who is now my husband.)

In spite of his troubles, Mast Stoltzfus Sr. persevered both emotionally and physically. Prior to World War I, he burned lime for nine years in four lime kilns—a dirty and difficult job. After loosening the limestone from the quarry by dynamiting and burning it, he loaded the finished product—powdered lime—on a wagon, hauling it to local farmers to sell. Of the hired help working for him, Mast said, "It's hard to find a man who can get along well with the customer, gets along with the mule, and lets the bottle alone." He hauled lime until the war began and it became too hard to get the coal needed to burn in the kilns.

While Mast Stoltzfus Sr. gained a reputation for unwavering tenacity, he was not known for his patience. To the contrary, he could be a bit harsh with his words. Elam experienced this when he was about three years old helping Dad make a cement porch and kept getting too close to the cement mixer. Grandpa Stoltzfus said, "We'll have to put him in if he wants to be so close." Elam stayed a safe distance away after that. And when Parke came roaring around the buildings on the little Jubilee 8N Ford tractor and turned sharply around the corner, careening sideways and shooting into the corncrib shed, who should be standing there but Grandpa? Parke hung his head, knowing he was in serious trouble. Grandpa gave eleven-year-old Parke what he thought he deserved—a tongue-lashing earful: "Suppose one of your little brothers or sisters would have been there? What would have happened!"

---

[2] When a cousin told Dad Ike's story, Dad did not believe him and went to his father. Grandpa told him it was indeed true. Oddly enough, Dad's steady girlfriend had also left him for another man. Grandpa had tried to console Dad by saying, "Life is sweet, but oh how bitter to love a girl and then not git her." Dad's response was, "Well, you should know." Like his father, Dad, full of heartache, also walked the fence row for many days.

Yet Grandpa Stoltzfus was not without compassion, and Mom's brother Omar, who had Down Syndrome, knew this. Every Sunday after church, he would seek Grandpa Stoltzfus out in anticipation of receiving the candy bar he knew would be waiting just for him in grandpa's pocket. Grandpa gave the candy to Omar not as a reward for his good behavior in church but simply to let Omar know that he cared about him and saw him as a valuable human being.

MARY BEILER STOLTZFUS: Dad's mother
May 9, 1870–December 19, 1953

Dad knew his mother, Mary Beiler Stoltzfus, as hardworking, courageous, and smaller than average with an unusual amount of spunk. She could outstrip Dad in the barn, milking seven to nine cows in a row with her sturdy hands. Before she got married, Mary had worked as a hired girl for her sister and brother-in-law. When their barn caught fire one day, she became a heroine to Dad, courageously running back into the burning barn to let the frantic mules out of their stables.

Grandma Stoltzfus was devoted to her family and made them her career, modeling much through everyday life. She read daily stories to her children from *Hurlbut's Story of the Bible* and sang *Begin the Day with God* in its entirety every morning while she made breakfast. Dad admiringly described her singing voice as a clear soprano. Maybe his love of singing came from listening to her sing every day.

When Grandpa and Grandma Stoltzfus grew older, they often came to visit the family in Oley, Pennsylvania, to help Mom and Dad. Grandpa drove an old '36 Ford. He would gun the engine, let the clutch slip, and spin out with a roar when they left. On their return home from one of these visits, Grandpa ran into a bridge abutment, injuring both himself and Grandma. After that, Grandpa did not drive again, and their visits to the family stopped.

Grandpa eventually developed pancreatic cancer and diabetes. Thereafter, when Mom and Dad took the family to visit and Dad went to greet Grandpa with a kiss, Grandpa would hold up a hand, palm outward, saying, "No, no—I might be contagious." At those same visits, Grandma handed out homemade sugar cookies. For Christmas, she gave her family white handkerchiefs.

3. Mom's Family

BARBARA KURTZ PETERSHEIM: Mom's mother

July 16, 1893–September 29, 1983

Barbara Kurtz Petersheim, young wife of Jonathan Petersheim

As children, when we fell down and looked up for sympathy, as children often do, we frequently heard Mom's confident, singsong voice admonishing us to "Jump up!" The interpretation of Jump up was, "When you fall down, don't stay down—get up and go on." And so we heard it a lot. Mom said it as needed when attending to our injuries, communicating care for us without feeding into self pity.

Mom likely heard the phrase Jump up from her own mother, Barbara Petersheim, whom we called "Grandmom." But even if Grandmom did not actually say "Jump up," she modeled how to do it. Grandmom, for instance, did not allow her husband's untimely death at the young age of forty-nine to keep her down. Picturing Grandmom with ten children to raise by herself, her acquaintances said, "She'll never be able to make it. She won't be able to keep the family together." To this, Grandmom staunchly replied, "We are staying together, and we are going to make it."

On her way to making it, Grandmom ran into more than her share of trouble. Not only did the crops have difficulty growing in the stony soil but the six dairy cows she was left with did not produce much milk. Praying for a better herd, Grandmom did not expect the answer she received. One day her cows licked some rocks in the pasture that had been painted, and the cows promptly all died. When friends and neighbors heard of this, they took good cows from their own herds and replaced Grandmom's cows with them.

Grandmom had a lot of debt, both from medical bills and the crops' failure to thrive, but she and her children banded together and paid off the accumulated farm debt. The first year after Grandpa died, they planted four acres of tomatoes by hand for Campbell Soup Company so Grandmom could buy a tractor and milk machine for her boys. Her theory was, "If you don't work, you don't have nothing neither." With her boys' help, she pulled the farm out of debt in three years, despite the fact that her children were a spirited and mischievous challenge to raise. Though she spent many hours on her knees agonizing over them in prayer, in the final analysis, her opinion of them was, "They done good—they stuck by me."

Grandmom and her children never talked about Grandpa's death, though her son Floyd, just two and a half years old, cried for his Daddy for seven months off and on whenever he saw a casket. "We didn't make a fuss about it," said Grandmom. "We just went on. I didn't want to make a fuss and make them feel bad that the Lord took him. Some people do, ja know." Someone told Grandmom they overheard some men saying at Grandpa's funeral, "Barbara—she'll get along with the farming okay," and that vote of confidence kept her going on the hard days.

When Grandmom later spoke about Grandpa's sickness and death, her voice took on a soft, reflective tone. She told how he had become sick with what doctors thought was the flu. But "the flu" would not go away. Three and a half years before Grandpa died, he had surgery. When the doctor saw the condition of his kidney, he said Grandpa surely would not live long. In Grandmom's words, "The Lord spared him three and one half years, which gave me and the children more time to get things together. If he had died sooner, I wouldn't have been able to keep the family together."

Grandmom's no-nonsense approach came complete with a strong accent all her own to match, and her authoritative tone sometimes came off sounding a bit edgy—as in her responses to my cousin Bob Petersheim's recorded interview with her: "Why, YES." "Ach, yes." "Why, sure." Or, "Oh, well, I guess too" (implying, "You ought to know that."). Her voice had its own unique inflection, her speech slow and distinctive, sort of like it was on a chopping block. And though she came across as very confident in her own opinions, she invited feedback from her listeners with, "Don't ja believe it?"

When Grandmom spoke to Bob Petersheim of her ledger in which she fastidiously recorded every little thing she bought for her wedding, she said in her lilting, high-pitched giggle, "I guess it was sorta silly—none of my sisters had one. Ja wanna hear it? Well, my coat was $8.90 … side combs for my hair, 10¢ … nightgown 39¢, underwear 96¢. Everything had to be new, ja know, and my prayer veiling was 10¢."

Grandmom spoke of "Yone" (Grandpa's nickname, pronounced Yōn) with fondness. She seemed to appreciate Grandpa's fine taste. With a look of pride and admiration, she told Bob, "When we were getting married, Yone couldn't find good enough fabric in local stores to make his wedding suit, so he went to Reading to find some." Bucking the system, Grandpa had bought brown fabric, not blue as was the custom then. The story according to Grandmom went like this: "Well, that one time, we got up early one morning while it was still dark. And, oh, we weren't supposed to go like that—ja know—much. We didn't drive together much, that way. Well, that one time, Yone said he would take me to Reading, and whatever color coat I bought, that's the color suit he wanted to buy. Here we went up Cherry Lane and passed Bishop Davy Kurtz's house, and he knowed it was Yone's horse because he knew the trot of Yone's horse, and he knowed we had went someplace. He had a nice horse. Davy tried to make a fuss about it to find out where Yone and me had gone, but he didn't find out. Afterward, he said he bets we went to Reading. Yone asked him, 'How do you know I went to Reading?' and the bishop replied, 'I could tell by the sound of your horse's hoofbeats on the road.'" Grandpa's high-spirited, high-stepping horse had a unique hoofbeat that set it apart from others. He drove it to church and into town, and on that day he wasn't going to church, so the sly bishop had his number.

Grandmom, too, had her own peculiar bent for the finer things of life. Usually women in her day wore black bonnets over their prayer coverings, but she made hers brown velvet to match the brown coat she bought for her wedding. Reminiscing, she mused, "It was pretty. They used to just get cashmere, but this was a bit prettier. Some fussed about it. Why, I just let people talk. I let them enjoy talking about it. I guess I had a little pride … I don't know. I was a pretty bride. Did ja see the picture of me and Yone?"

Grandmom also had a strong spirit of determination. When she set her jaw and got that special fire in her eyes, everyone knew she meant business. Her teenage son Joe experienced this the hard way with the baby raccoon he had found, bottle fed, and raised. Grandmom did not like having the raccoon around the one hundred pullets Joe was raising to sell, and when it did not come as called one evening, she was happy to believe it finally went the way of the wild. The next morning, however, upon inspection of the brooder house to check on the pullets, she found them dead— every single one of them, killed by the raccoon. That was the last straw for Grandmom. She'd had enough. When Joe refused to get rid of the raccoon, Grandmom took matters into her own hands. One day when Joe was gone and his raccoon was still in its cage, she opened the door of the cage and stuffed their Airedale dog inside. With her jaw set, she sealed her ears tightly with her hands and fled to the house so she wouldn't hear the squeals of the raccoon being killed.

Though resourceful and ambitious, Grandmom, for whatever reason, never got her driver's license, so when she found a ride to our house along the river, she usually stayed several days. When she came in the winter, she tackled Mom's huge pile of mending—sewing on buttons, darning socks, and doing other hand sewing. In the summer, she helped can food. She talked a lot about the news of the Conestoga Valley, telling Mom who did what—usually the gossipy sort of news about the vices of others, frequently inserting, "Ach," in a disgusted manner. Being very prim and proper, Grand-mom found things she did not approve of in Mom as well, such as going barefoot in the summer, and she made her disapproval known.

Grandmom Petersheim and the dresses she sewed for relief projects

Grandmom also helped many others out with her sewing. When she was in her seventies and eighties, she collected remnants of material from various factories and friends, using the remnants to sew hundreds of little dresses for relief work. The happiness in her voice as she talked about the dresses she was making conveyed the joy and fulfillment she found in doing this. When I look at the little yellow and white polyester dress hanging from a peg in my craft room now, Grandmom seems closer; the dress, slightly misshapen, is from one of the last batches she made.

Although Grandmom eventually started winding down physically, her spitfire personality remained intact. When Bob asked about her health, she replied, "Oh, I get short of breath. If I walk too much, I just can't do it." Asked her if she'd had her heart checked recently, she said, "Oh yes—they said it's good, but when I go to the doctor and sit up on the high thing … I told him it's just like sitting on a chicken roost. I go in there, and they take my blood pressure, and I'm relaxed. Well, why wouldn't my heart be good, ja know? Now if you get me right when I walk in … but I have to wait about twenty or thirty minutes."

JONATHAN (YONE) PETERSHEIM: Mom's father
September 27, 1889–December 18, 1938

Grandparents Barbara Kurtz Petersheim (1893–1983) and Jonathan Petersheim (1889–1938)

My mother's father was named Jonathan Petersheim, but the family called him "Yone." While we knew many things about Yone that were good, we also learned he was a complex human being with sides that were at least partly hidden.

To begin with, we knew that when Grandpa Petersheim was a boy, his family moved every year, which meant he attended a new school every year. While it was common in those times for people to move a lot, Grandpa Petersheim's family moved more often and farther than most— from Pennsylvania to Virginia, to Kansas and back, to Pennsylvania again. Maybe their moves were because his mother was a dissatisfied person, or maybe it was because his father did not manage his affairs very well. His father was not the best farmer or businessman, and the family was very poor. Is it any wonder Grandpa Petersheim had a liking for good quality things?

Living in a poor family did not deter Grandpa from creating his own fun, especially when he was bored. When he was just a young boy, he and some of his friends were sitting on a backless bench in church. The preacher had lost him soon after starting his sermon, and that was when Grandpa tacked the jacket of the boy sitting in front of him to the edge of the back of the bench. When it was time for prayer, the boy stood to kneel and took the whole bench with him, making a big commotion as Grandpa and his friends snickered.

Grandpa Petersheim grew to become a tall, dark-haired, handsome man, and Mom became the apple of his eye. He had a beautiful singing voice that carried my mother while they worked day after day in the fields together with teams of mules. The fields could be murderously difficult at times, but this father and daughter experienced a profound connection to nature and to each other. Turning up and discing large clods of dirt to smooth out the soil for planting, together they made space for nature to flourish. I imagine their bond as deep and silent, with each sharing appreciative glances around the fields amid moments of utter exhaustion, knowing they would later reap the fruits of their labor.

I wish I had met Grandpa Petersheim. Whenever we visited Grandmom, I couldn't help but gaze at the large portrait of Grandpa in the oval-shaped frame hanging in such a prominent place in her living room. He appeared young, with soft-looking eyes, gentle expression, and ever-so-slight smile. My mother talked about her "Pop" with quiet reverence. "He was easygoing and kind," she'd say with a slow languish of nostalgia. "He had both a masculine and gentle way about him." I wanted to experience him as she did.

Grandpa Petersheim's children experienced him also as lighthearted in manner. One day, they saw a column of mist rising from the ground and asked what was causing the picturesque mystery. "The foxes are cooking their breakfast," he explained.

Beneath Grandpa Petersheim's fun-loving demeanor lay firsthand experience with hard times. Growing up in a very poor family, he knew the meaning of grit, as did his ancestors before him. Mom recalled the tale of Grandpa's great-great grandfather, Georg Petersheim, arriving in America in 1811 with his wife and six children and having to borrow $50 from the church alms fund just so his family could survive. Georg Petersheim, a man of integrity, worked hard to build a life for his family, and according to a written note, six years later he paid back $80, which was every bit of what he had borrowed and more.

Grandpa inherited his great-great grandfather's work ethic and believed everyone else should do their fair share as well. When my mother was twelve, she had to stay home from school to help Grandmom with household chores because Grandmom was recovering from having given birth to Mom's brother Leroy. In those days, it was customary for the mother to stay in bed for about a week after delivery and for others to help out. Grandpa Petersheim watched approvingly as my young mother brought her work ethic from the fields into their home—

sweeping the floor, doing the dishes, caring for younger siblings, and washing clothes by hand, all without question or complaint "because it had to be done."

Grandpa also believed in rewarding people for their hard work. One day, he arrived home and handed my mother a tiny, silver wristwatch with a gray dial and stretchy band. I imagine my modest mother holding it in her hands like it was gold, rubbing it gently between her fingers to enjoy the luxury of it all. Not many girls Mom's age had a wristwatch, so I imagine she wore it with pride, walking about the house, laying her palms flat on every table she could find to look at it from yet another angle. She knew the exact cost of that watch in dollars and cents, and the way she spoke of it, you'd think that her father's love was wrapped around her little wrist. Perhaps it was.

To help out, Grandmom's unmarried sister Mary lived with Grandmom and Grandpa for a long time after they got married and started having children. Mary had a difficult time figuring things out and always seemed to be inside her head; Mom referred to her as socially awkward. Remaining unmarried longer than her sisters, Mary moved next door to her older sister Sade. During that time, Sade sometimes called Grandmom on the phone saying, "Your husband is over here again visiting Mary." Mom remembered a specific day when her father took her and her siblings to school in the morning and then went to Morgantown where Mary lived. Someone called Grandmom telling her that "Yone's" car had been parked at Mary's house for a long time, and Grandmom told the caller to tell him to come home. Mom remembered Grandmom being very upset, but Mom didn't know what about. Others gossiped and speculated about what was going on between Grandpa and Mary.

Then came some news that changed things. Back then, when two people were to be married they were "published," meaning their engagement was announced in church. Published engagements usually came as no surprise to anyone, thanks to the fact that close-knit communities were always in the know about one another. But when Mary and a man named Levi were published unexpectedly in church one Sunday morning, Grandmom's sisters Sade and Emma, sitting side by side, gasped loudly through wide-open mouths, nearly rising out of their seats with horrified looks. They took pride in knowing what was going on in everyone's lives and were peeved that they had known nothing about this. Yone and Mary were pregnant, and Mary, to cover over her "sin," had quickly become engaged to another man.

When Mom told us the story of her Aunt Mary's odd, quick marriage, it was apparent that to her the marriage seemed a mere reflection of Mary's quirky ways. As far as Mom and her siblings were concerned, Mary and her new husband were simply in a hurry to start a family (Mary was thirty-six years old when she married Levi), and Diane—the child Mary gave birth to—was just one of their cousins. It turned out, however, that Diane (not her real name) had the same kidney disease Grandpa Petersheim had. Referring to Diane's disease, Grandmom noted, "But we didn't know if it was like ours." Her voice became noticeably pensive, however, when she talked about Diane in the recorded interview with my cousin Bob Petersheim.

When my Uncle Leroy visited Mom a year before her death and told her everything about Grandpa's involvement with Mary and the polycystic kidney connection with Diane, Mom appeared surprisingly unscathed. I'm still not entirely sure how it affected her. Could it be she somehow knew in her bones the whole time of her father's wrongdoing? If so, I can't help but wonder how this affected her. Did she carry buried shame and internal conflict even as she defended her father up one side and down the other?

Grandpa Petersheim and Mary's past unraveled years later when Diane grew to adulthood and died from the same kidney disease that Grandpa Petersheim had. My cousin Martha, who had studied genetics back in high school and knew this kidney condition was both rare and hereditary, also knew both that Levi could not be the father of Diane and that Jonathan likely was. Others didn't believe Martha and looked askance at her as if she were digging into things that were "none of her business." The exception to this was Chris Kurtz, one of the church elders, to whom Grandpa Petersheim had confessed his sin.

Martha's suspicion was confirmed several years later when another cousin, Jennifer, was diagnosed with the same rare condition. When Jennifer went to a nephrologist, the medical staff mentioned that her "cousin" Marabelle, Diane's daughter, was being treated there too. They knew that on the family history form for polycystic kidneys, Marabelle had listed Jonathan Petersheim as her maternal grandfather. Jennifer immediately called Martha to confirm what Martha had already figured out. (These names have been changed to offer a level of anonymity.)

While Mom grieved the open disclosure that her Pop was "less than perfect," she was relieved and comforted to know that the man she looked up to, though flawed, had done the right thing and addressed his internal conflict by confessing his sin to the church elders and asking for forgiveness. Even at age eighty-seven, Mom remained strongly attached to her Pop, who seemed to embody for her everything good.

No doubt Grandmom, too, felt deeply the pain of her husband's betrayal, but she persevered in maintaining their relationship and even seemed to take partial responsibility for her husband's actions. Her admonition to Mom as a young bride was, "Never turn your husband down."

ISAAC KURTZ: Grandma Petersheim's father
October 12, 1862–November 11, 1922

Great-grandparents Isaac Kurtz (1862–1922) and Susanna Esch Kurtz (1865–1949)

Our family knew very little about Isaac Kurtz, Grandma Petersheim's father. From what Mom said about his death, I saw him as the poster example of someone who bore the consequences of drinking alcohol, though I suspect there was much more to him that we only saw glimpses of, such as the spirit of generosity he showed to mom and her siblings. Beyond this, we can only guess from the few photographs we have of him—jaw determinedly positioned, chin slightly protruding, and eyes deep-set, the same as his daughter's, my Grandma Petersheim.

Late one night in 1942, when Mom was about nine years old, Grandpa Kurtz went out to the barn to open up a new batch of alcoholic brew. Unfortunately, he didn't realize the fresh brew he had just mixed was bad, containing ethanol poisoning. After the first few swallows, he immediately became ill. Somehow managing to stumble back to the house, he crawled up the steps of the porch and collapsed just outside the front door. He called for his wife, who managed to drag him into bed, where he fell into a deep sleep. Three hours later he died. The newspaper described his death as a "paralytic stroke." But the story Mom and her family got from the person who banged on their door to tell them about her grandpa's death was that he died of alcohol poisoning.

I always wondered if Mom's strong aversion to alcohol was directly linked to the trauma she experienced over Grandpa Kurtz's death. She had a real soft spot for her grandfather, who seemed to know just how to make her childhood heart feel loved. About one of her visits with him, she recalled, "Why, he'd even walk a mile to get candy for his grandchildren. He really was a nice guy compared to his brothers." Grandpa Kurtz and his two brothers all had a drinking problem, but Mom always made sure to mention that her grandfather got mellow when drunk in contrast to his brothers, who were mean to their horses when they drank too much.

I'm guessing Mom must have felt torn in her young heart; how could someone so kind die so needlessly because of something "stupid" he did to himself? In my mind's eye, I imagine Mom and her siblings upstairs in bed just drifting off to sleep when suddenly interrupted by a loud, frantic knocking and someone yelling to open the door. They likely suspected bad news and had their suspicions confirmed when they heard Grandmom's cry of agony. I imagine they crept timidly downstairs and cautiously peeked around the corner, glimpsing Grandmom with her head buried in her folded arms at the kitchen table, crying quietly. Mom grew to equate alcohol with death and sadness, and something to be avoided at all costs. In a voice both strong with urgency and tinged with shame, she instructed us to stay clear of it.

As if to hold on to something dear about her Grandpa Kurtz, Mom always gave candy to the children after church. Candy seemed to hold the promise of something sacred, and this simple act seemed to connect her to Grandpa Kurtz in a powerful way. Unlike her grandfather, however, if she was out of candy, she did not walk a mile to the store. Instead, she scurried around the kitchen on Sunday morning before church with a plastic bag in hand, filling it with small marshmallows, chocolate chips, or whatever sweets she had on hand. Children flocked to her after church for their treat, which she gently, almost reverently, placed in their hands. Even though some parents mildly protested because their children got sticky from the candy, Mom paid them no heed. She knew the power of love and a precious little piece of candy. Grandpa Kurtz had shown her so.

AUNT IDA AND UNCLE LEON

Aunt Ida—Mom's sister—and Uncle Leon showed us what it was to Jump up! in spite of the heartbreak of losing several newborn infants to a rare blood condition. When their first child, Rachel, finally arrived, she was bedfast and not able to communicate. Though disappointed at not having a healthy child, Aunt Ida and Uncle Leon lovingly cared for her around the clock as if she were a rare treasure. Rachel lived to be a teenager. Despite their heartache, Aunt Ida and Uncle Leon always had a cheerful countenance and extended kindness to us in many ways. We had a special connection to them; they sort of adopted us. I looked forward to spending time with both of them. While I felt shy around most of the relatives I rarely saw, Aunt Ida and Uncle Leon's inviting warmth embraced us, and I came into their space unafraid. I felt safe and secure, knowing that if they could be so genuinely caring in spite of their losses, their tangible overtures of kindness must be real. After adopting three children, Aunt Ida and Uncle Leon's son Junior was born.

Jump Up!

For our family, the phrase Jump up! was more than a call to action. It was an invocation of the spirit of our family. It was about the mental toughness that life demands, about being uplifted. It was about fun and not allowing adversity to overcome our connection to one another.

Thanks to our parents, we knew how to Jump up! when we grew weary from working hard, when we faced fear of the dark and of chickens pecking us, when bicycle and motorbike excursions grew long, and when two of us experienced the death of our newborn babies. We learned to persevere as individuals whether it was going against the odds to attend medical school, getting up in the dark to check muskrat traps, hoeing a long row of tomatoes to completion, going alone out to the cow pasture in the wee hours of the morning, or pushing through the holdback of an eighth-grade education to become a successful businessman.

Mom and Dad learned to Jump up! from their ancestors. They showed us how to laugh, sing, and love in the face of exploding pressure cookers, floods, and freezing temperatures destroying tomato crops. As kids, we could always count on our parents to somehow not only keep going but also thrive. We knew we could do the same because we were not the first ones to Jump up! We had seen our parents and their parents before them do it.

As adults, we passed this knowledge on to our own children. I found myself using the phrase Jump up! many times with my children when they were young. I now hear them using it with their children. The sound of this simple admonition ripples all the way back to our ancestors. Perhaps they too used it as they headed down the Rhine River toward the Palatinate to Germany after being persecuted in Switzerland. Whether or not they said the exact words Jump up! our ancestors rose by personal determination to succeed against the odds, following their inborn understanding that jumping up is simply what one does.

When we are connected to community and encouraged and supported by others, we can surmount almost any obstacle. When the human spirit connects with another human spirit, something sacred and mysterious happens, giving purpose and meaning for our lives. It creates the ability to Jump up! passing the gift from one generation to the next.

Our family has become a river system—a tributary out of which nineteen other tributaries flow, each creating their own system, each shaped by the spirit of our ancestors.

I treasure the slideshow glimpses I have been given of my ancestors, while absorbing the knowledge that in years to come, others will refer to me as their ancestor. And the river of life that I am in will flow on ...

PART II

Our Parents

4. Mabel Kurtz Petersheim: Mom

"Each one is different."

My eyelids were heavy, everyone else had gone to bed, and I had finally turned off our dial-up computer after working late into the night. It was April 9, 2003.

Without warning, the loud ring of the phone cut through the nighttime stillness, jarring me wide awake. My sister Sue was on the other line. "We've been trying to get hold of you. Mom died tonight." "Oh nooooooo!" I cried out from somewhere deep within my soul. "I had unfinished business with her …" In despair, I knew for sure now that I could never have the relationship with Mom I had longed for.

Looking back, I realize I probably never would have been able to finish my business with Mom. She was a complex creature, part knowable and part mystery, as all mothers are. Though we tend to know them only as our mothers and less as women, they are both. Today as I was sorting through pictures looking for one of my great-grandfather Isaac Kurtz, I came across one of Mom. Tenderness and sadness welled up together inside of me as I looked at the woman in the photo— serene, warm brown eyes; cape dress and large prayer covering; abdomen thick and legs swollen.

"I never really knew you. I wish I could have," I thought longingly. I knew a lot of things about Mom but couldn't say I really knew her. The community knew her for the good things she did among them and in the lives of children, and they featured her in newspaper and magazine articles. First Lady Nancy Reagan wrote a letter to her expressing appreciation for the difference she was making. Her character and gifts were evident to many.

Where did Mom's character and gifts come from—taking motherhood so seriously; love of children; hard-work ethic; frugality; generosity; occasional playfulness; love of quilting, embroidering, crocheting, and knitting? And what about her often-guarded feelings, her inner longings, and the strict moral code she lived by—where did they come from?

THE WHITE HOUSE

June 23, 1986

Dear Mrs. Stoltzfus:

Someone recently sent me a newspaper article about you, and about your remarkable generosity in providing a home for so many children.

There is nothing more heartwarming than hearing of stories like yours. You are a living example of the great spirit that is the foundation of our wonderful nation -- generosity and love. I want you to know that you are a shining example for others to imitate. I thank you on behalf of everyone who's lives you have touched.

With my warmest best wishes,

Sincerely,

Youcy Reagau

Mrs. Mabel Stoltzfus
Route 3, Box 193
Lewisburg, Pennsylvania   17837

Mom's Early Years

Mom was born March 9, 1916, in Elverson, Pennsylvania, to Barbara and Jonathan Petersheim. At twelve years old, she developed a severe toxic abscess after her appendix burst, and wasn't expected to live. When her father came to visit her in the hospital, he hid his concern about her deteriorating condition, smiling and waving at her through the glass panel of the hospital window. Mom had a strong connection with her father, and the love she felt from him through that hospital window likely helped pull her through. During her hospital stay, her father wrote her a letter dated December 17, 1928:

Mom as a toddler and as a teenager

Hollow anabel Lu How are you? we got Home allright sunday. Well every one seems to be glat you can come Home this week. Yesterday when I was going down stairs from your room i met some People that asked me where the Petersheim girl is. i don't know who they were. it's soon Time you are coming Home i Believe the chickens wonder why you don't come around to hunt the eggs. We sawed wood saturday. samson wandered where's mable. the Pigens are cooing for you. Bute looks back and ada Bals for you. mach says whers mabel Tillie says Todloo. Mumsy and Daddy to. So much From Dad

Mom loved the camaraderie of her tall, dark-haired, gentle, fun-loving father, whom she and her siblings called "Pop." Actually, she idolized him. In her eyes, he could do little wrong, except for using tobacco. "He shouldn't have chewed tobacco," she said. She frequently shared his words with us, beginning each time in an adoring, wistful tone. "Pop used to say …" Perhaps Mom found refuge in her father's accepting manner in contrast to her mother's stubborn, determined nature and sometimes sharp and inappropriately crass tongue. Mom said she always got along well with her Pop but couldn't say the same about her mother. Mom's mother had clear expectations of her children and was somewhat intolerant of the foibles of others. Mom became a combination of the easygoing nature of her father and the stubborn determination of her mother, both of which were needed to meet the demands of raising all nineteen of her children.

Mom also had a strong connection with her sister, Della; as young children, they were best buddies. Fascinated, they used to watch their grandfather chew tobacco, coveting it for themselves since he seemed to like it so much. One day in a streak of luck they found a fresh wad of tobacco in his workplace. Dividing it in two, they each thrust half in their mouths and began chewing. Almost instantly turning green, the girls spit their wads out and ran headlong for the house, receiving their punishment as they threw up along the way. Grandmom, not knowing what was going on, was concerned and flustered. If she had just smelled their breaths, she might have guessed the cause of their sudden illness.

Mom wasn't always lucky enough to avoid parental discipline, and she learned the hard way how to be fair and take responsibility for her actions. One time she and Della each received a patch of cloth to embroider that would eventually become part of a quilt. While Della stayed inside doing fine embroidery work, Mom spent much of her time in the fields with her father. In the evenings after fieldwork, Mom sat embroidering her patch and couldn't help sneaking furtive glances at Della's patch. Growing increasingly jealous of her sister's fine stitches, Mom followed her destructive urge one day and grabbed a pair of scissors, demolishing Della's beautiful patch with a few swift snips. When her father learned of this, he marched out and bought another patch, bringing it home and telling Mom, "Now, you sew this for Della to repay the one you cut up."

It was a good thing Mom enjoyed working outside—indeed, preferred it—to inside housework. Before any sons arrived in the family, she was the oldest of six daughters and was expected to help her father with the farm work. Eventually the oldest of twelve children, she easily filled the eldest child role, shouldering responsibilities of hard physical work and caring for her younger siblings. For Mom, working with her easygoing father out in the open fields provided a welcome respite from the rigidity of her mother.

What did Mom think about and dream about out in the broad expanse of fields in front of the Welsh Mountain range as the sweaty, brown mules broke up hard sods of newly-plowed ground before her? Delighting in the outside air and the mules

Mom and Dad's first, little white house in the meadow

she loved so much, could she also have been envisioning being a wife and mother one day, the only option for the future known to her? What would she have thought if she had known she would become the mother of nineteen children, be pregnant for twelve years of her life, and have babies in diapers for twenty-six years?

Mom's new life started when she married my father in 1936 at the age of twenty-one. Suddenly, she found herself in a "strange land," expected to take on a clearly defined role as housewife in a little white house just over the hill from where she and her father had worked the fields. She soon began stretching the definition of housewife, balancing housework with going outdoors into the air she loved so much and making treks to the barn to check on the animals.

This didn't always sit well with Dad. One day early in their marriage, Mom found a sickly calf in the barn and alerted Dad to the matter, saying, "This one needs more milk." Not wanting Mom to start overseeing his work, Dad told her to stay in the house "where she belonged." As a young wife easily moved to tears, Mom started crying. Dad—a frustrated young husband who did not know what to do with a crying wife—told her to "stop crying." And she eventually did. Mom stuffed her feelings down deep.

During the time I knew her, Mom always had difficulty expressing her feelings. Maybe because Dad told her to stop crying, or maybe because she was quiet and reserved by nature. Or perhaps because her family of origin was not accustomed to expressing their feelings. Whatever the reason, Mom did not share her feelings easily.

Of course, that did not mean we never experienced her emotions. For instance, Mom let her anger be known to Dad in novel ways. Rarely lashing out with words, she sang her anger instead. This happened mostly when we were traveling somewhere together. Mom and Dad would have an argument, often using Pennsylvania Dutch, in which Dad seemed to take the upper hand with loud, harsh words overshadowing Mom's barely audible voice. Not to be outdone, however, Mom would break forth in a sing-song slurry voice and seal the argument. "I shall not be, I shall not be moved, just like a tree that's planted by the water …"; or, "I know the Lord will make a way for me …"; or, "Angry words, oh let them never from the tongue unbridled slip …" In the back seats of the station wagon, we children would quietly absorb the tension until Sue began singing with Mom, perfectly mimicking her way of singing. The moment Sue began this duet, the tension would quietly dissipate. How could Sue be reprimanded for merely singing along with her mother?

Mom and her first son, Parke

The soft way Mom showed her anger, and emotions in general, through singing, pointed to the gentle, giving person she was, formed first by relationships of boundless love in her family of origin and later by profound heartbreak. She watched not only her beloved young father die but also her cherished siblings, including her beloved sister Della. She lived as well with the knowledge that her grandfather had destroyed himself with alcohol.

But she also watched as her determined mother stood tall in the face of economic hardship. And when Mom spoke of her Esch ancestors who came to America in 1854 to start a new life, it was almost as if she was right there with them persevering and enduring, gaining the courage to raise all nineteen of us. Following the path of her ancestors, she did what needed to be done each day to care for us in spite of being emotionally drained and barely able to think by the end of the day.

Perhaps what gave Mom motivation to keep going was that in her children she found answers to her questions about her importance and her place of belonging. She made motherhood her vocation, saying, "I believe motherhood is the greatest career there is. Many people today think children are a bother, but I always felt my children were a gift from God." One wonders if this feeling was tested when twice she had three children in diapers at the same time—one growing out of diapers, one nowhere close to being potty trained, and one newly born. Pampers were nonexistent then, so her clothesline was full of yellowish-white cloth diapers flapping in the wind on wash days.

Top: Barb and Leona hanging out a clean load of never-ending diapers. Above: Pete and Edith delighting in baby Dale.

But Mom never complained about an unexpected pregnancy and instead gave us the impression that we were all wanted and valued. More than once, she said about her nineteen children, "I'm thankful for each one of them. I wouldn't want to be without any of them. I enjoyed my children." When one of my older sisters complained about there being too many children, Mom said, "Well, which one would you like to be without?" There was never an answer to that question.

All but six of us were born at home, with the help of a doctor who made a home visit to deliver us. Though Mom's labor and delivery was very difficult during the home birth of my oldest brother, Parke, she was undaunted by the experience and cherished the births of all her other children, preferring to give birth to her babies at home. I would catch her gazing lovingly at her newborn babies as if studying them carefully. She told me she knew which of us was going to be high strung and which was going to be easygoing by the way we cried and the way we postured our little bodies even at birth. She was usually right.

When Mom would take a new baby to church for the first time, she'd carry it as if she were carrying a treasure, quietly beaming when the other women eagerly gathered 'round to look at the newborn and "oohed" and "aaaahed" over it. I would stay close to Mom's side as she pulled the blanket back to reveal the swaddled baby's face. In the midst of the huddle, I'd quietly soak in the wonder of the newborn, seeking some recognition just because I was its sister.

Even with so many children, Mom was equitable in her approach to us. When Esther as a young girl asked Mom which one of us she thought was the prettiest, Mom replied, "Oh, you're all pretty in your own way." Recognizing us as individuals with our own worth, Mom gave careful thought to what she would give each child for Christmas from her limited resources. For everyday living, she assigned each of us a drawer of our own in the L-shaped corner cabinet—a unique piece of furniture with unending drawers—where we could put personal belongings. When we were sick in bed, we could count on Mom to carry a tray in to us containing a bowl with toast in hot milk, a soft-boiled egg atop, and tea. This special treatment gave me warm fuzzies (and still does). As we grew older, Mom made a quilt and comforter for each of us. When the girls became young adults, we were given a cedar chest, which Mom often bought at an auction. For any of us who lived far away from home for a while, she took the time to faithfully write letters to us. And when we got married, she generously provided us with canned goods and a rocking chair.

Giving things to her children seemed to be easier for Mom than giving us herself. Although I knew how much she loved all her children, I had a hard time understanding why I did not feel more loved by her. I couldn't understand how Mom could give off a warmth that drew others to her, yet I couldn't get close enough to feel that same warmth. For a long time as I was growing up, I thought the distance between us was evidence of something wrong with me.

Looking back, I'm guessing it was probably difficult for Mom to attend to my emotional needs when her own emotions were in an upheaval, especially during my formative years. I was one year old in 1953 when Dad decided the family would move from Oley to New Columbia, a three-hour drive from the life my mother knew well with her sisters and mother, a life in which she frequently quilted and canned food with women she knew well. Mom's struggle became my struggle; as she was having to figure out how to be farther away from her own mother, I was trying to figure out how to become closer to mine.

Parke, Dad, Elam, Mom, and Barb (baby) at our stone house in Oley

Leaving behind the familiar to settle in new, strange, unaccommodating territory was difficult for Mom not only emotionally but also physically. She had no say-so in leaving the large, beautiful limestone house built in 1799 with a cement floor basement, wide stone ledges for window sills, and an indoor bathroom in exchange for the large, rundown brick house along the Susquehanna River. The new house had only dirt on the basement floor, roof and shutters in a state of disrepair, a ramshackle kitchen, and no inside bathroom. The first commode was not installed until Mom was forty years old with twelve children.[3]

Outward Appearance

In the absence of an emotional connection with Mom in my growing up years, I knew her mostly by her outward appearance and behavior. One of the newspaper articles about Mom described her as "a rosy-cheeked, brown-eyed woman who looks far younger than her years." Appearing serene, calm, and patient, her facial expression rarely changed or gave away clues to her internal world. Her hands— their normal position halfway closed as if carefully guarding her feelings, and finger-nails chewed back as far as they could go—gave a bit of a different message, hinting at troublesome things inside.

In contrast to her hands, however, Mom's sturdy frame was supported by thick ankles and legs and seemed to reflect the inner strength she carried. Although the

---

[3] Placed behind plywood walls in the corner of the downstairs hallway, our first inside bathroom was just big enough to turn around in. Yet, compared to hurried runs to the weathered outhouse at the edge of the yard, the commode made us feel like royalty. We could now use toilet paper— "Only two squares," Dad would say—instead of pages torn from Sears catalogs or phone books.

blue and purple varicose veins of all sizes covering her legs embarrassed her a bit, she didn't seem phased by the deep, white cracks in her heels created by going barefoot in the summer. To me they were curiously ugly, but to Mom, going barefoot—cracks and all—was certainly preferable to wearing shoes.

As Mom worked throughout the day in the kitchen or the garden, she always wore an apron, usually sporting a brownish color on the front where the apron covered her protruding stomach. With the birth of each baby, her figure became more solid and round. I once heard her say in a whimsical sort of way that after the births of her first few children, she gave up exercising to get back in shape. Was this a sacrifice she made for us?

Mom's Inner World

Sometimes Mom called attention to "how nice" slender women looked, and I got the feeling she wished she were thinner herself. This fit with the general sense I had that Mom struggled with feelings of insecurity, inferiority, and self-consciousness, but I was puzzled by her apparent struggle because it did not seem to fit with her kind, generous behavior. I also did not understand how Mom often seemed to be so sure of what was the right thing to do—like when she took in other people's children—but could seem so lost about who she was as a person. And though she always wanted desperately to do the right thing, she seemed to have a difficult time acknowledging and apologizing when she was wrong. I did not understand why she sometimes sang to get her point across to Dad in the midst of conflict, sometimes overrode the wishes and desires of others, and sometimes took things into her own hands as if she could not trust others. Maybe her ardent zealousness about wanting to do the right thing made it harder to admit any shortcomings.

At the same time that Mom was a significant presence in our family, she also seemed significantly absent, appearing emotionally detached at times, not really letting many people in except children, even as she seemed to give out so much. She was like the blue and white chest on the landing at the top of our stairs that housed Mom's treasurers deep inside. Meaningful heart-to-heart conversation with Mom was difficult as she guarded a locked doorway to feelings in general, not sharing much of her inner self. Her laughter likewise only showed itself on rare occasions, and when it did appear, Mom would cover her mouth with her hand, letting out only a stifled giggle.

Where did this held-back laughter come from inside of Mom? It was a closed-off part I did not know and longed to experience more of. Wanting desperately to be known and approved of by Mom, I tried all my life to get into her mysterious inner world, even while fearing her rejection and wanting to stay safely distant. In spite of all my attempts, I did not feel accepted and approved of by her. Others appeared to have better access, like my sister Edith, who loved nature and seemed to have a good connection with Mom. So I tried an experiment. I got a book about clouds from the school library and brought it home. When Mom was cooking at the kitchen stove, I came up to her with the book in hand. Standing tentatively by her side, I opened the book and pointed. "Look, these are some cumulus clouds … ," I said, hoping to impress her with my knowledge of and interest in clouds. But her only response was, "Um hum," as she barely looked up from the kettle she was stirring. "Well, that one failed," I mumbled to myself in disappointment.

Fortunately for me, my older sisters provided much nurture and comfort when I was sad. They made sure I did not doubt that I was a valuable human being. In spite of this, I still felt something missing without Mom's explicit approval.

I did not voluntarily offer information to others outside our family regarding the things I did not understand about Mom. It seemed to me that we, as her children, took on the role of protecting Mom from herself, a task she seemed to have begun earlier herself. I believe, for instance, that she knew in her bones about her Pop's transgression but somehow managed to rearrange the reality in her mind, making her father into a sort of super saint about whom she could say nothing negative. I have to wonder now—did she defend her father so fiercely because she intuitively knew of his involvement with her aunt? Did she raise her own flag heralding the right way to live as a way to shut out the truth of the inconsistencies between her father's actions and the principles she believed in?

Several years after Dad's death, Elvin and Pete asked Mom if they could talk to her about her Pop. During that conversation, she could only talk about him with strong accolades. A week or two later, Mom said to Pete, "You know, there's something that doesn't make sense. I have a cousin on my Mom's side that died from polycystic kidneys. That was a disease that runs on Pop's side of the family."

Grandpa, it turned out, was not always a man of integrity. Surely the unresolved family agenda surrounding this must have impacted Mom at some deep level, whether or not she was consciously aware of it. Might she have been freer in her relationships with her own children and husband if she had not experienced this unresolved tension in her family of origin?

The Obvious: Love of Children

Any inner unrest Mom might have been carrying seemed to vanish when she was with small children. She was drawn to them and they were drawn to her, seeming instinctively to know that she understood and genuinely loved them. When one of my highly educated friends met Mom for the first time, he commented that she had a natural understanding of children even though she had not read psychology books about their needs. Placing high value on children, Mom forbade us to refer to them as "kids." "They're not baby goats," she'd say. "They're children."

Watching Mom with small children gave me a rare window into her soul. Babies and toddlers, especially, seemed to open the door of her heart and give her a sense of purpose. Lavishing love and affection on the little ones, Mom held them close, tenderly embracing them with a gentle smile. She quietly and soothingly sang children to sleep with a medley of songs: *Jesus Loves Me*; *Jesus Loves the Little Children*; and *Jesus Loves the Little Ones Like Me, Me, Me*. She did this for us when we were children and later for the children she took in after we were grown. Mom used music to communicate deep feelings that she otherwise seemed to find hard to express. Seldom do I remember her saying, "I love you," but when she wrapped the little ones in her lullabies, they knew they were loved—her children by birth, her grandchildren, and the children she took in.

Taking Motherhood Seriously

As her babies and toddlers grew older, Mom continued taking her role as mother very seriously, training us and teaching us life lessons. She went out of her way to make sure we learned self-discipline; coaxed us to take cookies to neighbors and "mean" people; had us memorize a weekly Scripture memory verse on the chalkboard; made us take turns going into stores with her on the way home from school; taught us how to cook and sew, helping us correct our mistakes; encouraged frugality by providing a penny bank for each of us in a "penny bank cupboard"; made sure my sisters and I dressed modestly; told us "not to laugh too loud" at friends' houses; and strictly enforced rules for our behavior in church, including no whispering, no chewing gum, no turning around, and no bathroom breaks during the church service.

All of this grew out of Mom's clear desire for us to grow strong spiritually. We heard her say on more than one occasion, "I have no greater joy than to know my children walk in truth." Stressing emphatically the importance of doing the right thing, of obeying God, of doing his will, Mom was the Guardian of Our Souls in following the letter of the law. In the summer when we drove past the outdoor theater after dark, she told us firmly, "Now look the other way." But the allure of the forbidden was strong. I tried to not let anyone see me peeking through the fingers of my hands to get a glimpse of "the evil on the screen." I'm not sure if the innocuous figures in color moving across the screen left me relieved or disappointed.

As part of her teachings, Mom faithfully read us bedtime stories from *A Hive of Busy Bees* or a Bible storybook every evening before we crawled into bed, even though she was usually dead tired by the end of the day. She'd sit on the edge of the bed with one of us on either side of her, sometimes falling asleep in the middle of the story. Once when I was about six years old, I made it my turn to sit next to her. I was surprised by how good it felt to snuggle up against her as she read, and I felt comforted. Following the story, Mom always instructed us to kneel by our bed and pray aloud, "Now I lay me down to sleep …" I hurried through the ominous-sounding part—"If I should die before I wake, I pray the Lord my soul to take"—hoping that part of the prayer wouldn't come true for me.

Mom modeled much of what she taught. She was very patient, able to withstand a lot of ruckus in the house, and rarely raised her voice at us. She was durable, hard-working, brave, stubborn, driven, determined, and willing to do the difficult thing to get a positive outcome. When she saw us doing something commendable, she praised us. Like when I changed Pete's diaper on my own at just five years of age, safety pins and all. She would brag to others, "Why, Rose changed Pete's diaper when she was only five years old." She also tried to keep us busy, even going so far as have my younger brothers embroider quilt blocks on the long ride to school to keep them out of one another's hair. (One day, Tim got so into his embroidering that when he tried to lift the sewing hoop with fabric off his leg as the station wagon pulled into the school driveway, it wouldn't budge. He had sewn a few stitches through his pant leg.)

Mom was also persistent. When her parenting methods failed, she simply became more resourceful, such as the time three- or four-year-old Ada kept sneaking off to the neighbor's house. Nothing Mom did to try to stop her seemed to dampen little Ada's adventuresome spirit. So one day Mom decided to introduce a bit of fear into the situation. When she saw Ada start out, determinedly walking down the lane toward the neighbor's house, she cut across the corner of the corn field, hiding in the corn next to the lane. As Ada passed by, Mom barked loudly in a deep voice like a big dog. Turning on her heels, little legs flying, Ada sped back home. Mom triumphed; that was the end of Ada sneaking off to the neighbor's house.

Courage

Mom's courage was obvious, especially when it came to cows. When we lived at Oley and a spark from the fodder machine started the barn on fire, Mom dashed in to rescue the frantically mooing family milk cow, ducking flames coming down through the upper level floor boards, while everyone outside—equally as frantic as the cow—yelled at her to get out. She did come out, leading the rescued cow.

What was it about cows and Mom? When we lived on the farm along the river, Mom had another incident with a cow, raising her to hero status of a different nature. Leading up to the story, Dad had sold his dairy herd, eliminating our automatic supply of milk each day. Mom, preferring milk directly from the cow rather than the store, was not satisfied with this arrangement. So, in spite of Dad's discouragement because he didn't want to be bothered with one cow, Mom persisted and saved up her money to buy a Jersey cow. (It had to be a Jersey because their milk was creamier.) But this particular Jersey had horns. One day when Mom walked into the barn to milk the cow, it met her at the door instead of the stall where it should have been. Without warning, it began attacking with its horns. Scrambling to a large, wooden feeding trough nearby, Mom fell to the floor in fear and barely managed to stuff herself into the small space under the end of the trough. Taking refuge, she braced against the legs of the trough so she could push the heifer's head away as it tried to reach her. Not put off by Mom's efforts, the heifer relentlessly pushed on, sinking down on its front legs for a better swipe. Tim didn't normally spend much time in the barn, especially at this time of day, but on this particular day he "just happened" to walk into the barn at the right time, as if guided by a guardian angel. Chasing the deranged cow away, he enabled an exhausted and terrified Mom to escape. It was a good thing he arrived when he did because Mom was wearing out and would not have been able to push the cow away much longer. She escaped with just a few heifer-inflicted scrapes on her legs, and broken glasses.

It took courage of a different nature for Mom to host a vanload of young adult males—complete strangers—by herself one January morning. That particular morning, a van broke down on I-80 close to our house, and one of the passengers climbed down over the highway embankment, knocked on our door, and asked for help. Mom and Dad invited the whole vanload for breakfast. However, it just so happened that Dad and some of the younger children were about to leave for the Pennsylvania State Farm show in Harrisburg. Not to be held back by a bunch of young men, they walked out the door, leaving Mom all by herself with them.

Strangers were not as suspect then as they are now, but it took courage nonetheless for my quiet mother to feed these strangers breakfast. Any misgivings she may have had about them in her kitchen were allayed, however, when she noticed one of the guys bowing his head to pray before he ate. Then, when it came time to open their soft-boiled eggs to scoop out the contents, Mom realized some of the guys didn't know how to proceed, so she demonstrated by cracking her own egg open with a spoon.

Mom was also quite stoic. One night, hard at work canning green beans after everyone else had gone to bed, she lay down on the sofa to rest while she waited for the next seven quarts of beans to come out of the pressure cooker. Falling asleep, she dozed past the time for the beans to come off the stove. When she awoke, she realized she'd passed the allotted time and hurriedly removed the lid of the pressure cooker only to discover there was no more water in the bottom of the cooker—just very hot jars of pressurized beans. In a state of dulled senses, she poured water into the canner. The instant the water hit the jars, they exploded with a tremendous bang like seven torpedoes, sending shrapnel of glass and green beans shooting to the white ceiling nine feet above and all around, blasting Mom's glasses off her face as well. Although somewhat in shock, Mom realized the pain in her arms and face was coming from scald burns and minor cuts. Over the next few days, she somehow handled the pain calmly and without complaint.

Hard-Work Ethic, Frugality, and Generosity

Canning green beans was only one of a mountain of things Mom canned. In her own words, "I canned about anything I could." It was not unusual for her to can up to one thousand quarts of food a year: tomatoes, tomato juice, tomato cocktail, peaches, pears, green beans, grape juice, and chow chow (a colorful mix of vegetables in season near the end of the summer, immersed in a sweet-sour, spicy base). But Mom's specialty was ketchup. She cooked the sauce from strained tomatoes in a large, copper kettle over an outdoor fire, stirred the thickening sauce as the tomatoes cooked down, then added pungent spices that our noses feasted on—the best part of all.

When it came to cooking, Mom stayed with what was familiar. Her go-to dessert was cornstarch pudding. Collecting many recipes, yet rarely trying them out, Mom tended to stick with her standard meat, potatoes, and vegetables. She approached meal prep as a necessary but unpleasant task and expressed relieved gratitude when one of her daughters would offer to make a meal. Mom would add that she liked it when we tried out new recipes.

On baking days, Mom mixed up a couple dishpans of dough to make ten to twelve loaves of bread and dozens of rolls. Baking for her family gave her joy. It was nothing for her to make eight pies at one time. Her specialties were pumpkin pie and mincemeat pie. When she took them from the oven, she usually cooled them on top of the freezer in the hall. On one occasion, after she had made seven large mincemeat pies and set them in the usual spot, she and Dad left for the day. Elvin and John, being the hungry, hardworking young men they were, discovered the pies and devoured every last one of them by the end of the day. When Mom came home and discovered the missing pies, her response was simply, "Well, that's what I made them for," and Elvin and John were instantly absolved of any potential guilt. Mom had made the pies for the boys knowing their older sisters weren't around to cook for them, but she probably had no idea they would eat them all in one day.

Though Mom's generosity was unquestionable, nothing in the kitchen went to waste when she was around. Strongly influenced by the depression era, she took the phrase "waste not, want not" to heart. We frequently heard her say, "Now, we don't want to waste anything." After making butter, for instance, she used the buttermilk leftovers to bake up a batch of buttermilk cookies—big and yellow with a raisin in the middle. They were best warm, right out of the oven, and neighborhood kids from "Newky" (New Columbia) walked a long distance for them, knowing that Mom would happily share.

Mom saved even the smallest leftovers. Without a microwave to heat things quickly, however, her frugality often led to the very waste she was trying to avoid. The small bits of leftovers accumulated in the refrigerator would lie there forgotten and collecting mold in a corner. When Mom occasionally rescued one of these containers to heat up for a meal and we protested, she would say, "A little mold won't hurt … just scrape it off." My younger brothers got in the habit of sniffing their first bite of food at mealtime to make sure it wasn't partially spoiled. Sometimes they find themselves still doing this as adults.

Wash day pulled Mom out of the kitchen one day a week. Every week, she put the Dexter double tub wringer washer through its paces. She used the same wash water—first heated in an iron kettle—for all eight to ten loads of laundry, starting with whites and ending with jeans and other dark items. She didn't have a clothes dryer until her fifteenth child was born and Dad bought a stable cleaner. At that point, Barb told Dad abruptly, "If you can afford a stable cleaner, Mom should have

Running A Small Assembly Line, Mrs. Stoltzfus shapes dinner rolls and passes them on to daughter, Edith, who places them in the pan and pricks each with a fork. Tantalized by the operation are Miriam 3, and Dale.

Everybody Must Help

Cooking For Family Of 16 Children Poses Special Problems, New Columbia Mother Find

Mrs. Mast Stoltzfus of New Columbia copes every day with a family cooking problem that might reduce many women to tears if it came once a year. Blessed with eight girls and eight boys, she cooks every night on a scale that most of us can manage only when an occasional tureen supper calls up our greatest powers of endurance.

We stopped out at the Stoltzfus farm last Saturday and caught her in the midst of her weekly baking, serene in spite of a preponderance of children, cats and dogs. Sitting down at the long kitchen table with her youngest, Miriam, we took a quick survey of the little jackets hanging in a row on the kitchen wall and asked how many of her children were home this year.

"Why, let me see," reflected Mrs. Stoltzfus. "The four oldest are married now. That leaves just fourteen of us at home, altogether."

How does she manage? "Well, of course, it all came gradually. I just got used to cooking more and more. And then," she smiled, "I do enjoy cooking. We do a lot of canning and freezing in the summer from our garden, and then of course we have our own milk, chickens and eggs. I only have to shop once or twice a week.

I just do the same as everyone else, but in larger quantities. Instead of baking one pie, for instance, I make twelve or fourteen of them together."

We directed our attention to the baking at hand. On the table was a huge pan of dough that she was pushing down. This was, it turned out, the basis for the week's supply of rolls. Some would be frozen for future use, the rest cooked right away. Assisted by her daughter, Edith, Mrs. Stoltzfus deftly molded the dough into various sizes and shapes: a pan of dinner rolls here, cinnamon buns there, confections for school lunches, and finally the childrens' favorite, sticky buns.

Several of the little boys who had been playing with a six weeks old collie puppy in a corner of the big kitchen came into help the assistant when we came to the sticky buns. "I don't think you've got enough syrup there, Edith." Ten year old Edith beamed and added a generous dollop. "More pecans," advised another. "Why don't you show the lady your Siamese cat, boys," suggested Mrs. Stoltzfus, coming to Edith's rescue.

"I like to have the girls start in cooking young," she explained, "but sometimes the boys get a little jealous and want to help too."

Watching Edith show an absorbed Miriam how to sprinkle brown sugar on the buns, we felt a little jealous ourselves. It was easy to understand why cooking for fourteen in the Stoltzfus household is not a chore but a delight.

Mrs. Stotzfus' Sticky Buns

1 cake compressed YEAST dissolved in 1 quart warm water
1 large cup LARD melted in 1 scant quart warm water
1 tablespoon SALT
2 cups SUGAR
enough FLOUR so that dough can be easily handled.
Knead dough, roll into a ball, cover and let rise in a warm place. When it is twice its original size, push it down and let it rise again. Now pour SYRUP over the bottom of your pans and sprinkle PECANS on top of it. Roll out the dough and sprinkle it with BROWN SUGAR and CINNAMON. Roll it up like a jelly roll, and cut into pieces about 3/4 inch thick. Place pieces horizontally into the pan with the syrup and bake.

a clothes dryer." Until then, Mom had pinned the wash on the clothesline, in warm and cold weather alike. She told someone, "Sometimes my wash pile got pretty high … My wash basket was always full, but I just asked the Lord for strength for the day. I couldn't have done it without him."

Occasional Playfulness

Mom was more comfortable with work than play. So we'd laugh especially hard when, after a lot of heavy-duty begging, we occasionally got her to stick out both her top and bottom dentures together while we all sat around the table after mealtime. We'd laugh hysterically, probably in relief that our mother was able to provide us this kind of fun, and Mom's belly shook along with our laughter.

One year at our cabin, where Mom was out of her normal routine, we went a step further. We managed to convince her not only to take out her false teeth but also to don a wig of long and stringy hair, a green cap, and a pair of sunglasses. When we got her to laughing without her teeth, she really looked like she had come straight from the hills of Appalachia, needing only a cigar to complete the effect. Of course, we got a picture of her, and one of us showed it to her brothers, who likewise got a good laugh from it. They welcomed her burst of playfulness as much as we did, but Mom did not appreciate us showing this portrayal of herself to them. Others' impressions of her were very important to her, and I suppose she wanted to maintain a dignified image in their eyes.

But Mom laid dignity aside when she put the cat in the washer early one morning. Kenyatta watched her do it, then hightailed it into Siobohn's room yelling, "Siobohn! Wake up! There's something wrong with Mom—she put the cat in the washer!" Siobohn bounded out of bed and joined Kenyatta behind the couch on the other side of the house to watch Mom from a safe distance. Mom was still in her nighty with her night slip hanging at least half a foot below, her hair in shambles, and her night covering hanging from her hair by one straight pin. There she was, trying to stuff the cat in the washer, appearing to have lost her sanity. "What are we going to do?" Siobohn asked Kenyatta. "I don't know!" replied Kenyatta. Who would have thought that Mom was just trying to get the cat to eat a mouse in the washer!

Every bit as unlikely was Mom causing her children to double over in laughter from an unexpected quip. One day when she was driving Siobohn and a friend to a school football game, she made a quick stop at Weis Markets. As they were leaving the parking lot, Siobohn's friend said, "Look at those hot guys," motioning to some guys standing outside the door of Weis. As the distance between them narrowed, Siobohn's friend said, "They are looking at us!" Usually quiet and reserved, Mom begged to differ as she drove over the curb. "No, they are just looking at your hot mom." Siobohn and her friend about died laughing!

Mom sometimes also surprised adults with her occasional playfulness. Like the time friends of Mom and Dad came to visit and brought with them their baby, who was a little older than newly born Parke. While Dad and his friend went out to the barn, Mom and her friend conspired. "Hey, let's trade our babies and see if they notice." When Dad's buddy came in, they called him over to look at "Masty's new baby," which was actually his own child. As he checked out the baby, they asked him, "What do you think? Who does he look like?" "Oh, I don't know," he replied. "They all look the same to me." Mom and her partner in crime laughed uproariously. "What are you laughing about?" he asked. "I meant what I said!" "We believe you!" they howled.

Was it this same playful spirit or an indignant reaction that led Mom to chase Dad upstairs with a broom on another day? I'll go with playful spirit, but either way, her reaction was unusual. Dad had headed upstairs for the night and found some laundry on top of the covers, blocking his side of the bed. Seeing one of Mom's bras in the pile, Dad got a naughty idea. He slipped his arms into the bra and traipsed downstairs wearing it. Appearing in the doorway, he asked in an innocent, plaintive-sounding voice, "Mom, where do you want me to put the wash on the bed?" "Masty!" Mom fired back from across the room. Looking up from the kitchen, I spotted Dad at the bottom of the winding stairway leading to their bedroom, grinning from ear to ear, the bra hanging from his arms across his chest. I wouldn't have believed it, but with my own eyes I saw Mom grab a broom and chase Dad up the stairs, with Dad laughing as he dodged her swats. We never knew how the story ended, but from what we saw, Dad had managed to coax a bit of historic playfulness out of Mom.

Feistiness

Mom did not usually find it so funny, however, when Dad teased her. Such was the case when Dad and Mom went to see Esther and Glenn in Maine and Dad discovered he could get the car to backfire by stepping on the gas then jerking his foot off the pedal. He enjoyed seeing Mom's startled reaction each time. Mom, on the other hand, told Dad to stop, but he kept doing it, and Mom lost her cool, pummeling his right shoulder with her fist. This must have startled Dad, because he said, "Mabel—get ahold of yourself."

Code of Life

More than anything, Mom wanted to do God's will. Maybe it began as a twelve-year-old girl when she nearly died from a burst appendix but recovered instead, and then, as though paying a debt she owed, promised God she would never read comics again. As I reflect back, it seems that even as an adult Mom had unrealistic ideas of what God expected of her. She had a deep devotion yet seemed to desperately need to do everything just right to please him. I wish she had experienced more of God's love and grace instead of this difficult struggle.

In her interpretation of what it meant to do God's will, Mom seemed to live by her own set of guidelines. Appearing to wrestle with inner turmoil, she took the counsel of others into consideration cautiously unless the counsel was clearly in line with her belief. Did she feel not good enough? Did she need to prove her opinion as worthy? Paradoxically, she seemed afraid of not pleasing God while also seeming to feel she had a direct line to God, frequently underscoring the rightness of her ideas with, "It came to me in the middle of the night," as though reporting a prophetic vision. Or she would find evidence in Scripture to back herself up. When we were selling our farm to Pennsylvania Power & Light Company but were asked to lease it from them and continue farming it—a good arrangement financially—Mom protested strongly and at first refused to sign the papers, invoking a passage in Psalms about "the children of Israel 'leasing' against God."

Following what she felt was a correct biblical code of ethics, Mom wore her prayer covering religiously—even at night. Since women were to cover their heads for prayer and "pray without ceasing" (I Thessalonians 5:17), it made sense to Mom to wear her covering at night as well as during the day. After all, what if she needed to pray at night? I can still see her kneeling in her nightgown, praying with a crumpled up old prayer covering on her head before she crawled into bed.

Mom raised us also with her own personal code of ethics. For instance, having had a brother with Down Syndrome, she forbade us to make light of any mentally challenged people. In addition, she would not allow us to get a piano for a long time in spite of our begging, defending her position by saying, "As they say, when pianos come into the home, it's not long until they come into the church," a situation that she viewed as worldly and unacceptable for the church. Anyone who came on our property couldn't miss the two big signs with glow-in-the-dark lettering that Mom had posted to the front of the corncrib. One of the signs said, "Prepare to meet thy God," and the other, "Christ is the answer." She left no doubt about where she stood.

Mom made her stance on things clear to her children as well. She saw to it, for example, that we did not become prideful. When Barb and Leona were teenagers, Mom made it her mission to enforce a lack of pride when they were in their bedroom getting ready for church. Leona dreaded the sound of Mom's footsteps because it meant the thick, black, wavy hair she had just carefully combed was about to be altered. Upon entering the room and seeing Leona's waves piled way too high, Mom would march over and squash the pride right out of them, flattening Leona's hair to the top of her head. Leona, whose spirits were likewise flattened, didn't dare protest.

As part of keeping us properly in line with her beliefs, Mom saw to it that her daughters began wearing the prayer covering at about eight or nine years of age whether we wanted to or not. It would have felt better if she had explained ahead of time why we didn't wait to wear it until baptism around age eleven or twelve as was the church norm. Allowing us to be part of the decision might also have been helpful. One day without warning, Mom announced to Sue that, come Sunday, she would need to start wearing a covering. Sure enough, when Sunday morning arrived, Mom took Sue's hair, bound it up into a bun and pinned a homemade covering over it. Furious, Sue refused to get out of the car when we pulled into the church parking lot. Instead, she removed the covering, released the confined bun, and braided her hair in the two long braids with which she was familiar. I walked into the church that Sunday feeling that Sue had been terribly wronged by this violation of her free will. Then, because she had refused to wear the covering, she was not allowed to go with the family to visit friends that afternoon. During the wait at home, Sue's conscience got the best of her and she apologized to Mom when the family returned from visiting friends, saying that next Sunday she would wear the covering. From this point on, I began braiding my own hair and determined to never be alone with Mom lest I also became a victim of her prayer-covering coercion. Because I could not seem to get Mom's approval anyway, it seemed prudent to at least protect myself from her.

All too soon, however, I let my guard down and found myself alone in the living room with Mom while holding Mim, who was a baby at that time. Shortly before this, we'd had revival meetings at our church, where many of my friends had responded to the invitation to "confess their sins and accept Jesus into their hearts." Wondering what, exactly, I was supposed to feel, I had not responded. Mom had noticed. Sure enough, she now queried, "Well, I see that your friends have decided to become disciples of Jesus. What are you going to do?" Aiming to appease, I quickly landed on what I thought would be my best option—"I'm going to join the instruction class." That seemed to suffice. Soon after, I began wearing a prayer covering and cape dress but still combed my hair myself.

One of the few times I felt close to Mom was the day I sat in the front seat of the station wagon with Dad driving, Mom in the middle, and me on the passenger side. I had on the prayer covering and cape dress I had just begun wearing, and I had the strange sensation that Mom approved of me while I sat close to her. It felt good. Still, I wondered—was it me she approved of or the clothes I was wearing?

Mom enforced her beliefs with the boys as well as the girls. She wouldn't allow them, for example, free access to Dad's hunting magazines, such as *Sports Afield*, *Outdoor Life*, *Pennsylvania Game News*, or *Field and Stream*, because she objected to the beer and cigarette advertisements and "didn't want them to fill their minds with hunting all the time." Only the most recent editions were on Dad's desk. The attic housed boxes of older versions of such magazines, with vivid hunting and fishing scenes on their covers and stories designed to stir the red blood of any male. Only with special permission did Pete get to spend some wonderful hours up in the attic transported to distant times, places, and adventures hunting mule deer, elk, grizzly bears, and huge midwestern whitetails.

A few years later when Pete had a nasty cold, he stayed home from school because he was afraid of spreading germs to the other students. Mom, conceding her stance on too much hunting, took him up to the mountain to go turkey hunting. Being out in the fresh mountain air was just what he needed to get rid of the cold. Mom must have seen how much good hunting did for Pete since it seems that when she saw the benefits to being outside, she modified her aversion to hunting somewhat.

Mom's high moral standards matched her high ethical standards. She was strong and clear in her teaching about not having sex before marriage, using "Keep yourself pure" as her motto. After she said this one too many times for Sue, Sue asked with conjured-up innocence, "What do you mean by 'pure'?" intending to pressure Mom into elaborating. But Mom skillfully avoided the question. "Oh, you'll understand when you get older," she said. Mom also placed a book on sexual standards in an obvious place on the bookshelf in the living room. As she hoped, our curiosity got the best of us, and we checked it out, learning what we could. Who knows—we may have even gotten some insight about what "keeping ourselves pure" meant.

Strategically reinforcing the message, Mom put a pamphlet about sexual behavior on a stand beside my brothers' bed. It may have been comic relief or it may have been protest at having yet another teaching about morality thrown at them, but one of my brothers drew tongues touching on the man and the woman pictured on the front of the pamphlet. If Mom had felt more comfortable with the topic of sex, we might have had some enlightening teaching about it being a gift, normalizing it as natural for the right circumstance.

An enigma about mom was that while she held the line in some areas, she was flexible in others. She consistently disciplined us for out-of-line behavior yet bent the rules and gave us crackers or cookies before mealtime when we were hungry. She had a strong moral code yet seemed almost relieved when one of us—namely, one of my brothers—pushed her boundaries out a bit with something earthy, at which times she giggled. And then there was the seemingly contradictory time near Christmas when Mom coaxed us to sit on Santa's lap in a department store. At age seven, I already knew how strongly Mom felt about us understanding the true meaning of Christmas, so it took me by surprise when she stopped beside the line of children waiting to sit on Santa's lap and quietly yet confidently nudged us into the same line. Dreading the moment, when my turn came I approached Santa slowly and shyly. This Santa was not overly friendly, and I sat stiffly on his red, velvet lap until my time was up. But it was worth it to see that Mom seemed pleased I had met with Santa.

Taking in More Children

Driven by something many of us did not understand, Mom could be counted on to take in anyone else's children. Sometimes she did it publicly and sometimes privately, but always she sought out children, whether the eight New York City children from Fresh Air—a program offering city children the experience of living in the country for two weeks—or children from the community for a few weeks during the summer; or children from poor families in the community who found it hard to take care of them for a period of time.

Over the years, Mom took in seventeen foster children on a temporary basis. While this appeared quite admirable to others, when I was young we secretly resented Mom taking in the needy children of others when she already had all of us wanting more of her attention. It seemed she loved these other children more than us. One of them, a toddler, stood at the side of his crib wailing, "Ednaaaa" for his mother. Sue, seeing this as her perfect opportunity, stole into the bedroom and pinched the toddler, smug about expressing her jealousy and dislike of him so well.

Barb, Leona, and friend, with two children (2nd from left and sitting) from the Fresh Air program

The times when Mom went on campaigns to adopt more children were also times when her emotional vulnerability seemed especially great. My sister Barbara said she always knew when Mom was pregnant because that was when Mom would unfurl her adoption flag. Mom said she wanted to adopt more children because she wanted to start an orphanage, but I wondered if she was actually combating the oh-no-I'm-pregnant-again feeling by trying to communicate, "I'm good with this, and just to prove it I'll take in a few more."

One time Mom campaigned to take in a set of biracial twins from an acquaintance who was placing them for adoption. I had seen these twins only once or twice, but that was all it took to know I disliked them. How could Mom want them so much when she already had so many of us, and there wasn't enough of her to go around as it was? I was bewildered this time and each time Mom pursued adopting more children against the wishes of the rest of the family, and I lived in constant fear about what Mom might do next when it came to taking in more children. I could never understand why it seemed we were just not enough for her.

My feeling of desperation regarding adoption of the twins dissipated somewhat when Barb went on strike about the situation, telling Mom, "If you adopt these twins, I'm leaving." Surely this would get Mom's attention. I found refuge in the company of my older sisters when we gathered in a huddle to put our heads and hearts together to try to figure out what was going on with Mom. Where did her need come from to take in or adopt more children? What was it that made her enjoy her foster children so much—that gave her an extra spark to take care of other children? Was it her "missionary" mentality?

I do not know exactly when Mom stopped trying to adopt children on her own, but when she was in her seventies, with Dad's approval she took in newborn babies born to incarcerated women at a nearby prison. The babies were placed in private homes by a lawyer who made it his mission to reunite the mothers with their children after their term was finished so the babies would not be placed in the hands of social services. Many of these babies came from drug-addicted moms, making them restless sleepers. Mom would hold the babies close and calm them, singing *Jesus Loves Me*. Mom loved every one of these babies, sometimes torn inside when she had to place a child in the arms of a mother it hardly knew. This was especially true for little William, who cried and reached out for Mom—the only mother he knew— as his birth mother walked away with him. For several weeks after that, Mom wondered out loud how William was doing.

Kenyatta and Siobohn

Thankfully, two of the babies Mom did not have to give up; they became my two youngest sisters, Kenyatta and Siobohn. The time was right at that point for Mom to take on the additional responsibility for their care, and her inclusive, welcoming, caring nature drew them right into our circle. When they came to us—Kenyatta first, Siobohn next—they were embraced with open hearts and waiting arms by the whole family. They were ours and we were theirs.

When Siobohn and Kenyatta were able to understand, Mom and Dad explained that their mothers loved them very much. When one of Siobohn's classmates said, "Her mother just didn't want her," Mim, standing close by, intervened by saying,

"Birth mothers love their children very much, when they realize they can't take care of them and allow them to be placed in a loving home."

Kenyatta

Kenyatta was a smiley baby with dark curls covering her little head and dark eyes to match shining out from under the curls. We

L-r: Kenyatta, Mom, and Siobohn

placed her bassinet in the family room, where she was surrounded by sounds of family even as she slept. When she awoke, she would raise herself up as high as she could on her belly, trying to see whoever was next to her in the room. One day she strained to make eye contact with Dad and Dale but was unable to raise her head high enough. Her smile spread up through her barely visible eyebrows, however, and it didn't take long for Dale to go over and pick her up. Who could resist that pleasant, winsome personality of hers? Clearly not Mim, who loved bringing Kenyatta into bed with her in the morning so she could talk to her and cuddle with her.

When Kenyatta was about five months old, her mother was released from prison and came to pick her up. That was a sad day for our family. I had already been married and lived in Virginia, but I felt the family's grief across the miles. The next three years of Kenyatta's life were a myriad of crisscrossing paths between multiple caregivers after her mother was again incarcerated. Kenyatta was allowed to visit us periodically but always had to leave again, crying and protesting, pulling at Mom's heartstrings, desperately pleading for Mom to intervene.

Mom kept in touch with Kenyatta's grandfather, who became a more permanent caregiver just before Kenyatta returned to Mom and Dad again three days before her fourth birthday, subdued and less trusting. Wondering what all she had experienced in the first four years of her life, we just hugged her more tightly and loved her. Mom and Dad were finally able to adopt Kenyatta when she was nine years old. This was a day of celebration for us for sure.

Siobohn

Siobohn, with her big blue eyes and fun personality, found her way into our hearts about a year after Kenyatta had left as an infant. Mom and Dad kept a watchful eye on her when they learned her mother had made an escape from prison. Her mother was soon found and returned again to prison. When she was finally released, she wanted to spare Siobohn being uprooted, so she allowed Mom and Dad to adopt her.

Siobohn grew into a very active toddler, climbing onto the chair at Mim's desk and scribbling on her papers, then grabbing a pile of magazines and throwing them into the bathwater like a flash of lightning, too quick to stop.

She was also, you could say, innovative even at a young age. One day when her older sisters were upstairs with some visiting friends, she wanted to go join them in the worst kind of way. Dad tried to keep her from going up to the girls. At first he thought he had succeeded, only to discover that she had quietly slipped by him when he got absorbed in reading the paper. He just laughed kind of proudly and said, "She'll be able to figure out how to do things."

Tina

About fifteen years before Kenyatta and Siobohn joined our family, we experienced the joy of adoption for the first time. It all started with our neighbor lady, Bev, excitedly calling Mom one day, saying, "Mabel, you've got to come up here to see what I have!" When Mom arrived at the house, Bev motioned her into the next room and pointed at a dresser drawer on the floor. Peering in, Mom

At left: Tina at her birth mother's house. At right: Taken after Tina started living with us.

laid eyes on the face of a baby girl just a few months old. She fell in love instantly. The baby's name was Tina.

Tina ended up staying with Bev for days at a time whenever her mother and stepfather asked Bev to babysit. When Bev felt she could no longer keep Tina for such long stretches, she called Mom, who then began babysitting Tina. Tina stayed for extended periods at our house also. During these times, she was embraced within our family circle.

Because Mom and Dad wanted to give Tina a permanent place of belonging and security, they approached her mother and stepfather a couple of times about adopting her. But each time the answer was no. It was apparent that Tina's mother loved her very much and seemed to be having a hard time giving her up. Mom contacted a lawyer to be on standby just in case Tina's mother and stepfather changed their minds. The lawyer, who wanted the same thing for Tina as Mom and Dad did, tried his best to facilitate the adoption.

This went on until Tina was about five years old. At that point, Mom finally had enough. She wanted Tina to have the security of knowing where her home really was. I still remember the day Mom came to tell me she was taking Tina back to her mother and stepfather. I was in the attic, and I recoiled in anger so strong I couldn't see straight, fearing for Tina's well-being and feeling Mom was being heartless in taking her away. Tina belonged to us! And what about how Tina was feeling? Did Mom not even consider that?

Although Tina had expressed her wish to live with us, Mom went ahead and got her things together. What Mom was doing didn't make sense to me, because I knew she loved Tina very much. Staring through a window in the attic, I watched Tina walk in front of Mom down the sidewalk toward the car, my eighteen-year-old soul churning with anger and anguish as Mom put Tina and her belongings inside the car then drove away.

What I didn't know was that Mom had called Tina's mother and stepfather ahead of time saying she was bringing Tina back and unless they were willing to sign adoption papers they were not to bring her to our house anymore. When Tina's mother realized Mom meant business in bringing her back to stay, she quickly agreed to sign the adoption papers. Mom, it seemed, had been exercising the wisdom of Solomon.

And finally, because of two mothers loving their child enough to give her up to the other, Tina became legally what she had already become in our hearts—a full member of our family.

Self-Care

This poem by Mary F. Butt (slightly different than the original) that Mom hung in her room bore witness to her life:

Build a little fence of trust

Around to-day;

Fill the space with loving work,

And therein stay.

Look not through the sheltering bars

Upon to-morrow;

God will help thee bear whatever comes

Of joy or sorrow.

As the burdens accumulated of birthing so many children and of working so hard in her body, soul, and spirit, Mom sought renewal in quilting, sewing circle, reading her many devotionals, and talking to other women. At times, she would go into great detail about things she found traumatic, such as the death of someone dear to her. She seemed to enter another world as she recounted events like the death of little Jamie, a handicapped girl for whom she had provided care for several months.

My young self found some of Mom's self-care methods incomprehensible. Of those was her visits with Bev, a neighbor who lived on a farm near us. Bev sought Mom out, showing up randomly at the house, and Mom welcomed her, appearing to find soul food through their deep conversations, though after Bev left, Mom would make comments giving the impression she was trying to influence Bev with her faith. They were an odd pair, sitting close together on the porch, talking in hushed undertones—Mom in her modest cape dress and covering and Bev in tight, red shorts and sleeveless top, smoking a cigarette. Bev knew what was going on with all the other neighbors, so maybe listening to her was one way Mom kept up with what was going on around her. Or maybe the draw to Bev was in connecting with another woman, albeit very different from Mom. One connection the two held in common was deep affection for a family member with Down syndrome—Bev with her daughter and Mom with her younger brother Omar.

In spite of all the things I did not understand about Mom, I drew comfort from believing that in her heart she wanted to do the right thing. Her stack of devotional books—blue, brown, and red—on the bathroom windowsill told me so, and I drew comfort from them. Sometimes during the day Mom would retreat to the bathroom

and her books. Annoyed at having to track her down, I'd call to her from the bottom of the stairs and catch a barely audible, "What?" wisping out from under the door. But I couldn't hold this against Mom, because I believed those devotional books somehow kept her going. And the way she fervently sang *Be Still My Soul* during the middle of the day as she went about her work was like she was holding on to something for dear life.

Another place Mom found calming stillness was in the quilting and knotting that she so loved to do. She could quilt or knot comforters for hours, by herself and with other

Mom crocheting a baby cap

women, quietly creating beauty in the midst of chaos. Maybe it was because she liked to quilt and knot or maybe it was a survival tactic that prompted Mom to make each of us a quilt and a comforter. Either way, we reaped the benefits of her sewing.

One of the women from church hosted sewing circle once a month in her large living room. Some of my younger siblings and I joined Mom in this monthly gathering, playing with our friends as our mothers sewed. Traipsing down the long, cement walkway to the front entrance of the stone farmhouse, paper bag lunches in hand, we were like little ducklings following their mother. Mom, carrying her little portable Singer sewing machine, led the way, her steps quickening as she approached the house. Soon, the quiet hum of sewing machines and women's voices joined together, filling the room. Women sewed clothing or knotted a comforter, its edges sewed onto cloth strips tacked onto a four-piece wooden quilting frame with corners held together by aluminum clamps. Everything Mom helped to make at sewing circle went to relief work, a cause close to her heart.

Mom also knitted bandages for lepers in Africa, crocheted yellow caps and sachets, and sewed pink and blue kimonos for Christmas relief projects. The caps, sachets, and kimonos, along with a baby rattle, were wrapped into a soft, yellow, flannel blanket and held in place by blue and white baby safety pins. Mom sewed a label onto each blanket and had each of us write our name on one of the labels, identifying us as the one giving the bundle. My heart and my own importance swelled as I helped send my bundle to a baby somewhere across the world. The satisfaction Mom got from being involved in relief work as well as from getting us involved was definitely part of her self-care.

One time, however, Mom's mission mind went rogue. Her need to be involved in missions grew so compelling that she began talking to a mission agency about going abroad on a mission assignment by herself. Somewhere along the way she dropped the plan, probably because the agency would not bless a mission assignment that involved leaving behind a family. What was she thinking?? My guess is that she was emotionally unstable at the time and thought God was leading her to do that. I wonder how much pregnancy hormones, postpartum depression, and menopause impacted her responses. She once said she didn't experience menopausal issues like some women did, but I wonder if she was simply unaware of the issues that can come with menopause.

Later, it seemed Mom came to see her own children as her mission field. As a speaker at a 1999 Mother's Day meeting, she gave this advice:

"I would say to the young mothers, having children and raising them for the Lord is the greatest career you could choose. The daily duties of raising children sometimes seems to be a heavy burden keeping us from serving the Lord in more important ways. But if we keep standing in the right position to the Son, our shadow of influence will have the right effect on our children. They will go places and do things for the Lord we never can. Which is more valuable? The doing or the influence? The first will not happen without the second."

Many years earlier, when I was about ten years old, Mom went to a summer women's retreat. She returned home looking genuinely peaceful and refreshed, mirroring her report of the event. I wish she could have gone every year. What might that have done for her? If I could rewind life, I would strongly encourage her to do just this. Perhaps we overlooked the fact that we all have limited inner resources, and when those resources are not replenished, we are more likely to behave in unacceptable ways—Mom included.

In the Final Analysis

We all have light parts that we shine for others to see and shadow parts that we try to hide. This was true of Mom. It is also true of me. It is true of all of us. I have carried on Mom's legacy of being known yet unknown, for I have light parts that I want others to see and shadow parts that I try to keep hidden from others. It was probably the unpredictable, unknown part of Mom that I, as an adolescent, reacted negatively to. Propelled by fear that I would become like her, I obsessively did everything I could to prevent myself from turning into her. In spite of my best attempts, however, it happened. I am just like her in the way I love kids, in the way I persevere, in the way I am undaunted by hard work, and, I admit, in the way I try to keep certain things about me hidden from others.

I live in a time when introspection and searching one's soul for both the light and the dark are encouraged. Not so for Mom. If she had lived in such

Mom

a time, how might it have changed things for her? I don't know. The unknown about Mom has forced me to do my own self-examination. Who am I? Why do I do the things I do? Undoubtedly the people in our lives as we are growing up influence who we become. It was true for Mom, and it is true for me.

One such influence in my life came unexpectedly from a seminar speaker I heard when I was eighteen years old. The speaker challenged the audience to try to "see a particular person you are having trouble relating to as God sees them." It was an "aha" moment that freed me to approach Mom in a different way—to consciously reach out to her to try to bridge the gap between us. I knew that my siblings, her friends, Dad, and so many other people experienced Mom in a completely different way than I did. The speaker's reminder allowed me to embrace and love the fact that she was a many-sided woman, a complex woman who was indeed a remarkable person demonstrating remarkable resilience and strength in the way she lived her life. I am deeply grateful that my younger siblings experienced Mom when she was at her best and that they did not know the mother I experienced during my growing up years—a time when Mom had some of her greatest personal struggles.

In spite of all I do not know about Mom, I now know that in her times of fragility, she really was a strong person. Even when she seemed to be barely holding it together, she was held together by a strength beyond herself that she reached out to. And though we were confused and put off by the way she went about trying to adopt more children and go into mission work by herself, six of her children have brought children into their own families through adoption and foster care, and many of us have been involved in mission work. I guess you could say we are carrying out her vision. Maybe it's because we saw how very important it was to her and have now taken on its importance ourselves. It seems right that in 1997, six years before her death, Mom was able to go to Russia with her granddaughter Bethanie Burkholder to spend time at an orphanage.

When asked near the end of her life if she would do it all over again, Mom responded, "Yes, the hard part is letting go and not being able to do it anymore." She could very well have written the following song herself, as its message seems to express her inner longing and experience.

How Can I Keep from Singing?
My life flows on in endless song,
Above earth's lamentation.
I catch the sweet, though far-off hymn
That hails a new creation.

Chorus:
No storm can shake my inmost calm
While to that rock I'm clinging;
Since Love is Lord of heaven and earth,
How can I keep from singing?

Through all the tumult and the strife,
I hear that music ringing;
It finds an echo in my soul.
How can I keep from singing?

What though my joys and comforts die?
The Lord my Savior liveth.
What though the darkness gather 'round?
Songs in the night he giveth.

The peace of Christ makes fresh my heart,
A fountain ever springing!
All things are mine since I am his!
How can I keep from singing?

—Robert Wadsworth Lowry

5. Mast Beiler Stoltzfus: Dad

"If you're with your honey and your nose is runny,
you may think it's funny, but it's snot."

One fine spring day, Dad was bringing a pickup load of us children home from school. Pulling out onto the main road from a side road, he did not see a closely approaching vehicle in his lane. Who knows where his mind was—maybe he was talking to us, maybe he was correcting one of us, maybe he was preoccupied with how he was going to make ends meet—no one knew, or at least no one remembers. But we do remember what happened next. As luck would have it, it was a state policeman in the approaching vehicle, who had to slam on his brakes and swerve into the right lane to avoid hitting Dad. Whipping in behind Dad, he flipped on his flashing red lights. When Dad stopped and rolled down his window, the policeman, probably a bit rattled, hotly interrogated Dad on why he had pulled out in front of him. Not getting the reaction from Dad's calm responses that he seemed to be wanting, the policeman finally let loose. "Don't you even care about your kids, pulling out in front of me like that?!" That did it. Dad lost his cool. In a passionate burst of anger, he told the cop off. "How dare you accuse me of such a thing?" As Dad drove away down the road, he complained loudly and at length, spouting off about the audacity of the cop to ask him a question like that. Not care about his children?? That was the last straw!

A study in contrasts, Dad was both transparent and complex. He did not give pat answers, yet he voiced strong opinions. He was quick to express his feelings yet remained able to contain strong feelings when necessary. He was impatient yet tolerant, tough yet tender, compassionate yet harsh. He lashed out verbally yet spoke encouragingly. He was very clear about what he thought and felt, yet remained a puzzle with some of the pieces not seeming to go together at times. Shaped and formed by forces perhaps unknown even to him, Dad lived his life as authentically as he knew how. This we knew—he had a touch of earthiness, loved humor, and laughed easily. Dad was passionate about a lot of things but most of all about us.

The Early Years

Born May 23, 1913, one mile south of Morgantown, Pennsylvania, my father, Mast Beiler Stoltzfus, grew up as the second youngest child in a family of eight boys and four girls. His parents expected him to work hard, and he learned the meaning of endurance at an early age. As a little boy, he walked a mile to and

Dad in elementary school

from school each day, morning and evening. On cold winter days, he ducked into Hartz's Feed Mill to warm up. Barely getting time to play, Dad milked cows by hand, hoed acres of thistles, and planted, cut, and husked corn by hand. He cut wheat with a cradle, tied it into sheaves, and pitched the sheaves on a wagon one by one with a pitchfork while someone on the wagon put them in place. Then he rode on top of the pile of sheaves into the barn where they were thrashed. In the barn, his job was to watch over the four horses walking in a circle, each pulling the end of a pole attached to a shaft that turned the threshing machine at the center of the poles.

When the family got their first hay loader, Dad was relieved. No longer would he have to heap rakes full of hay into a large pile on the ground and pitch it onto a wagon by hand. But he did still have to manually pitch wheat sheaves on a wagon with a fork.

Such outdoor labor carried its share of risk. One spring day, Dad's twelve-year-old brother, Paul, who was the fourth child and second son, died from a tragic head injury while rolling grass in a field. Good with horses for his age, Paul was using a log roller pulled by horses—the primitive forerunner of the present day cultipacker that crushes and levels dirt clods in plowed fields—when one horse started running and kicking. The other horses joined in, and as they all ran together down over a hill, Paul fell forward under the roller. Five days later he died. Dad was born two years after Paul's death, yet the sadness his family carried about their tragic loss trickled into Dad's young soul.

Some of the stories Dad told us about his life made me wonder if he was carrying other hurts all the way from boyhood to becoming an adult. For example, in elementary school, his classmates made fun of him about the clothes he wore; today it would be called bullying. I imagine that Dad put on a tough face at the time, acting like his schoolmates' taunts didn't affect him, but as we could see, they lodged deep enough in his memory to survive and surface decades afterward.

Another experience that went deep for Dad happened with his beagle dog Daisy when he was about twelve years old. Daisy and Dad were tight. She was Dad's hunting buddy, wagging her tail furiously whenever she saw him coming with gun in hand, ready and eager to join him on yet another adventure of hunting squirrels or rabbits. One day, for reasons unknown to Dad, his mother told him he needed to get rid of Daisy. I imagine Dad already crying inside as he obediently got his gun and walked outside to find Daisy. Daisy wagged her tail at him as she saw him approaching, but this time she would not be going on a hunting expedition with him. Dad told her to stay, which she did obediently while Dad backed up a distance from her, raised his gun, and shot one bullet. The floodgate of Dad's tears broke, and he cried as if his heart was broken. Probably it was. Not only would he miss his best friend terribly, he had also betrayed her. Sadly, there was likely no one there to comfort him.

Dad's heart was broken deeply again when the girl he was about to ask to marry him cheated on him. Dad never talked about this much; he just sort of mentioned it in passing as if he were talking about what he'd had for dinner the night before. Apparently one of Dad's brothers had come to him one day telling him there was something he thought Dad needed to know—that Dad's girlfriend was seeing another man. This was a betrayal for which there were no words and only time could heal. Dad found an outlet for himself by walking the fence row like his father had before him, crying day after day until the pain lessened.

Dad was about moving forward in spite of losses. His losses were part of him, but they did not hold him back.

The Obvious: Outward Appearance

When we spread Dad's belongings among us after his death, we realized certain articles of clothing had been immortalized—his green cap being one of them, with its grease-marked band lining the inside. It matched his green work clothes and smelled just like Dad, a distinct smell, maybe of hair that held the honest sweat of his brow from many days' work outside.

Just a whiff of that much-loved cap brings a slideshow of heart-filled memories—Dad's hard work, companionship, laughter, compassion, and passions; Dad walking outside around the farm buildings with a distinct, purposeful gait, always appearing to be on a mission, his upper torso tilting slightly

forward and arms swinging lightly at his sides. His muscular body accompanied an angular, tanned face; bushy, dark eyebrows (which mom often trimmed while giving Dad a haircut) that claimed their spot above his glasses; and thick, dark hair. That lush hair would eventually turn into a beautiful white as he grew older, even as his eyebrows remained defiantly dark.

The smell of Dad's cap also brings into focus his broad, calloused hands—hairy on top with large, raised veins, and long fingers ending in wide fingernails with an ever-present bit of "hard work dirt" under them. We'd often catch a glimpse of Dad's tough, calloused palms and we came to know them as evidence of years of disciplined and diligent labor.

Dad also used his hands to talk—fingers spread wide open, filling spaces between the words with "Okay," "Why uh," and "Yeah, well," while

Dad in his familiar, green work clothes

sitting in his chair discussing history, the church, and anything else of particular interest to him.

And always, Dad's cap will bring the sound of his hearty laughter springing up from somewhere deep down inside of him, his whole face breaking into a broad smile with the flash of his infectious, white-toothed smile. Elvin now owns the cap.

History

When Dad would come home and take off his cap, he'd sit in his chair and read with legs crossed and work shoes protruding. Reading was one of his favorite pastimes; he was insatiable, reading every chance he got. He had a lifetime subscription to *Hoards Dairyman*, a couple other farm magazines, and various hunting magazines. He also subscribed to *National Geographic* and *Reader's Digest*. And we got *The Daily Item* a day late from the mailman—it was secondhand and nearly free that way.

Dad also loved history. He knew facts, times, and places liked the back of his hand. And when he told stories of times past—whether it was his own family history, American history, or the history of the Buffalo Valley—his listeners were transported with him on a journey of bringing the past into the present.

When he was thirteen years old, Dad picked up the *Mast Family History* book and noticed that "Stoltzfus" Amish and Mennonites mentioned in the book had been buried in a cemetery in Union County in the Buffalo Valley. He asked his parents about this and learned there had been an Amish/Mennonite settlement there beginning in 1830 and ending in 1890, the cemetery being the only remaining evidence of that Amish/Mennonite church. He listened as his mother told him about the beauty of Buffalo Valley, the time she herself once visited the cemetery, and the story of the trouble in the church that led to it falling apart. His curiosity was piqued when he learned of several people in the Conestoga Mennonite Church, where he was attending at the time, who had actually been born in the settlement at Buffalo Valley. Their stories drew him in—how they loaded all their family's belongings into three railroad cars and moved back to Lancaster County, Pennsylvania, leaving the settlement behind. As an adult, Dad wished he had learned more from these people about life in Union County. Could it be that part of him was already there in their stories?

In the summer of 1937, Dad stepped into his curiosity about Union County and decided he would experience it personally. So he, Mast Beiler Stoltzfus, took his young bride, Mabel Kurtz Petersheim, and her parents, Barbara and Jonathan Petersheim, with him to the Dutch Masters Hunting Club (later to be known to us as "the Cabin") in northern Pennsylvania, where he was then an active member. On their way home, Dad turned off Route 15 to make a stop in Buffalo Valley. He wanted to see it for himself. He asked people questions about their experience of living there, and as they talked, he turned his head to gaze with longing at the fertile fields of grain and corn stretching along valleys through long mountain ranges. Taking in the details of the farms, he noted that hog raising and dairy farming were popular and that barns were built in an L shape, with vents instead of windows, unlike those he was accustomed to.

During his visit to Buffalo Valley, Dad was also drawn to the Susquehanna River and its tree-lined banks winding through the area. Though there was no Mennonite church in this "untamed" region, Dad was not able to get Buffalo Valley out of his mind. So he explored the possibility of moving there, checking with his parents and Mom's parents. All their responses were a resounding "No!" Nevertheless, his fascination with the area grew, and his connection with it became stronger. In the spring of 1953, Dad moved his family—which included nine children by then—from Oley to the Buffalo Valley in Union County, and the stream of history that had stopped could begin flowing again.

None of the relatives were happy about the move to Buffalo Valley. In fact, when Dad's good friend and sister, Miriam, and her family came to visit for the first time, Miriam disdainfully kicked the dirt beneath her feet and said, "This dirt looks like shit!"

Personality and Character

Like Miriam, Dad had his own form of earthiness and did not pretend otherwise. He endeared himself to us through his humanity—his awareness of it, comfort with it, and struggle with it, wanting to be better, and most of the time succeeding in doing the right thing. We watched him cry, throw back his head in laughter, be mischievous, self-preserving, opinionated, quick-tempered, and in the end, ask for forgiveness. We learned what it was to be human from watching Dad.

Dad's no-nonsense approach anchored our family. He maintained a stance of holding life together even when things were falling apart around him. He drew me into his circle of warmth even while sometimes confusing me by his responses. On the one hand, I knew I was loved by him, and on the other hand, I never knew when he might lash out at me or my siblings. But the magnetic pull of his heart was greater than the threat of his intense emotions. In spite of the things I did not understand about Dad, I noticed he was comfortable inside his own skin. This made him more approachable to me.

Sense of Humor, Playfulness

Dad's sense of humor was a big part of his amiability. It was tinged with earthiness and allowed us to relax, lay aside our cares for the moment, and allow joy to bubble up from our inner being. His laughter, and ours joining his, lifted our souls and spirits like an electrical surge. When someone's nose was running, Dad would quip, "If you're with your honey and your nose is runny, you may think it's funny, but it's snot," putting us in touch with our humanity, teaching us to be comfortable with ourselves at a deeper level.

Dad's quips popped up in all sorts of places. Ada was a little runner. She ran and ran without getting tired. Noticing this, Dad would sometimes chant, "Ada-potato, my little spud, she ran so fast she fell in the mud." And we siblings would chime right in with, "And she couldn't get out until Paul (a boy we teased her about) came along and pulled her out with a cheery song."

Creating little ditties was just one part of Dad's quick-witted humor. One day when Pete was about eight years old, he was standing out by the corner of the barn beside Dad, who was engaged in conversation with a fertilizer salesman. Buzzing in upon their conversation, a small-engine airplane flew overhead. Our collie dogs, as they usually did whenever a plane interrupted their afternoon naps, leapt off the porch in hot pursuit across the fields. The fertilizer salesman exclaimed, "Wow, look at them go! They took off like rockets!" Dad responded in his droll sort of way, "Well, you ought to see them when a jet goes over!" Dad and the salesman both laughed heartily, while Pete beamed, proud of Dad's quick comeback.

Dad's hearty laughter had a way of lightening the atmosphere around him. One solemn day, Sue, Esther, and I were having a funeral for one of our beloved farm cats—a tri-colored black, brown, and white cat who had died of unknown causes. Aiming to give it a well-earned proper funeral, we lowered it carefully into a shoe box lined with pink cloth and placed the lid securely on top. With shovel in hand, we filed out to the orchard, stopping at a weathered old apple tree where we dug a hole deep enough for the box to fit into. But just as we were starting to shovel the dirt over our beloved companion, our bull, who had been standing with a herd of cows in the corner of the orchard, lowered his head and began walking with alarming and purposeful speed away from the herd and toward us. Bringing the ceremonious burial to an abrupt halt, we fled to the nearest escape route, scrambling frantically to crawl under the electric fence without getting shocked. As the bull—now standing on the side of the fence we'd just escaped from—shook his head and walked away, loud laughter erupted nearby, and we realized Dad had witnessed the whole thing. Our rapidly beating hearts slowed a notch or two as we watched the menacing bull change course and Dad's laughter dissipated the scariness of it all.

Dad found humor in many places, including the comics in our "secular" newspaper, *The Daily Item*. We loved it when he shared the "By George" daily comic with us. With the newspaper spread open in front of him at the end of the table after a meal, he would turn to the comic strips and start laughing as we sat in expectation, smiles beginning to spread around the table, waiting for him to tell us as he always did what the cartoon was about. He didn't pass the newspaper around for us to see for ourselves; he just told us about it as he laughed, but we got the picture. Dad especially liked "By George" because he enjoyed humor that "turned something on its head," which this particular comic strip frequently did.

Sometimes Dad's humor took an odd twist. Once, for example, a male dog came to our farm paying a call to one of our female collies who was in heat. The male dog persistently hung around, paying no heed to our efforts to make him leave. Dad proceeded to tie a string of cans to the dog's tail, chortling like a kid when the startled dog took off like a streak, high-tailing it for home with the cans rattling behind. It worked. The male dog got the point and did not return. But the dog's owners probably wondered who the scoundrel was that tied cans to their dog's tail. Leave it to Dad.

Even when it came to difficult things, Dad knew how to use humor to ease the situation. We never liked to ask Dad for money, and he must have sensed this, because he sometimes made it into a playful thing, sparing us the awkwardness of having to be straightforward in our request. This happened to Barb when she was finally able to drive by herself and Mom asked her to go to the grocery store to pick up some things. But first, Mom told Barb, she needed to go out to the field where Dad was working and ask for money to buy the groceries. When Dad saw Barb coming, he somehow knew she was on this difficult mission and pretended to hide behind a wagon where he was working, in order to make her "find" him. By the time Barb came face-to-face with Dad, she was laughing, and the difficult task had turned into a fun thing.

Dad found humor also in a mischievous sort of way, such as the time Barb bought a Mitch Miller record and Mom said Barb was only allowed to play it in the living room—separate from the main living area—since she didn't want to take a chance of it negatively influencing the rest of us. Sometimes when Barb was listening to it, Dad would listen to it with her, laughing at the song *Sweet Violets*, whose lyrics took unexpected twists such as:

There once was a farmer who took a young miss

In back of the barn where he gave her a …

Lecture on horses and chickens and eggs

And told her that she had such beautiful …

Manners, (etc.)

Dad used every opportunity he could to have fun with his friends as well. It was common for us to have company on Sunday evenings when we didn't have church, and sometimes when a family was just about to leave, Dad would reach through the open car window and quickly tap the arm of the man in the driver's side, saying with a twinkle in his eyes, "Last tag!" This always meant the other man, even if he was shy or quiet, got out of the car to chase Dad to give him back "last tag." Two grown men laughing, running clumsily across the yard … now this was a wonder to behold.

I loved seeing Dad's no-nonsense approach to life give way to playfulness, bringing it out even in other grown men.

Other times when a family visited us on Sunday evenings, Dad would turn the clock back an hour so that when the family started talking about needing to go home soon, it was actually an hour later than they thought. When the family found him out and learned what time it really was, Dad would laugh in great delight. I recently saw a friend I hadn't seen since my youth, and one of the first things she said to me with a big smile was, "I remember when we were visiting you one time and your Dad turned the clock back …"

On evenings when we did have church, occasionally one of us would be left lying asleep on a hard church bench after succumbing to a service that had seemed to go on forever. To make sure we were all accounted for, after one or two times too many of someone being left behind, Dad started doing roll call on the way home from church. "Sue … Rose … Edith … John … Pete … Tim … Elvin …" One evening after we left church, Tim, about four years old, did not respond during roll call. It didn't take long to discover he was not in the car. Dad turned the station wagon around right in the middle of the road and drove back to church just a little fast, relieved to find Tim sleeping soundly on a church bench, oblivious to his solitary state in the totally dark building. One of Dad's friends, who was still talking to someone on the church porch when Dad came back for Tim, was quite amused to see Dad carry his sleeping son out of church, and he gave him a sound ribbing about it.

But Dad got even with his friend when he discovered one evening after church that this same man, who also had several young children, had left one of his own children behind sleeping on a church bench. As we pulled up to the boy's house with the boy in tow, the friend stepped into his doorway with a quizzical look of, "What on earth are you doing here?" He didn't have to wonder long as Dad opened the back car door. Letting the awakened child out, he walked him down the sidewalk to his befuddled father, laughing with immense satisfaction. "Here you are," he announced. "We brought one of your lambs home!" Leaving as quickly as he had come, Dad drove away still laughing as he left his friend standing there shaking his head in disbelief.

Playfulness was just part of how Dad related to people. As a rule, he related better to us as teens than when we were younger, but he also made a special effort to put himself out there and play with us as babies and youngsters, too. When we were able to sit up by ourselves, he perched us on one of his big, broad hands and lifted us high above his head, with a big grin spreading across his face as everyone else smiled but held their breath. After we grew too big for this, he allowed us to climb up him like little mountaineers as we grasped his hands and found footholds on his body, starting on his feet, gradually moving up to his waist, and ending by standing on his shoulders. Sometimes when he came home from a long, hard week of trucking, we all mobbed him at the door, eager to tussle with him. Not once did he say, "No, I'm too tired for this." Instead, he obliged by giving us "horsey rides" on his shoulders, running and jumping around the long kitchen table as the rider squealed with delight and the rest of us, awaiting our turn, made a train behind him.

We also loved it when Dad jumped rope with us. Sometimes we would jump in the middle of the family room on the hardwood floor to break up long winter evenings, one person at either end of the rope turning it for the "jumper" and Dad and Mom smiling quietly with delight in the background at us. If we begged Dad hard enough, he sometimes joined in. As if no longer able to resist, he would get up with a big grin on his face, walk over to the turning rope, and jump in to take his turn. Sometimes he even jumped hot pepper style as we cheered him on, but not for long, as he inevitably came to a sudden, laughing stop. We were impressed that he even tried at all. Unprompted, Dad even did a high jump one evening and was actually pretty good at it, though I'm guessing he did it just to prove he could.

Dad also played with us outside. When the I-80 bridge across the river right by our house was under construction, it was a perfect place to run races. Joining us there one day, Dad challenged Sue to a race. Sue won easily, with Dad fussing about how fast she could run. I doubt he really expected to win; I think he just wanted to play with us. It seemed as though Dad looked for these opportunities, and having him play with us made everything right with the world.

When Dad swam with us, he made memories. For starters, we couldn't help staring at his "farmer's tan" and visible muscles as he came down over the river bank to swim with us. Tina has a vivid memory of this when she was swimming with Mim one day and Dad came down to join them. Only after she was finally able to take her wide-open, disbelieving eyes off of her first-ever view of Dad in his swimming trunks was she able to enjoy swimming with him. One of Fred's first memories of Dad was of sitting on his back at Dad's insistence when just a little tyke, scared stiff while Dad swam all the way across the creek at the Cabin. John remembers riding on Dad's back while Dad dog paddled where the water was too deep for us to go by ourselves. Tim remembers Dad carrying him on his back while Dad swam all the way across deep holes in the river where our feet couldn't touch the bottom, and around the piers of the bridge spanning the river. Would Dad have taken the time to go swimming by himself? Maybe. But it seemed he only went swimming when he got to go with us. Knowing Dad, he probably enjoyed it more with us. In any case, whenever Dad took time out of his busy schedule to swim with us, we were immersed from head to toe in the good feeling of our obvious importance to him.

Proving what a good sport he was, Dad also allowed us to play with his hair. Many times on winter evenings, he sat in the chair next to the stove in the family room, dozing with the paper in his hands while we combed his hair. We'd part it many different ways and put numerous barrettes and tiny pony tails all over his head, then stand back to look at the final outcome with satisfied peals of laughter. Eventually, he could be heard to say above the sound of our laughter, "Okay, that's enough." And then we'd pull out all the barrettes and dismantle all the pony tails and attempt to comb his hair back to the "right" way. I always wondered at Dad, a grown man, allowing us to play with his hair. Maybe it was partly because he enjoyed us being near him.

Dad seemed to understand our need to cavort and play. He would sometimes call it to a halt if it got out of hand, but at other times he was long-suffering. Like the time Tina brought some school friends home overnight. They were "carrying on" and whizzed past Dad as he sat on the recliner reading the paper. Whoosh! Tina backhanded the paper unto Dad's chest, and he was left holding his hands at half-mast. Unperturbed, he gathered up the paper and continued reading. Tina's friends were amazed. "I could never do that to my Dad," one of them said.

Compassionate

Dad's responses weren't always so easygoing (more on that later), but one of the reasons we could so easily forgive him at those times was that he let us know he felt compassion for us when we were hurting. When I went through a time of deep depression in high school, for instance, Dad let me know he understood how I felt. One afternoon as I was sitting behind closed doors in the rocking chair by the living room window, gazing out over the river and wondering what the purpose of my life was, Dad gently opened the door and said softly, "When my mother was a young girl and she had to work very hard in the potato field in the hot sun all day, she said she wished then she could just die." Then he asked, "Is that how it is for you?" I slowly nodded my head. Without saying a word, he closed the

77

door as gently as he had opened it and left, not telling me why I shouldn't feel what I was feeling or that I should be grateful for what I had. In that moment of Dad's reaching out to me, I felt a deep connection to him because I knew he understood and felt compassion for me. The tenderness in his voice overrode any harshness I may have heard from him at another time.

Though it was unusual to see Dad cry, when he did it was in response to another's pain. I watched him cry as he stood in his gray suit by the grave of Elam and Miriam's infant son Philip Brent—one of three of their infants who died[4]—as we buried Philip's tiny coffin. I knew Dad was deeply feeling the pain of their loss.

I also watched Dad cry with Edith the day she sat in the kitchen telling him the doctors thought Merle, her fiancé, had leukemia. Dad felt her turmoil, and she was deeply comforted because she knew he did.

In September 1978, Fred, Rhoda, and their four small children left behind everything at their home in Minnesota and fled for Pennsylvania. Fred's depression had been deepening, and Rhoda was searching for solutions. When Dad took Fred to be evaluated at Philhaven Hospital, the hours that day crawled by for Rhoda. Dad finally appeared in her doorway that evening—without Fred. He sat down at the kitchen table with Rhoda and explained that the staff at Philhaven wanted Fred to stay for a while. With the birth of their fifth child only weeks away, it was more than Rhoda could bear. She broke down and cried, and Dad cried with her. It was comforting to Rhoda that Dad was willing to let her know it hurt him too.

Dad wrapped us in compassion when we were young as well. When Barb was a little girl, Dad bought her a brand-new tricycle as a reward for quitting her thumb-sucking. The tricycle became her pride and joy, so when Dad accidentally ran over it, she cried inconsolably. But when Dad took her to the store that same day and bought her a new one, she knew he felt her broken heart, small as it was.

Barb also knew Dad cared about her desire to be included when she begged to go along with him, Parke, and Elam to climb the mountain across the road from the Cabin and Dad relented even though he knew her small, five-year-old body

---

[4] While Elam was a missionary doctor in Belize, Miriam went into premature labor with Lydia, who died in utero and was delivered stillborn. Their second child, Eva Lynn, was born with toxoplasmosis and lived two months. Philip Brent died from complications during birth and was buried beside Eva Lynn. When Elam came back from Belize he went into pediatric medicine and set up the first pediatric clinic in Lewisburg, Pennsylvania. He was recently celebrated for forty years of being a much-loved doctor of children. Undoubtedly, losing his own babies shaped him into the compassionate doctor he became.

would have a hard time keeping up. Sure enough, Barb soon got too tired to go any further. So Dad handed her a stick and instructed her to hold on to one end while he held onto the other end and pulled her up the mountain.

Mim was likewise on the receiving end of Dad's caring when her little feet got freezing cold on a winter hike with Dad and the younger boys. Hoisting Mim onto his back, Dad sheltered her feet in the warmth of his coat pocket.

When Leona grew into her early teens, she was away from home for a week or two and got very homesick. Seeming to sense her need for reassurance, Dad gave her a warm, welcome-home hug, sparing her any feeling of embarrassment about being homesick. Leona loved him for that.

Outgoing and People-Oriented

Dad's warm-hearted spirit also radiated out beyond family. He loved to interact and visit with a variety of people—like him and unlike him—making friends far and wide. Leona quickly learned as a young girl that she did not want to ride along with Dad if it meant she would be stuck waiting in the vehicle when he stopped to talk to someone. It was her first inkling of what eternity might be like. Leona's self-conscious teenage shyness, nowhere close to Dad's free-flowing social comfort, clashed with his expectations one day when some relatives stopped in unexpectedly. Leona had just come in from doing field work and was embarrassed about her appearance and a messy house, and was feeling inadequate about carrying on a conversation with these relatives she hardly knew. Not knowing what else to do, she disappeared upstairs until they left. When Dad learned where she had been, he took her to task, telling her that her disappearing act gave an appearance of being snobbish to the relatives. Dad's scolding along with his ease in conversing with these relatives, even in his dirty farm clothes, made Leona resolve to make more of an effort to forget herself and think of the needs of the other person in settings like this.

Hard-Work Ethic

I suspect that all of these characteristics of Dad helped him persevere through the hard times. When Mom and Dad moved from Oley, the barn on the "new" farm along the banks of the Susquehanna River was in very bad shape. There were holes in the walls so big that a cow could have walked out through any of them. Before the move, Dad, Parke (age fourteen), and Elam (age twelve) made many trips back and forth from Oley to Lewisburg—approximately ninety miles one way—working hard to put new sheeting and boards on the walls of the barn and main barn doors, and doing a lot of hard work to get it in shape for moving day. An extension to the barn was built out over the barnyard from birch trees that Dad and the boys had cut and then pulled up over the river bank and made into boards; but the water birch wood did not weather well or handle moisture well, and the roof did not hold up. All that hard work—for what?

Crop failures in Buffalo Valley provided additional challenges. To help ends meet, Dad took up truck driving. He drove many long hours from Monday morning to Thursday evening while twelve-year-old Barb and thirteen-year-old Elam milked cows morning and evening. Barb could hardly wait until Dad came home on Fridays, not only because she was weary of milking cows all week but also because she could lay aside her worry for another week when he was home safe, particularly after having overheard Dad say he got very sleepy while driving truck.

Above: Tomato harvest. Below: Dad and John Everitt, tomato field man for Chef Boyardee.

Though Dad worked hard driving truck, he was more at home in a tomato field than in a truck cab. In the fields, his children could also be part of what it took to provide for the family. As I was growing up, in the late summers Dad, Esther, and Fred worked together relentlessly in the tomato field night after night until 10:30 or 11:00 doing the hard work of loading tomato baskets onto a wagon in a tier formation, or emptying them into a low-walled wagon. One evening after dark as they left the house to load yet another wagonload of tomatoes, Dad sensed Fred was very weary and quietly encouraged him.

"Hang in there, Fred. We'll be done after a while." Fred heard in those words, "We're in this together."

During tomato harvesting, Dad hauled wagonload after wagonload to the Chef Boyardee's processing plant in Milton. As he drove slowly down the road for about six miles and across the narrow bridge spanning the Susquehanna River to get to Chef Boyardee, traffic piled up behind him. Drivers clearly communicated their anger and frustration at him for slowing them down, but Dad appeared undaunted. He was on a mission, and nothing was going to stop him. He was working hard to provide for his family and paid no mind to those drivers.

Through the years, Dad continued to work hard with strength, stamina, and determination, always doing more than his fair share without complaining. From childhood to adulthood, work was a part of living for him. Our tomato field man, John Everitt, told Dad on more than one occasion, "Mast, you act like you're not tired, but I know you are. You're just too bullheaded to admit it! Stop and take a rest." Rarely did Dad heed his counsel. No doubt he kept working so hard throughout the spring and summer months to provide for his family, but he was likely also keeping his eye on the big game hunting trip to Canada or the West that he rewarded himself with every year. We knew these hunting trips were important to him, because he always went self-assuredly, no questions asked. It was as if he knew this time away to renew and rejuvenate was a means of personal survival.

Courageous

Hard work coupled with courage was an integral part of who Dad was. His courage showed his true character in the face of disasters—fires, floods, and droughts. He never took on a victim role but stood unflinching, resolving to pick up and move on. We watched him and learned from him.

The first disaster came the year we moved to Buffalo Valley. That year, Dad competed with bludgeoning weather as he planted the tomato crop not one time but three. Green tomatoes on the vines of the third planting—one last attempt to defy mother nature—froze in early fall. But even though the tomatoes yielded only two tons to the acre, not enough to pay for the fertilizer, Dad gave Elam the profit from an allotted acreage of tomatoes as payment for doing all the farming that year. (Elam had plowed with a two-bottom plow, filled the silo with hay using the manure spreader, shoveled wagonloads of corn onto the elevator by hand, and picked tomatoes.) Dad didn't give up but planted tomatoes again the next year and the next.

Neither did he give up when Hurricane Agnes unleashed her floodwaters upon us in early summer of 1972. Instead, he stood tall on top of the bank of I-80 where it went by our house, watching his bountiful tomato crop sweep away. His heart had to be heavy, but he simply said in a low voice, "Well, there goes our new station wagon …" After the waters receded, Edith, a teenager, stood with Dad beside the grape arbor by the path leading to the barn. She does not remember his exact words to her, but it was clear that he was accepting the terribly discouraging situation and choosing to get up and go on.

Rather than defeating Dad, discouraging situations brought out his "We're going to make this work" attitude. In 1969, Dad and sixteen or seventeen other farmers in the area purchased tomato harvesters in cooperation with a promotion by the local Chef Boyardee, the purchasing agent of their tomato crops. The harvesters were large, dinosaur look-alike machines pulled behind a tractor, which scooped up the whole tomato plant from the ground and shook the tomatoes onto a conveyor belt that elevated them onto a wagon driven alongside. But the machine couldn't live up to the disappointed farmers' dreams of being freed from having to round up humans to pick their tomato crops, which would have allowed the farmers to raise more tomatoes. None of the tomato harvesters worked.

Late that fall, a group of disgruntled farmers met at our house. As they huddled together in our driveway, voices rising and falling in animated discussion with hands gesturing frustration, my younger brothers listened around the corner. They heard the men trying to persuade Dad that they had every right to sue the manufacturer and Chef Boyardee for damages and the tomato harvester's failure to deliver as promised. They listened intently as Dad heard them out, sometimes threw in his two cents, and in the end stated emphatically, "No, we're not going to sue them, we're going to make this thing work!" At that moment, a burst of inspiration coursed through my brothers' veins, quickening their imaginations. They joined with Dad in an excited, determined declaration of "Yes! We're going to make this work!"

It was a challenge they were up to—and besides, loading tomatoes and picking them by hand was getting old for them. Not long after this, Elvin and one of his friends, learning from what didn't work about the original harvester, built a tomato harvester that actually worked. Other farmers soon placed orders for harvesters, and Elvin, though only having gone through eighth grade, eventually built a very successful business—Pik Rite Inc.—which today manufactures many other kinds of equipment in addition to tomato harvesters. All this from hearing Dad say, "No, we're going to make this work!"

Opinionated

Dad approached the tomato harvester fiasco like he did most of life; he knew what he believed and exactly why he believed it, holding up his end of an argument or discussion. He also invited our opinions even while clearly stating his own. But if we insinuated that Dad did not know what he was talking about, or if he thought we were making him out to be a fool, he usually had a strong knee-jerk reaction.

I saw, for example, how sharply he responded to Sue when she was driving us in the blue station wagon and chose to follow her own directional instincts instead of Dad's. Dad had told her where to turn to get on the interstate, but Sue had driven right on past, saying, "No, I think it's up here." When Dad was proven right, he said to Sue in a loud voice, "Now see, if you had just listened to me in the first place …"

Sue was one of the children whose outspoken personalities clashed with Dad's strong opinions. Others of us were easily hurt by Dad and didn't dare speak up to him, especially when we saw his reaction to those who did. I was in this latter category. If something of a conflictual nature was being discussed and I could see that Dad had a strong opinion on the matter, I hardly dared voice my own opinion. This "reactionary Dad" also exposed a seemingly fragile side of him that I felt I needed to protect and reassure that his opinion mattered.

In areas that Dad was passionate about—two of which were children not "sassing back" at their parents and not being "picky about your eats"— he both commanded and demanded our respect. If Mom's tolerance level for backtalk was near zero on a scale of one to ten, Dad's was negative thirteen. It was definitely your unlucky day if you talked back to Dad.

The same went for animals and Dad. He was very indignant when our collie barked at him for no reason. And when the sheep buck caught him by surprise from behind and butted him, Dad wheeled around and kicked it, showing it "who was in charge."

Dad's Inner World: Harshness, Quick Temper, and Asking Forgiveness

Dad's angry eruptions were a puzzle to me. In spite of my best efforts to figure them out, I remained clueless about where they came from. How could he respond in this way, I wondered, when it was clear he loved us and would do anything for us?

Dad's strong reactions formed one of my first memories when I was about three years old standing by the corner of the washhouse, overcome by diarrhea. Diarrhea filled my gray-striped flannel bloomers and ran down my legs. As I stood there in my misery, Dad came down the walkway, grabbed me up by my waist, dangled me from his arm, and marched me into the washhouse. The next thing I knew, cold water from the pump was running down over my bare bottom, and a stiff prickly brush was scrubbing my skin. As Dad set me down angrily, he told me I was "too big to poop my pants." His harshness scraped my spirit more than the bristles of the scrub brush scraped my skin.

When I was about eleven or twelve, my spirit was bruised again by Dad's response. The snowmelt from the spring rains had created a backup of water running into the stream in the meadow in front of our farm buildings, and the swelling waters had created a small lake crossing the lane, making it difficult to pass through with vehicles. When the water was at its deepest, we kept our rowboat in the meadow just in case. Rowing around the trees in the orchard made us big-time adventurers. One day I invited Edith and John to go exploring with me in the boat. As I rowed them across the meadow, I lifted the oars to bring them back down on the water—hard—for a big splash and a more fun ride. But as I did so, the oar on the right side popped out of the oar lock and landed in the water with a kerplunk. I panicked. Without thinking, I jumped in after it. The cold water up to the middle of my chest took my breath away, and all I could do was cry out in a terrified, gasping sort of way. At the top of the meadow a distance away stood Dad and one of my older brothers watching. Dad yelled, "Rose, you dummy, get back in the boat!" I did, fighting the resistance of my water-logged, thick blue coat, somehow managing to swing my leg up over the side of the boat.

I do not remember how I got the boat to the shoreline. I only remember sort of staggering into the house, shivering in my heavy, dripping coat as I walked into the kitchen to the warm cookstove to shed the coat. There I cried silent tears. I don't know if it was because I was so cold or because I felt so ashamed at being such a "dummy." A few years later when we were telling stories around the dinner table, I told this story. When I got to the part where "Dad called me a 'dummy,'" Dad got a remorseful look on his face, shook his head slowly, and said, "Awck— I did?" Although he did not speak the words "Please forgive me," I knew he wanted to be forgiven, and I forgave him.

I wilted when Dad's harsh words were directed at me but not when they were toward one of my younger siblings. One day when he lashed out at one of them at mealtime, I saw how his tone deflated their spirits, and I was angry, infuriated.

Not knowing how to voice my anger, I instinctively slammed my utensils down on the table. Though Dad could not have helped but notice, he never responded to my demonstration of indignation.

Mealtimes with everyone sitting around the table were usually pleasant, but Dad occasionally had other harsh outbursts that everyone witnessed. These were often directed at Sue, who when reprimanded responded by smiling. Dad could hardly stand this and reacted by barking, "Now wipe that smirk off your face!"

Dad also reacted strongly to disrespectful comments. One day when he reprimanded one of the boys about something, Mim, who was just a whippersnapper at the time, made a comment about it. Dad said to her, "I didn't ask for your two cents." In the adjacent hallway, Tina quietly added, "I didn't ask for yours either." Uh oh. They knew there was trouble when they heard Dad get up out of his chair in a hurry; he had heard Tina. Wide-eyed, she froze on the spot. Mim whispered frantically to her, "Run!" Like a gazelle she bolted up the stairs with Mim only a few steps behind. When they reached the top of the stairs, Mim whispered, "Hide!" Tina flew into the closest in Mom and Dad's bedroom and hid behind Mom's dresses. But Dad saw her legs sticking out below, pushed the dresses aside, and gave her a smack across her mouth. Tina had never even gotten a spanking from Dad, so the smack was devastating to her.

Dad was usually quick to apologize, however, when he realized he had accused us wrongly. When John was about twelve years old and Dad was "a little extra harsh" with him about the careless mistake he had made, Dad came back to him about half an hour later, told him he was sorry, and asked for forgiveness. And when Dad blamed Esther for something she did not do and later realized his mistake, he walked into the barn where she was helping with chores and kind of gruffly said, "Sorry for the misunderstanding." Esther doesn't remember the incident for which she was blamed, just Dad's apology.

What Dad Was Passionate About

HIS CHILDREN

Being a person of intensity, Dad loved his children fiercely. He let us know he was proud of us and made us individually feel like we were the only one, even with all the other siblings. We felt treasured and valued by Dad—up close and personal. "Let's see now," he would say. "Parke was born at plowing time … Ada was born at potato grating time … Dale was born at wheat harvest time …" Dad could remember all our birthdays and what was going on of importance in his world when we were born, even though he could not remember the few groceries Mom asked him to get. This showed us how special and important we all were to him. The matter was clinched when a visiting evangelist came for dinner and Dad went around the table recalling each of our birth dates as well as significant happenings on those days, such as what the weather was like, what crops were growing or being harvested, and so forth. We proudly took it in as Dad went down the line.

It was hard to fathom the visiting evangelist having only one child—a daughter—whose birth date he was not quite sure of.

Dad showed us how much he loved us in so many ways.

❋ When someone made a comment to Dad about something one of us had accomplished, such as, "I bet you're proud of that one," he replied, "Yes, I am, and I'm proud of all of them."

❋ He always waited up when someone was away at night. We could count on him to be sleeping in his chair near the phone until we were all home and accounted for. When Esther worked the three-to-eleven shift at the hospital, she would walk through the door and say, "Okay Dad, I'm home now," and Dad would get up from his chair and go to bed.

❋ He was very generous with us as teenagers, even in our inexperience, unselfishly giving us unlimited access to the "run-around" car and gas tank on the farm.

Top: Dad giving William a bottle
Above: Sue's graduation from Harrisburg Hospital School of Nursing

❋ He loved spending time with us, taking us with him in his truck to run errands. Some of our earliest memories are of going with him in the truck somewhere. For Parke, it was sitting next to Dad on the motor cowl so he could see better in the old, 1941 Ford truck when Dad hauled corn or potatoes. For Elam, it was when he had his first taste of coffee ice cream—liking it ever since—when Dad stopped at an ice cream shop during a ride in the truck together. For Barb, it was being treated to a hotdog, the best-tasting one ever, when she was out with Dad and they stopped at a luncheonette. It was also being allowed, after considerable begging, to go all the way to Virginia with Dad by herself to get beef cattle. For me, it was going with Dad in the old, beat-up pickup truck in winter to get sawdust for the cows' stalls. I still love the smell of sawdust.

✳ He took us to the Farm Show every year, making us feel important by giving us spending money for the day.

The depth of Dad's support was particularly evident to many of us during tumultuous teenage years. Even though Elvin, by his own admission, treated Dad unfairly and took him for granted, Dad related to him in a way that did not alienate him. In his early to mid-teens, Elvin had a job catching chickens that required him to work a distance from home. Without once mentioning what he was doing for Elvin, Dad drove thirty miles a day to transport him to and from work, even while Elvin made it obvious he was trying to distance himself from Dad, speaking disrespectfully to him and hanging out with friends he knew Dad did not approve of. But Dad hung in there through it all. If Dad had stood up for his own rights and not been unselfish and caring, who knows where Elvin would be today.

Dad allowed us to tell him when he frustrated us, holding his tongue as if what we felt was more important than what he felt at that moment. When Dale was in his teens and angry with Dad, Dad entered into a long conversation with him on their way to an auction and, without defending himself, let Dale express his feelings. This left Dale feeling very close to Dad.

When Barb questioned and challenged Mom and Dad's beliefs, Dad listened and did not say much, but his answer was usually well-thought-out, brief, and effective in addressing her challenge. When she spoke her mind in an abrasive fashion and he got frustrated with her, he said, "Honey child," in a tone that conveyed, "I love you, but you don't have to act and talk like this."

Tim knew Dad did not approve of the things he was doing as he went through a rebellious stage in his late teens, having to learn everything the hard way. But he also knew deep down that Dad was trying to be patient and understanding, and he did not want to disappoint Dad. Later when Tim changed course and asked Dad to forgive him for the trouble he had caused, Dad replied, "All forgiven, Tim, all forgiven." Tim knew then that Dad had forgiven him even before he had asked.

In spite of the grief we gave Dad, he defended us even in the face of the law. One day a sheriff came knocking at the kitchen door, startling all of us while we were sitting around the lunch table. He had come to collect a fine that Elvin owed. Dad stood up, pulled his wallet out of his pocket, and asked, "How much is it?" He took out some bills, handed them to the sheriff, and said in an annoyed tone of voice, "Okay, you can go now."

Dad's caring came through in our common, ordinary life as well. Often while he worked with us—loading heifer manure with the boys, for instance—he showed he cared by discussing our teenage ideas with us, using teachable moments to make comments, rather than preaching at us or lecturing us. There was something about talking as we worked together that made a lasting impact. Dad inspired the boys to "be a better man" as he talked and worked together with them just as he communicated to the girls that he delighted in us as we worked alongside him, calling forth a desire in us to be the best we could be.

When Dad expressed his deep feelings, these were also times for teachable moments. Like when Fred and some of his classmates in the fifth- through seventh-grade classroom were giving the teacher a hard time. Dad was on the school board at the time, and the board asked him to talk to Fred and his classmates. So he sat on a desk in front of the group of boys and said, "I'd rather take a beating than come here and talk to you." He told them that when he was a young man some of his friends refused to submit to authority and that today they are out in the world not living for God. When Dad started to cry and had to stop for a while to regain control of his emotions, Fred was embarrassed, but his classmates were impressed. In that moment, Dad modeled for the boys strength through tears.

Dad often seized the moment like this, taking advantage of opportune times to show us unwavering support. When Elam was just nine years old, someone wanted to give him a mutt. He cried when Dad wouldn't let him have it, but Dad didn't give in, telling him to get a good registered dog to earn money instead. Elam followed Dad's advice and got a registered collie, selling many collie pups over the years, which partially financed his way through college. Dad later supported Elam in his big decision to go to college and medical school by providing employment on the farm for him during summers between spring and fall semesters, allowing him several acres of tomatoes as a source of income.

Dad's support often came in the form of spoken affirmation. During my sophomore year of high school when one of my friends had just been crowned homecoming queen, I was up on a stepladder outside washing the kitchen window when Dad walked up to me and said, "I want you to know this means more to me than being homecoming queen." In that moment, I heard him saying that what I was doing meant a lot to him, that I was valuable to him. In those few words, he told me he appreciated my work and did not take it for granted. So I worked even harder because, as I saw it, my work equaled my value. In reality, I'm sure Dad did value my work, but most of all he was trying to show me support.

When Fred became a budding teenager, Dad would introduce him by saying, "And here's my right-hand man." Later, Fred grew two sizes taller when Dad would ask his advice on the order of work for the day or what he would rather do, given a choice between jobs.

When the tomatoes in the field along the river beyond the orchard could not be sprayed one year, Dad told us he would pay us a certain amount for every row we weeded—and they were long rows. Although Edith would have preferred to keep her nose in a book or go out in nature, she got up early before it was hot and worked at her row until she had it finished. But the best part for her was hearing Dad tell a man who stopped by what she had done. "She worked like a grownup," Dad said, and Edith beamed with pride.

Dad connected with Dale in their common love for music. Since Dale didn't share Dad's love of hunting, he spent a lot of time playing piano. Sometimes when he was in the living room playing piano, Dad would come into the room, comment on his playing, give suggestions for improvement, then compliment Dale on improvements he had made up to that time.

When Tina got married, she stepped out on a limb and wore a full-length wedding gown, breaking tradition with the mid-calf gowns that her older sisters had been expected to wear. When she asked Dad to walk her down the aisle—something he had never done for the other girls—Dad conceded. To Tina, Dad walking her down the aisle was one of "the greatest things about her wedding." She knew his comment about her gown having "enough dress dragging behind her to make dresses for a set of twins" was his way of supporting her in the midst of using humor to acknowledge that this was a stretch for him.

Tim spent a lot of time in the basement where he set up a workroom of sorts, tinkering and making little projects. When Dad came through the basement after tending the furnace, he often said to Tim, "I would never have the patience for that," letting Tim know his tinkering had value.

These were some of the ways that Dad said, "I love you," something he rarely said directly. He also said it through kisses that he saved for special times, like the week when he was going away for several days, leaving in the middle of the night. On that night, John was awakened by the light coming on in the bedroom. Pretending to be asleep, he watched Dad circle around to the beds of the five sleeping boys, giving each of them a goodbye kiss. John thought he was too big for that, but he secretly loved it.

And then there were Dad's hands. There was something about his big hands that also held special meaning of love and support for us. When we were little and our hands got cold, big strong Dad warmed our cold little hands by tenderly rubbing them between his large, warm hands. Dad's hands could clench tightly together, too, when necessary. When Sue was little and squirmy and had to sit with Dad during church, he held her firmly on his lap, his fingers intertwined so she would sit still. Sue tried to pry open his large fingers but could not. These same hands held her hand years later when she awoke from unconsciousness after the car accident she and Esther had been in. The feeling of Dad's strong, rough hand holding hers was the first thing she became aware of as she lay bewildered on her hospital bed, trying to understand where she was.

Dad stayed the course with us as we grew up and went through hard times as adults. When Fred and Rhoda moved to Slate Falls, Ontario, immediately following their marriage to work with Northern Light Gospel Mission, Dad chose to go moose hunting at Slate Falls not once but twice. Fred thinks Dad knew he needed him for moral support and encouragement. On the one hand, Dad probably experienced vicariously through Fred the challenges of his life—surviving in the great outdoors and working side by side with the people living in the bush— since he told Fred that going to Ontario was something he would have enjoyed doing when he was young. On the other hand, when Dad and Mom loaded Fred's younger siblings into the station wagon and headed for Ontario, Dad must have known that having them there to romp and play with was just what Fred needed. Later, when Fred and Rhoda moved to Montana, Dad went with them, giving moral support and helping entertain their children during the many miles they traveled in an old bus to get there. At one point, the brakes gave out and the bus barreled down a hill toward a red light. When Fred yelled for help, Dad sprang to the front beside him to grab the emergency brake.

Dad's love for us was sealed one evening when he was in the hospital for heart surgery and Elvin asked him what one thing in his life he would do differently if he could. To this question, Dad replied, "I would have spent more time with my children."

This was something Dad was able to do with my two youngest sisters because he was retired when they were growing up. Often when Siobohn and Kenyatta woke up in the morning, they climbed sleepily up on Dad's lap as he sat in his chair reading. With his lap and heart big enough to contain them both, he held them close, saying, "These are my girls."

After Dad's death on May 18, 1994, we each contributed to a collection of memoirs about him. Siobohn, ten years old at the time, wrote:

Thank you for taking me to the cabin to go swimming and to go to the candy store. I liked when you took us to look for deer. Thank you for picking the place for the cabin to be. I liked when you took me out to eat. Thank you for letting me sit on your lap. Thank you for reading books to me. I will miss you but I will see you in heaven. I love you. Goodbye Dad. Love, Siobohn.

Kenyatta was eleven years old when she wrote her memoir:

It is with much joy that I write this letter. Because even if you're not here at the cabin with the family we all know where you are. We are very glad for all you have done. For example having gatherings and finding this cabin for the family. Although you were the kind of man that tried to get well fast, you lost. But we're still glad you could be with us as long as you were. Dad thanks for taking me into your family. I was never really cared for until I came into this family. I appreciate it. Thank you. Love, Kenyatta.

SPIRITUALITY

Dad was both very human and very serious about his faith. He often quoted Ecclesiastes 12:13, which seemed to sum up the way he wanted to live his life: "But let us hear the conclusion of the whole matter: fear God and keep his command-ments: for this is the whole duty of man" (King James version). He didn't preach at us but lived out his faith consistently. I can imagine he had frequent, long talks with God.

Dad's humanity was tightly interwoven with his spirituality. Connecting with him meant connecting with his spirituality. Seeing him pray by his bed at night drew us close to him because we knew he was praying for us. He said he prayed for us regularly. Probably included in his prayer for us was a request for wisdom about how to raise us, as he coached us about the importance of asking God for wisdom daily. Dad believed in the power of prayer, saying things such as, "Don't ask God to make you humble unless you really mean it."

We grew to connect spiritual nourishment with being close to Dad. During family devotions in the morning, we fought to take turns sitting on his lap. When it was Edith's turn and she was kneeling with Dad at his green, wooden chair during prayer, she tried hard to hold still and not let him see her peek through the spread of her fingers held tightly to her face, only the green chair visible through them. It felt good to Edith to be close to Dad.

Dad made church attendance with his family a priority. We went to church Sunday mornings and Sunday evenings and to prayer meeting Wednesday evenings. Even when hay was on the ground ready to bale with imminent threat of rain, or the tomatoes were ripe and ready to be picked, Dad stopped what he was doing in the fields to go. But when he got to church, it was often hard for him to stay awake after being so physically active. When Barb was a little girl and sat with Dad in church, Mom told her to keep him awake. Only too happy to do so, Barb crawled onto his lap and pulled his nose when he dozed off.

As a little girl kneeling at a church bench, I sometimes peeked over the top of the bench when Dad took a turn praying during Wednesday evening prayer meeting. I could hardly hear others when they prayed, with their faces to the back of their bench, but when Dad prayed, his voice was loud and clear. I was fascinated with the way he raised his head clear of the pew with his elbows on top of the back of the bench where he was kneeling. I assumed this was so others could hear what he was praying, since he sometimes complained on the way home that "so and so mumbled when they prayed, and they talked so fast I couldn't even understand them." At those times, Mom would try to get him to hush up, as though she didn't want us to hear him criticize another person.

HUNTING

Dad was at his best in the fall, hunting in the woods. Maybe it was because it was something he enjoyed doing so much. When he went to Slate Run to hunt when Elam and Parke were little, he sent them postcards with notes about the eight-point bucks that Dutch Master members, including himself, had bagged. Elam and Parke were excited and proud of Dad and his hunting success. This was just the beginning of a special bond Dad formed with each of his sons through hunting. Each of my brothers has a special story about hunting with Dad. His contagious love of nature and hunting transferred something from his soul to theirs. Hunting was about experiencing nature together, working together to bring a prized deer out of the woods, and just being together enjoying one another's company.

It was in the great outdoors that my brothers learned about an important part of manhood from Dad—braving the elements of cold, wind, rain, and snow with diligent tenacity; determinedly meeting the challenges of hiking rugged terrain head-on with stamina and endurance; disciplining themselves to wait quietly with patient persistence for the sound of a snapping twig; posturing themselves in readiness for the deer, bear, or turkey to appear. As I listened to the sound of pride in their voices and exhilarated laughter as they told their stories of suspense and conquest, of narrow misses—shooting a turkey from an unbelievable distance and hitting a deer when it was running "wide open"—I knew this much to be true: my brothers experienced a rite of passage into manhood by hunting with Dad.

Dad's passion for hunting was no doubt connected with the survival of his soul. He relaxed when he was in the mountains, breathing in deeply the smell of the woods; feeling the cool fall air; stopping to take in the magical scenery of snow-dusted evergreens; hearing snaps and crackles of wildlife in the brush beside him; and crawling on the ground tasting teaberries. These things filled Dad's often nearly-empty reservoir of soul food. It also gave him a chance to sit back and think through things. But best of all, it gave him a chance to have quality time with his boys. Dad gave his sons a lot of freedom when he took them hunting, and he made it obvious he was proud when they got something.

Each of my brothers has a special memory of going on their first hunt at age twelve, with Dad coaching them and speaking quiet words of encouragement. When Parke went on his first deer hunt, Dad picked him up at school in Oley on a Friday, and they drove all the way to Slate Run, one hundred and sixty miles away. Dad shot his own doe the next morning then tutored Parke for several hours. A whole box of shells later, Parke finally got a tiny doe weighing about as much as he himself did.

One year on the first Saturday of buck season, Dad took Elam and Parke, budding teenagers, to Clinton County to hunt, about a four-hour drive from home. On the way, Dad said to them, "If one of you gets a buck today, I'll get you a new 32 Winchester special rifle." Elam, who was at his post and had just answered nature's call, said, "If I get an eight-point, will you get me a 300 Savage?" Dad said, "No. That's just what you would do." Sure enough, as Elam was buckling his belt, he saw three deer coming up the trail toward him, the last one a spike buck. He put the gun to his shoulder, and with one shot hit the spike buck. True to his word, Dad rewarded him with a brand-new 32 special. When Dad handed the rifle (now a collector's item) to him, Elam just about burst with pride. To be fair to Parke, Dad bought him one also. The tradition of each of the boys getting a new rifle and shotgun at age twelve started with this hunting trip.

When Fred turned twelve, he went hunting with Dad at a place in the mountains close by called the Big Basin. Dad told Fred, "You stand here, and I'll make a big circle around you. Maybe I'll chase something in to you." It was cold, and Fred had been standing there a long time as the sun sank farther in the west. Fred thought, "Maybe Dad can't find me! I'll break a stick or two so he knows where I am." A little while later, Dad walked up to him saying, "It's time to go. I was standing a little way over here the last while, and I heard you break some sticks. The deer won't come if you make noise."

Pete went on his first hunt with Dad at Lick Run during doe season. He thought hunting with Dad was boring since he had been hunting small game by himself since age ten. By the second afternoon of no doe being shot, Pete had had enough and asked Dad if he could hunt by himself. Dad agreed, and Pete walked quietly off to the side of a ridge. He proceeded to shoot a doe that had been startled and confused by Pete's first missed shot. When Dad came down Lick Run in the evening, he asked a hunter at the bottom of the ridge if he had seen a boy. "Yes," the hunter said. "And he was dragging a doe that was bigger than he was." Dad was proud of Pete and let him know it.

One year in doe season, Pete had a nasty cold with a fever that wouldn't go away. Mom didn't think he should go hunting since she had established an irrefutable law that if we had a fever we were not allowed to go outside. Pete desperately wanted to go, however, fever or not. Dad knew it and quietly suggested, "Why don't you drink some cold water?" Pete whispered, "I already did." When Mom checked Pete's forehead again, "strangely" his forehead felt hot while his temperature was just a little below normal.

Not to be outdone by her brothers, Mim went hunting with them and Dad soon after she turned twelve. By then, Dad was seventy years old. At the end of a long day, Mim shot a doe on a steep mountainside. Dad heard the shot and climbed slowly up the steep grade, huffing and puffing with each step. As Mim saw Dad coming toward her, she could see he was tired and was afraid he might have a heart attack, but her fears were put to rest as he congratulated her with a big smile.

Dad was not one to pick a fight, but he knew how to stand his ground when challenged, especially when it came to hunting. One year he shot a little deer in Lick Run and was hauling it to his truck when, to his chagrin, whom should he meet but Mr. Breon—a loud, arrogant man from Milton who operated a welding shop. Mr. Breon took pleasure in telling anyone who came into his shop and would listen, about Dad shooting this "teeny deer." One day Mr. Breon made the mistake of poking fun at Dad when Dad walked in to have some welding work done, and asked him about his "teeny deer" in front of a bunch of men who were standing around in the shop.

Locking eyes with Mr. Breon in a fiery gaze, Dad calmly and deliberately stated, "I have shot eight, eight-point buck in my time. How many have you shot?"

Dad must have told this story at least fifty times, and each time he came to this part of the story, he would get a twinkle in his eye and triumphantly report, "That was the last time I heard from him!" Of course, the listener was expected to ask, "How many eight-point bucks did Mr. Breon shoot?" To which Dad, with a big smile, would exuberantly reply, "Why, none!"

Somewhere in his hunting ventures, Dad began making yearly trips to hunt big game, sometimes to Canada and sometimes to Colorado. We liked the scruffy beard he had when he came home from long hunting trips, dressed in his wool, red-plaid Woolrich pants and coat. One time Dad went to Canada to hunt moose by himself with no guide. When he went to step out of the canoe, he misstepped and fell into the lake where the water was over his head. Fortunately, he was able to get out in spite of having his heavy Woolrich hunting clothes on. It was a sobering time for him, offset by managing to get a moose with prize-sized antlers. Today the antlers are hanging in Elam's den, reminding him of Dad.

Usually Dad went on big game hunts by himself, but the time he went moose hunting in Ontario when Fred and Rhoda were in voluntary service there, he left home with Mom and a carful of youngsters (the five younger boys and Mim). As they were driving out the lane, Dad asked, "Now, are we sure we have everything?" And after only a few miles down the road, some of the youngsters began fighting. Dad looked around and said, "I sure hope we don't need to go on this whole trip fighting like this; now straighten up! We'll go right back home if you don't stop!" They stopped. To break the boredom of the long trip, the younger ones held contests to see how much gum they could put in their mouths at a single time. The winner shoved in two packs.

As they finally entered Canada, a huge moose crossed the road in front of them. But Dad's gun was in its case packed away, and before he could get it out, the moose walked into the woods. Dad fussed about that for a long time.

His ego was bolstered considerably when, on one of his week-long hunting expeditions to Colorado, he shot a running bull elk in the aspen with one shot on his first time out. This was a story he told with great enthusiasm.

As the younger set of brothers grew up, Dad took them with him in the fall from the small mountains of Pennsylvania to hunt in the monumental mountains of Colorado. Horses were loaded up at the point of arrival at the hunting area to carry supplies and hunters back to the campsite, where a large tent complete with a small stove and chimney was set up several miles from civilization. These hunting trips became a yearly tradition. Eventually, friends and acquaintances were invited to join. The trips created a close camaraderie between those who went, with everyone sitting around the campfire outside the tent in the evening. They helped dress out one another's wild game, then loaded it on horses that followed the trail back through the back country to camp six or seven miles away. Dad was clearly the leader of this group of men as long as he was able to be.

The first time Elam went to Colorado to hunt with Dad, they went with a bunch of guys who offered to pay Dad's way, including his license, if he would show them where to hunt. The hunting season consisted of ten days of elk, then a three-day intermission with mule deer season to follow. After the guys hunted elk for about a week, they wanted to come home. Dad reluctantly agreed; however, after a day or two at home, he announced he was going to drive back out to hunt mule deer because the he didn't want to waste the

Dad hunting out west

deer license the guys had bought for him. He drove his little blue Ford Escort right back out to Colorado all by himself. At that time, Dad was in his late sixties. Mom wasn't very impressed, to put it mildly. Several days later, Elam received a call. "Elam, where did you see those buck during elk season?" Dad never did find them and drove back home without a deer.

The trips west from Pennsylvania to Colorado were long enough to create plenty of memories on the road. At a pit stop on one of those trips, Dad was standing at a urinal in the men's bathroom when Elvin walked in and said in a high-pitched voice, "Excuse me sir." Dad's head spun around, and when he saw it was only Elvin, he sputtered in exasperated relief, "You rascal!" On another trip, they got to a gas station at 3:00 a.m., almost out of gas, only to find it was closed. Dad got on the pay phone and called the cops, who called the station owner, who begrudgingly came out and pumped gas for them.

One time, when Dad was in his seventies, he was frustrated that he couldn't get around like he thought he should be able to. He called Myles, their hunting guide, and rented a horse to ride over the mountains. A lot of the guys were apprehensive about Dad riding a horse, but he had made up his mind. As he and his horse were headed up a trail, he came to a low limb hanging overhead. Thinking he could clear it, he ducked under as the horse proceeded. But the limb barely even cleared the saddle, and it knocked Dad off the horse except for his foot that got caught in the stirrup. Fortunately, the horse stopped immediately and just stood there while Dad worked his way over to a bank and managed to get his foot free.

The next year when Dad announced he was going to rent a horse again, Elvin

quietly called Myles and asked him to tell Dad he didn't have a horse available. Dad seemed to suspect a little behind-the-scenes work going on; nevertheless he hunted on foot that year! Dad and Myles always had a close connection and high regard for each other. It was amazing to watch them interact—a tomato farmer

Dad and Myles, a Colorado hunting guide with whom Dad had a special connection

from Pennsylvania and a wild cowboy from Colorado so committed to each other.

Other signs of Dad's slowing down continued to show up here and there. One year, when Tim jumped rope to get in shape for the Colorado hunt, he walked into Dad's shop to find Dad also jumping rope but with clumsy and painfully slow jumps. Looking up rather sheepishly, Dad said his knees hurt. It seemed to Tim that Dad had to work as hard to jump fifty times as Tim did to jump sixteen hundred.

The last few years he went west, Dad began walking at the Dark Canyon up the trail to the campsite before the others to get a head start. He moved ahead slowly and stopped often to catch his breath and give his knee a break. Elam usually walked with him, and as they sat, Dad repeated numerous hunting stories, some of which Elam had heard before, but he didn't mind. It was just good to hear Dad telling them again.

Dad loved being out in the Colorado mountains with his boys, so he did what he could to keep going. On his last hunting trips west, he stayed closer to the tent and hunted at the campsite, sitting on an upside down bucket scanning the hillside for elk whenever his eyes were open (he usually fell asleep). But he didn't seem to mind that he couldn't go out into the mountains to hunt anymore. He was so happy to just be there. Many evenings when the hunters returned to camp, Dad would be sitting by the campfire in his folding chair, his legs crossed, reading his Bible. It must have gotten a little lonely for him sitting back at camp by himself, because he would grumble when the hunters got in too late, "My ... what took you so long?" Then, as they sat around the campfire, he would ask them all about their hunt and inform them, "I used to be able to climb those mountains like that," as he shared his memories. He slept by the tent door because, as he said, "I just have to answer the call of nature more than I used to." The last time Dad hiked the trail back to the camp, he was eighty years old. That was after he had had an aortic valve replaced and a segment of his colon removed because of colon cancer.

During his last few years of hunting deer in Pennsylvania, Dad seemed to prefer hunting with the younger guys in the mountains close by than with the Dutch masters at the Cabin at Slate Run. On one of these hunts, in a cold, penetrating wind with the temperature twelve degrees below zero, Dad shot a doe running wide open across the field in front of him. This, plus the nice, eight-point buck Dad shot during one of his last drives made him "feel right good about showing the younger fellas how it's done," as he grinned from ear to ear for a long time and declared confidently, "The old man can still do it." When asked, "How many eight-points does that make for you, Dad?" he replied, "Ten." Now it was time for Dad's sons to be proud of him.

Two weeks before Dad died, he told Elvin he had this feeling he would never go to Colorado again. Elvin responded, "Dad, I will pack you in on a horse if I need to." Dad replied, "No, I don't think I will ever go again." Elvin went home, lay on the couch, and cried his heart out because what Dad had said felt so real.

And it *was* real. While trips west with Dad are only memories now, a group of my brothers and friends continue to go west every fall to hunt elk and mule deer, keeping the tradition Dad had started alive and well.

In the Final Analysis

Dad was influenced and inspired by those he looked up to as he grew up: his parents were great storytellers; Grandpa Beiler demonstrated boundless physical strength, even in the face of adversity; David Mast modeled both emotional and physical strength; Grandpa Stoltzfus modeled command and compassion; and all of these ancestors modeled the value of working with their hands. In turn, my father, Mast Beiler Stoltzfus, modeled all of this for us in his daily living.

Just as Dad talked about his family of origin and the past that shaped him, we now talk about Dad and the past that shaped us. Though gone from us in person, Dad is still very present with us—in the mannerisms and voices of his sons as they joke, laugh, and tell stories; in their strides as they walk; in their love of history; and in the values we all hold dear. Dad had a big impact on each of our lives, and he remains ever near.

The spirit of the Johnny Cash song *These Hands* pretty much sums it up for Dad: his hands raised a family, built a home, and filled a task. Today, it seems as if Dad still holds our hands.

6. Mom and Dad in Their Final Years

Dad came out of the house and ambled slowly to the car in the driveway just outside the front door, where he waited for Mom to come out. They were getting ready to go somewhere. As Dad saw Mom open the door, he reached over to her seat and fluffed up the little pillow on it. Mom's hip hurt her when she sat on the car seat, and the pillow eased her discomfort.

I would have given almost anything when I was younger to see this. As I was growing up, Mom and Dad's relationship was probably at its lowest ebb, and I felt the

Mom and Dad in later years

threat of its fragility. That was also the time period that Mom seemed the most emotionally fragile. I always wanted Mom and Dad to really love each another, and I looked for any shred of evidence to confirm my hope. Looking back, I would guess that they both desperately needed affirmation from the other and didn't know how to give it. I wonder how different their relationship might have been as I was growing up if they could have found ways to openly encourage one another.

The great differences in Mom and Dad's personalities surely played a major part in the misunderstandings between them. In some ways, they were like oil and water together, the contrasts in how they were raised and formed as persons widening their natural differences. For instance, Dad, in general, wore his feelings on his sleeve while Mom kept hers inside. A visiting minister once quite unintentionally highlighted this difference. Speaking against conventional wisdom, he said it's healthy for children to occasionally see their parents openly disagree and experience what marriage is really like so they can learn how to resolve conflict. In classic form, Mom disagreed and Dad said appreciatively, "That's what I always figured."

At times, it was as if Mom and Dad did not speak the same language. Because of this, I liked hearing them talk to each other in their native Pennsylvania Dutch, a language only the two of them shared in a rather mysterious sort of way. Though I could not understand what they were saying, it was enough to know they understood each other.

Finances were also an obvious tension between Mom and Dad, especially when they experienced financial difficulty in spite of their best efforts. They didn't necessarily try to hide the obvious from us, however. Fred remembers that when he was about fifteen or sixteen, Mom and Dad were having a hard time making ends meet and called the five oldest children together for a family counsel. Being

At Easter get-togethers, Dad would emerge with a big, brown bag of peanuts, gather the kids, and toss the peanuts as the kids scrambled to retrieve them. The first Easter after Dad died, we were missing him and especially so when there was no one to do the peanut scramble. Feeling his absence, Mom bravely stepped forward and did the scattering in his place.

included in the meeting and having his advice sought made Fred feel valued and needed.

What is amazing is that Mom and Dad managed to stick together through all their differences and struggles. Their connecting points must have been strong enough to take them through their tough times. Their children, undoubtedly, were their strongest link to each other. In us, they found a reason to keep going. They gave a lot to us, and we gave back to them pride and joy.

Two things that especially bonded Mom and Dad together while raising us were singing and family devotions; they gave these practices a place of profound importance in our family life, and I found reassurance in the solidarity of Mom and Dad's togetherness in this. Even though we sometimes resisted the call to come for devotions, not wanting to stop what we were doing, I actually soaked that time up when it came down to it. Seeing Mom and Dad function as a team in this was wonderful; being part of it was even better. When we were asked to take turns reading the Bible and praying, we felt like we were part of something greater than ourselves.

In later years, Dad closed his prayers with "Forgive us where we have sinned and have come short of doing Thy will," while Mom would always end her prayers with "When our life's work is over, gather us all home to be with Thee, without the loss of one." Their prayer of inclusion drew us all in.

Mom and Dad were also a united front in their expectations of us to do our best (particularly in school) and to treat others with respect—especially them. So we knew how they felt about backtalking, but we also knew just as deeply that they loved us. With open hearts, they invested in us personally and spiritually, modeled sharing their faith, expressed confidence in us, encouraged us, and built us up. They accepted us and cared for us regardless of what we did, even while teaching us to conduct ourselves in such a way that we would not have a lot of regrets later in life.

They did this not only for us but also for the fresh air children from New York and the foster children they took in over the years. They also loved the babies they cared for whose mothers gave birth while incarcerated at the Muncy women's prison. In an interview for a newspaper article, Mom said,

Back row, l-r: Ada, Leona, Parke, Elam, Barb, Fred
Front row, l-r: Edith, Esther, Mom (holding baby Pete), Dad (holding John), Sue, Rose

"We believed these babies should be given loving, warm homes. [They] needed homes so we took them in. We're happy. It's so thrilling to go up there and pick up a little baby, take it home, and see what you can do with it." They unselfishly loved each of these babies as little individuals, all the while knowing they would have to relinquish them at some point. "It takes healing," Mom said, remembering the pain of letting go. But she and Dad felt they were serving the Lord "by taking care of his little ones."

Mom was in her late sixties and Dad his early seventies when they adopted my youngest sisters, Kenyatta and Siobohn, whose mothers were incarcerated at the time of their births. (See page 57 for the stories of their adoptions.)

Hospitality and treating others with respect was something else Mom and Dad did well together. They frequently hosted people in our home as guests, and living along I-80 gave them even more opportunities to be hospitable. They never locked the house, and one Sunday they came home from church and found a rather unkempt-looking man in it. Though this might have raised an eyebrow, they were not terribly put off upon finding him there. They believed it was their duty to reach out to those less fortunate. Dad, in his hospitable way, invited him to stay for dinner. Sometime later that afternoon, after the young man had eaten heartily of Mom's cooking, he said he had a confession to make. He had noticed fresh peaches in their basement and had eaten some because he was hungry. Mom and Dad just smiled and assured him it was okay.

Another I-80 guest was a stranded young man who came to our house late at night. Mom and Dad said he could spend the night on the couch and they would get help in the morning. The next day Mom and Dad were in the kitchen where Mom was cooking breakfast. They spoke in Pennsylvania Dutch about the young man, thinking he couldn't understand. They were startled to look up and see him in the doorway as he began speaking German—his clue to them that he understood what they were saying. Thankfully they weren't saying something he would have been offended by.

Mom and Dad would be the first to say they don't want recognition for the many times they saw needs and willingly did what they could to show love and care. But their influence will long be felt through their selfless giving, sharing, and parenting. Laboring harder than anyone else I know, they devoted their whole lives to their spirituality, the welfare of their family, their work, and maintaining their own sanity.

Our parents both ruled and served, and sometimes that worked beautifully and other times not so much; sometimes they handled life better than others. Sometimes the river carried us gently downstream together, and other times we bumped into logs and stones and each other along the way. Yet even then, in the midst of their shortcomings and our own, Mom and Dad were strong and ultimately fair and caring, their intentions and love for their children deep and true.

Of the fifty-seven years Mom and Dad were married, the last ten were some of their best together. Maybe there was not as much everyday stress of working

INTELLIGENCER JOURNAL, Lancaster, Pa., Friday, May 9, 1986 –

Mabel Stoltzfus Is Called 'Mom' By Lots Of People

LEWISBURG, Pa. (AP) — Mabel Stoltzfus, who turned 70 on March 9, will be getting Mother's Day greetings from a lot of people who call her "Mom."

Mrs. Stoltzfus and her husband, Mast, have reared 16 children of their own, adopted a 17th, hosted 12 Fresh Air children from New York City and taken in 13 more youngsters on a temporary basis.

Three of these foster children remain today with the Lewisburg couple, who will mark their 50th wedding anniversary Nov. 5.

She feels strongly about her role. A Mennonite, she opposes abortion. She stands firmly for warm, loving treatment of children, a belief that led her to accept youngsters in need of temporary care into her home.

Siobhon Fusaro, whose first name is pronounced Sa-bon, has been with the Stoltzfuses since she was 6 days old and a tiny five pounds. In two years, she has grown from a premature baby who was fed every two hours to become bigger than other children her age in the Buffalo Mennonite Church. Siobhon, who entered the terrible twos May 3, is the daughter of an inmate in the Muncy State Correctional Institution.

She is the couple's second foster child from a mother incarcerated at Muncy.

Mrs. Stoltzfus learned of the need for foster homes for babies born to prisoners through her involvement in a volunteer program at the institution. The Kelly Township residents also are foster parents to Marie and Jacob, 9 and 7, respectively, who came to them from a broken home in August 1984.

They attend the Maranatha Christian School, Watsontown, meaning Mrs. Stoltzfus is up packing lunches and getting them ready to meet the 7:16 bus each morning.

"Some people may think it's funny that we're involved in this," said Mrs. Stoltzfus, a rosy cheeked, brown-eyed woman who looks far younger than her years. "But we believe abortion and the killing of babies is wrong.

"We believe these babies should be given loving, warm homes. These babies needed homes, so we took them in. We're happy. It's so thrilling to go up there and pick up a little baby, take it home and see what you can do with it. To be married and have children is the greatest challenge there is."

True to her religious beliefs, Mrs. Stoltzfus is quick to shun glory or praise for herself.

"I want Christ to be exalted," she said. "I couldn't do this without him. I feel that if he calls on us to do something, then he'll give us the strength to do it."

"I'm thankful for good health. I think a lot depends on your attitude. Two different times I had three in diapers at once. It didn't seem bad."

Mrs. Stoltzfus, who became a great-grandmother a month ago, said she still babysits occasionally for her grandchildren, who number 48, but "I have my hands full with these three." At one time, the more than 30-year Union County resident used carbon paper to duplicate parts of letters, since some of the children are scattered and most have families of their own.

Lately, she said she has started photocopying letters and leaving space at the bottom for a few personal remarks or observations.

The Stoltzfus children are:

Parke, Lewisburg, a chicken farmer; Elam, Lewisburg, pediatrician; Barbara Metzger, New Columbia, does day-care in her home and decorates cakes; Leona Graybill, Granville Summit, minister's wife; Esther Metzler, Winthrop, Maine, minister's wife; Fred, Lewisburg, trucker; Ada Longenecker, West Milton, part-time nurse; Susi Horst,

Associated Press Wirephoto

Mabel Stoltzfus holds foster daughter Siobhon Fusaro at their home.

Palermo, Italy, minister's wife and trained as a registered nurse; Rose Huyard, Newport News, Va., schoolteacher and design artist; Edith Burkholder, Dryden, Canada, minister's wife and freelance artist; John, McConnellsburg, dairy farmer; Paul David, known as "Pete," Lewisburg, dairy farmer; Tim, Lewisburg, manager of a silo-building crew; Elvin, Mifflinburg, farmer; Dale, Reading, teacher; Miriam, Rosedale, Ohio, elementary education student at Rosedale Bible Institute; and Tina Weaver, New Columbia, a housecleaner.

Mrs. Stoltzfus said she and her husband, who still helps farm even though he will be 73 on May 26, treat the foster children as they did their own:

"We correct them like our own," she said. "You have to, or you couldn't handle them. You not only have to treat them like your own, but we want to."

to provide for their family and not as much economic difficulty. Maybe they had both come to accept their differences. Or, maybe it was a little bit of a lot of things.

Whatever it was, it was a gift. After Dad passed away, Mom said, "One of my hardest times was when my husband died." Perhaps the books about marriage I had put out for them were not necessary after all.

PART III

Together

7. Seasons

Each spring, I ran first thing in the morning to the lilac bush at the corner of our yard, eagerly sinking my nose into the dew-covered clusters of lavender lilacs. I inhaled deeply, and the heavenly fragrance transported me to a magical realm.

In summer, I licked the creamy, cold, vanilla freshness dripping off the metal paddle from the ice cream maker barrel. Its taste was sublime goodness.

In fall, I listened raptly to the symphony of crickets playing violins in their insect concert hall.

In winter, I curled into a ball, snuggling into the soft, fuzzy, flannel sheets that had replaced the cotton summer ones. I floated luxuriously on a warm, cozy cloud.

In each of the seasons, I saw beautiful, shifting colors—soft pink, light green, and yellow pastels in spring; bright crayon-box colors of blue, green, orange, red, yellow, and brown in summer and fall; and silhouettes of blacks and whites in winter.

Nestled within each of the seasons were our family's annual rituals, the singular rites of passage, and the repeated routines of ordinary time. From the gardens we planted to the food we ate and the clothes we wore, to the births of babies and celebrations of milestones, we found comfort and strength in the rhythm of our life together.

Then came the flood of 1972, a season all its own, brutally interrupting any sense of rhythm we had built together up to that point. The surging waters created a season of both destruction and rebirth, calling forth new inner strength and resources as family and friends came together to help rebuild our lives from the devastating chaos.

Spring

The things we could count on about spring set the pace for the rest of the year. The burst of new life in those early months shored us up for the blazing heat of summer, the hard toil of fall, and the bitter cold of winter.

By April Fool's Day, spring had officially arrived. Without fail, every first day of April when Dad woke Fred in the morning, he would yell, "Fred—the cows are out!" And Fred would bolt out of bed from a deep sleep. Dad would chuckle as Fred's head cleared from sleepy fog only to realize that once again he had fallen for it. Mom, on the other hand, didn't allow us to say "April Fools" when we played jokes; instead we were to say "First of April" because in her interpretation of Scripture, we were not to call someone a fool.

With the coming of spring, we could also count on fresh sand for the sandbox. Scooping up the new, loose sand, I would notice how the grains felt on the palms of my hands. Next, I'd take off my shoes and wiggle my toes down deep, knowing the looseness would not last long; with the next rain, it would become hard and packed down.

Opposite the sandbox, the winter-hardened ground in the fields gradually transformed into fine dirt. Brittle, dead stalks from last year's corn disappeared under dark-brown, clumsy mounds of soil turned up by the blades of the small plow, and seagulls appeared mysteriously, flying after the tractor and plow and dive-bombing for worms wiggling on the unearthed clumps. Their plaintive cries added to their mystique. When the disc and cultipacker broke the rugged, plowed earth down into softened, fine soil, the seagulls disappeared just as quickly as they had come.

Like the sand in the sandbox, the fine soil would not last. Rain would soon come and flatten it out, but meanwhile, the fresh expanse of brownness begged exploring. Edith and I ran in the new tractor tracks in the field behind the barn, holding hands across the span between them, not stopping until we reached the distant fencerow marking the border of the field. Panting as we caught our breath, we turned to look back at the barn in the distance, which in its smallness appeared as if on another planet.

The garden soil also turned powder soft in the spring. When Mom said, "Dad, it's time to plow the garden," the tractor and plow would exit the distant fields and make their way to the garden on temporary assignment. Looking strangely out of place so close at hand, the plow would turn over the first furrow of the previous summer's garden dirt and simultaneously release a fresh burst of excitement in me. We were about to plant a brand-new garden, a ritual all its own.

First came the pounding of stakes into the ground at each end of the garden, with a taut stretch of baler twine between the stakes. These lines of twine served as guides for hoeing straight rows of small trenches to drop seeds into.

Making the rows was part two of the garden-planting ritual.

Planting was part three, when Mom, with packs of seeds in her hands, called us out to the garden. As she gave us our own pack of seeds, she'd say almost reverently, "Now, these are beans … these are corn … these are radishes … and this is how you plant them … this far apart …" I loved carefully covering the seeds with the soft soil along the sides of the trench, trying to imagine what they would become. The day I discovered small, green sprouts peeking through the tops of the rows, I was too excited to think about all the upcoming work this meant. They were new plants in our garden, part four of the ritual.

Mom allowed us to have a little section of the garden to plant our own seeds so we could sell the produce. When we didn't have a market for the radishes we grew, she bought them from us.

Tomato planting was also a springtime rite. After the last frost, when temperatures got warm enough to plant tomatoes, it was time to come together in a concerted effort to get the job done. Dad drove the tractor, pulling the two-seater tomato planter as he joked, smiled, and looked back at us every so often. He gave the impression that he was enjoying himself immensely. When he started a fire at the end of the row for us to warm ourselves on those mornings of lingering cold, a spirit of camaraderie encircled the fire as we stretched our hands out above the flames.

Planting tomatoes was a team effort. It began with pulling bunches of closely packed tomato plants from a wooden, thin-slated crate; taking off the rubber band holding the bunch together; shaking out the dirt to loosen the roots; gently separating the plants; then stacking our tray on the plant-laden tomato planter in front of our seat. While we did this, Dad would fill the water tank fastened to the tractor, then dump bags of blue fertilizer granules into it. Now we could finally take our seat on the back of the planter to laboriously make our way to the other end of the long field, where we repeated the tank- and tray-filling process.

Alternately revolving metal planting arms circled round and round, keeping us on our toes as we tried not to miss our turn to slap a tomato plant into them. The squirt of blue, fertilized water released for each plant placed in the ground sounded good to me. When one of us ran out of plants before we reached the end of the field, the person beside us would hurl a bunch of plants over into our empty tray—a simple act of team spirit.

Sitting on the planter in the midst of tomato-planting concentration with the earth under my feet, I'd hear the distant cry of wild geese flying north, and I couldn't help but take a sneak peek at their V-shape weaving slightly in the sky above me. I may have missed a plant or two as their honking pulled my eyes upward, but I didn't want to miss this display of "spring in the air." Camaraderie on the earth, camaraderie in the sky.

In contrast to the peaceful, leisurely pace of planting tomatoes, spring was also a time when I sprang into action whipping the outside into shape, raking in the yard and around the farm buildings, planting and weeding flower beds. I took this task on as if my life depended on it. (Maybe it was one thing I felt I could do that I had control of when I couldn't control other things, such as Mom and Dad's often conflictual relationship.) Observing my frenetic activity one day, Dad said, "Rose, you are running around here like a chicken with its head chopped off."

While the outcome of what I accomplished outside pleased me, the inside was a different story. Relentlessly I organized closets, cupboards, and anything else out of order. Other family members, however, didn't seem to understand my system of order, so, much to my dismay, closets and cupboards usually returned to their original dishevelment in short order.

Summer

As spring gave way to meandering days of summer, we settled into a different kind of rhythm. With the garden in front of the house and the tomato fields planted in the distance, I felt a strong urge to plant my bare feet on the earth. I searched the yard diligently to catch sight of a bumblebee and eagerly watched the thermometer, because the first buzzing bumblebee or temperatures reaching eighty degrees meant I could finally go barefoot. When one of these would happen, I'd race into the house to tell Mom, kick off my shoes, leap over the three porch steps, and run through the yard with the exhilarating tickle of grass on my tender feet—feet that would soon grow so calloused on the bottom I could barely feel the grass anymore.

In early summer, a morning saunter out through the wet grass to the bed of poppies—brilliantly red, velvety, and open-faced—and fragrant, pink-and-white, ant-covered peonies (I was told the ants helped them open to full bloom) would get my day off to a wide-awake start. The simple joy of feasting my eyes on flowery splendor in the morning deeply satisfied my young soul.

With the arrival of the warmer days of summer, the routine of our sleeping arrangements changed. The most coveted space was a balcony just over the kitchen porch entrance, tucked into an L-shape corner of the house. When Mom finally gave in to our begging and put sheets on the bunk beds on the balcony, we had only to figure out who got to sleep there first—girls or boys. With decisions of paramount importance such as this, Mom exercised fairness by grasping a slip of paper in one of her hands behind her back. The boy or girl who correctly guessed which hand the paper was in earned first sleeping-on-the-balcony rights. Waking in the balcony's open air to the morning sounds of the farm—dogs barking, Dad and the boys conversing in the distance, Mom talking to a cat in the yard below as she hung wash—both excited and calmed me.

My brothers found ways to create excitement before they even made it onto the balcony. On several occasions, they stretched their legs precariously from the window sill of their bedroom over to the outside banister of the balcony a few feet away. The span was quite a reach, so it's no wonder they didn't consult my parents first. Leave it to my brothers—no getting bored with doing things the same way. Why should they simply walk when they could engage in breathtaking risk instead?

Summer evenings also beckoned us outside to experience the insects up close and personal. Lightning bugs in the yard or a nearby field signaled an invitation to grab a jar and capture as many as I could to create a blinking lantern or to light up the tip of my nose when I went so far as to remove the light from one of their bodies and rub it there. And as soon as it got dark enough, green and brown moths with fuzzy wings, body, heads, and antennae flopped on the screen door and outside windows toward the inside light.

The day I discovered a green caterpillar with black stripes circling its body on a bean plant in the garden, I felt I was holding a miracle-in-the-making. I dropped the caterpillar into a quart jar, punched some holes in the screwed-on lid, and put it in my bedroom, curious to see the changes that would transpire. Daily I replenished fresh, green leaves for the caterpillar to eat, until it transformed into a hanging, green chrysalis. Each day after this, I eagerly examined the jar. The morning I discovered a beautiful monarch butterfly fluttering inside, I couldn't take my eyes off it. Finally, I released it and watched it take wing. From crawling green to winged orange-and-black—nothing but a miracle.

Newly hatched, fly-sized frogs covering muddy rocks at the edge of the river also seemed a miracle to me, no less so than the frogs plaguing Egypt in the biblical story of the exodus. The teensy critters made their surprise appearance at the beginning of every summer; they came, and then they went almost as quickly. I only found them if I just happened to go down to the river the right day to explore. Because they were profusely scattered everywhere, I thought I could easily snatch one up. But they would fool me by springing out of my grasp on their miniature legs. When I finally managed to catch one in my cupped hands or in an upside down can, I'd throw it into the water for its first swimming lesson, usually short-lived because a fish would spot it immediately, surface, and devour it all in one smooth motion. When this occurred, I felt only a tinge of disappointment, knowing the frog's demise was a part of the natural cycle of life.

The cycle of living things was no more apparent than in the garden. Tiny brown, black, and white seeds sprouting into seedlings gave rise to a garden full of green plants growing rapidly under the warm, summer sun. On the bean stalks, I watched for the blossoms that would become minuscule green beans. As weeds began to emerge in the rows and between plants, Mom would instruct us to dig the garden worker out from its place of winter storage. The garden worker—a contraption with a large wheel in front, two long handles spreading out in a V-shape behind it, and three small, plow-like pieces of metal attached at the bottom of the wheel—was most effective with teamwork. The small plows dug deeper into the soil between rows if one person pushed down on the handles from behind the garden worker and another person, with a rope of baler twine tied around their waist, pulled from the front, in horse and driver style. If I was the "horse" and walked too fast, the "driver" would yell, "Hey, slow down," which meant the garden worker was just skimming the ground, not digging deep enough into the soil to uproot the weeds. When we had done all we could with the garden worker, we'd lay it on its side at the end of the garden and pull weeds between plants by hand or dig them out with a hoe. The long task of weeding the whole garden went more quickly when someone else worked close by to converse with.

The planting, the weeding, and then the picking. Mom was often in the garden early on summer mornings picking lima beans and green beans. She seemed to enjoy the task of gathering in basket after basket. When we'd get up and see six or seven full baskets sitting on the porch, we knew they had to be empty by the end of the day. That left us no choice but to pull up a chair or find a spot on the porch swing as we circled 'round the baskets, regardless of what we may have wanted to do instead. The lima beans with their tough, unyielding shells were the hardest to shell. But we were in this together, so the hours we spent shelling baskets of lima beans or snapping off the ends of green beans and breaking them into small pieces didn't seem quite as laborious as they might have otherwise.

We sang silly songs, held races to see who could finish their basket first, and passed the time by reciting little ditties. One of which was taking turns describing something gross—such as a squashed skunk in the road with maggots on it— then going around the circle beginning with the "describer" saying, "I one it" and continuing on … until the eighth person said, "I eight it!" followed by a chorus of "Eeewwww." The moment two of us said the same thing at the same time, we stopped doing beans to interlock little fingers and alternately recite, "Pins." "Needles." "What goes up the chimney?" "Smoke." "May yours and my wish never be broke." Each then made a silent wish, not telling the other what it was lest the wish be broken.

We kicked our feet a lot to keep the sticky, buzzing flies from landing on our skin as they circled determinedly around us. Our reward for finishing the task—jumping into the river for a swim—could not come fast enough.

It was the girls who assisted Mom with the beans, but making homemade ice cream at the end of hot summer days required everyone's help. We made it on the porch. First came the crushed ice, layered alternately with large grains of salt in the space between the wooden barrel on the outside and the small metal canister inside. Then we poured the creamy liquid mixture into the canister and placed the paddle in the middle. And finally, we crowned the whole bit with the gear mechanism and handle topped with a burlap bag to keep the cold in. The process itself built anticipation. We each had a chance to turn the handle—the younger ones first while it was easier and the older ones when the mixture began to thicken and the handle turned harder. At this stage, we knew the ice cream was just about ready to eat. If Mom saw the mixture clinging to the sides and paddles when she opened the metal canister, she would nod her head, signaling the long-awaited moment—it was time to bring out bowls and line up to receive our dollop of ice cream. Whoever got the paddle could start eating first since it had to be pulled out before the ice cream could be dished out.

Most tasks on the farm needed all available hands, from oldest to youngest. For haymaking, the younger ones' contribution was the best one from my perspective. Mom would hand me a plastic container of lemonade with sliced lemons floating on top and ask me to carry out it out to the field where Dad and the older siblings were making hay in the heat. Holding my head high, I'd take on a posture of importance and walk confidently with the sloshing lemonade while another sibling toted paper cups and still another candy bars. Carrying that heavy vessel all the way out the lane and across the field was no small feat, and I always felt like I had saved the day and that it was worth every bit of my effort. Maybe because I picked up on the importance of this job from Mom or maybe because of the way Dad and my older siblings smiled when they saw me coming.

Back then more of us had to work together to make hay, because we didn't have highly mechanized farm machinery. Someone drove the tractor and baler while another person on the wagon in back grabbed the square bales of hay exiting the chute of the baler. That person then passed the bales off to one or two others who stacked the wagon so tall that it appeared like a giant, hay-bale pyramid. Sometimes I ran alongside the wagon just so I could climb to the top of the pyramid with those who did the loading while the tractor and wagon slowly made their way down the lane and into the upstairs barn. Those in the house who were assigned the job of unloading the hay headed to the barn when they saw this procession coming.

When evening arrived, we'd use the bales from the barn to feed the heifers at the end of the long, half-mile lane. I often jumped on the back of the pickup truck with a couple siblings and sat astride the bales. It was a carefree time to end the day as we talked and laughed both going out and coming back.

In late July and early August, the corn on either side of the lane grew to about five feet tall. Who knew this could pose a threat to younger siblings? One evening when the family sat down to supper, Elvin's spot was empty. Mom asked, "Where's Elvin?" (Elvin and Tim were about three and four years old at the time.) Tim nonchalantly replied, "Oh, we were playing in the cornfield. He's still out there." Several of us sprang up from our seats to search for him. Hearing Elvin's crying, we ran in the direction of his sobs. As we called him, he followed our voices and burst through the tall cornstalks, desperately flailing his way out.

Summer days ended with a feet-washing ritual. As it was getting dark, Mom would call out, "Okay, it's time to come wash your feet." Standing by the blue plastic basin of warm water she had set on the second step of the porch, she would casually supervise the process while we took turns dipping our dirty feet into the water. "Now make sure you put soap on the washcloth," she'd say. If I was first in line, I'd dry my feet with the towel so I'd have time to finish whatever I had started just before this while all the other feet, big and small, were washed. The croaking of bullfrogs in the river, the fragrant bar of soap, and the flash of lightning bugs at hand made this feet-washing ritual a rather pleasant way to end the day.

Fall

The monotone sound of crickets and other insects ushered in a melancholy note of fall approaching. But the colorful display of trees along the riverbank, the big tub of multicolored chow-chow, the copper kettle of red tomato ketchup, and the multiple jars of canned yellow peaches, green beans, and red beets lining the cellar shelves were anything but monotone.

Fall was a closing out of summer and preparing for winter. Vegetables from the garden were already frozen and canned to feed us in the months ahead, field corn was gathered in and put in the corncrib or made into silage to feed the cows until spring, and the tomato fields were left with sprawling, dying remains of plants.

The garden, now finished offering up its summer fruit, sat barren with just dry stalks remaining. After we gathered in the final vegetables from the garden, Mom would take the galvanized metal tub down off its nail in the washhouse and dump chunks of carrots, celery, tomatoes, corn, and all manner of chopped-up vegetables into it to make chow-chow. After adding vinegar and other flavorings to the colorful mixture, she would can it and add it to the nearly overflowing basement shelves.

As if to say a final farewell to the summer garden, Dad would build a small fire at the garden's edge, under the huge, copper kettle, to make ketchup or tomato cocktail. The kettle, black on the outside and shiny on the inside, received the last of the season's tomatoes and soon became a boiling cauldron of mush, not looking anything like ketchup or tomato cocktail. But after we put the concoction through a sieve and inundated it with pungent spices, the final product looked and smelled tantalizing.

The last thing Mom would cook in the copper kettle was apples to make applesauce or apple butter. Making applesauce was a cinch compared to making apple butter. Apple butter required a long time of stirring until it finally boiled down to just the right thickness. When I was called on to take a turn, I felt like I was an important part of something bigger than myself. The spicy smells of cloves and cinnamon added at the end hung in the air around the copper kettle, and I stood back and inhaled.

With canning finished for the season, Mom could take a breath and fold her arms across her chest, deeply satisfied at the sight of all the jars she had canned— enough food to take us through the approaching winter. As if on cue, birds flew south in droves. Wild geese flew the opposite direction they had come from at the beginning of spring. And now it was time to butcher chickens.

Chicken butchering was a day I didn't want to miss. It was strangely awful and good at the same time. The night before butchering, Mom would gather up a few of us to go out to the barn with her to capture chickens roosting there that had escaped from the chicken house. Finding them with her flashlight, she'd point them out to us. We'd grab them, carry them upside down by their feet with their wings flapping, and throw them into the chicken house with all the other chickens.

The next morning, Dad would bring out the chopping block, which had two nails about two inches apart on the top, and plunk it down in the garden. Mom would put a large kettle of water on the stove to heat while Dad and the boys caught random chickens. They brought them, two in each hand, to the chopping block. With sharpened hatchet close by, Dad would retrieve a chicken from one of the boys, carry it to the chopping block, and put its head between the two nails. Mom couldn't bear to watch what came next. Though she ran away as fast as she could to avoid seeing the inevitable, she could still hear the sound of the axe hitting the block. One mighty thwack severed the chicken's head and left the body flopping around on the ground. We were careful to avoid getting in its way. Though this was gruesome, I did not think it to be cruel. I knew it had to be done so we could eat.

My siblings and I gathered up the scattered, beheaded chickens by their feet, careful not to let their bloody necks get against our clothes, and brought them to where Mom was waiting with scalding-hot water. There we laid them in a pile on the ground, and Mom lifted them one by one, dipping them quickly into the hot water then laying them on a table for us to begin the unpleasant task of plucking the wet, hot, smelly, stick-to-your-hands feathers off the chickens.

We couldn't pull the hairs off the skin of the chickens, but Mom got rid of them quite effectively. She lifted one of the heavy, round lids from the kitchen cookstove, placed a crumpled sheet or two of newspaper inside the lid, held a match to the paper, and dangled the chickens one by one over the leaping flames to singe off any remaining hairs. With each chicken, the repugnant smell grew stronger.

When Mom showed me how to butcher a chicken, I was amazed at what I found inside: coils of intestines, heart, liver, lungs, gizzard, and sometimes partly formed eggs in different stages of development, from tiny clusters of yellow balls to a large yolk that looked like a ball of sunshine. Sometimes there was a soft shell around one of the yolks that was getting ready to be laid. Cleaning out the gizzard with its grit-filled inside pocket fascinated me. Butchering a chicken was a great lesson in anatomy.

With chickens in the freezer, we were finally ready for winter, which was just around the corner. Part of rounding that corner was returning in September to the two-room Buffalo Creek School, flanked by the creek itself. As I'd step inside the door on the first day, the greeting of freshly oiled, wooden floors would put me in the mood for a new school year. Cursive and manuscript letters of the alphabet lined the front of the room. It was within these walls that I learned the basics of math, grammar, history, and how to get along with people different from my family.

Each day, Mom and Dad drove a total of sixty-four miles—two round trips—to haul us to school. It was sixteen miles from home, but Mom and Dad made it a part of their normal routine and never complained about how much time it took. The rides back and forth were no big deal for us; that is, unless Dad took us in the pickup. That meant we crowded into the cab of the pickup, three across beside Dad and two deep. Being on someone's lap or holding someone made the ride seem unbearably long. This was especially true for Fred, who accused Sue—the sibling who usually ended up on his lap—of intentionally digging her tailbone into his leg. Sue denied the accusation.

When Mom hauled us and stopped to get groceries or do other shopping, it was a test of patience for those whose turn it was to wait in the car, unless Mom happened to leave the keys in the ignition. In those instances, we seized the opportunity to change the radio station to one that played "worldly" music. When we saw Mom leave the store, we quickly changed back to the original station. After all, she had never told us we couldn't change it.

When Mom got groceries, I always hoped she would get something special for our school lunches so I could flaunt my open lunch box, with the chance that my school friends would see the chips or baked goodies in store wrappers. Rarely did we have anything store-bought in our lunches, since homemade food was common-place then, especially for my family. Hopefully the food wouldn't be tainted with the smell of paint, given that we used the same repainted metal lunch box year after year, unless we were in first grade and got a new one or the one we were using rusted through.

The task of packing our school lunches in the morning usually fell to one of the older siblings. The exception to this was when it was our family's turn to take advantage of the "cookstove" heat from the school's furnace and bring baked potatoes for our lunch. (The school created a schedule for the families to bring potatoes on different days—Stoltzfuses on Monday, Weavers on Tuesday, Sharps on Wednesday, etc—to keep the number of people cooking on any one day manageable; we attended a two-room school house with grades one to four in one room and grades five to eight in the other room, which meant that families could have as many as four children in different grades in one classroom.) We'd pick out medium-sized potatoes, wash them, rub butter on them, wrap them in foil, and put them in our lunch boxes. I liked having baked-potato day because then I didn't have to worry about my lunch looking acceptable to my classmates. A baked potato was a baked potato. When I arrived at school, the first thing I did was take it out of my lunch box and place it carefully on the inside front ledge of the large, round, hot furnace at the back of the room, confident it would be soft by noon.

Occasionally there was nothing to put in our sandwiches except canned pickles. I didn't especially care for pickle sandwiches myself, and it didn't help when Miriam, one of my classmates, saw me eating mine and exclaimed, "Ewwww, a pickle sandwich?!" I felt annoyed that she had checked out my sandwich in the first place and embarrassed that I had it.

In warm weather, we ate our lunches on the bridge over the creek. I often lingered there a bit longer than the others when my lunch was finished, to peer down into the water below and observe fish swimming slowly around stones and rocks, mesmerizing me into a calm, relaxed state of mind.

Pupils took turns carrying a large, yellow, plastic bucket with a lid to the Brocious' house on the other side of the bridge, who generously allowed us to draw drinking water from their kitchen sink. When it was my turn, I felt uneasy. The terrier dog barking furiously just inside the door intimidated me, and I couldn't comprehend how Mrs. Brocious could sit on her easy chair in the next room in the middle of the day, smoking a cigarette and watching black and white TV. Who did this? Mrs. Brocious rarely acknowledged us and might not have been aware we were there but for her yipping dog. I tried my best to align myself so I could watch TV while the water was running, hoping the bucket wouldn't fill too quickly. My partner and I heaved the bucket out of the sink together, trying not to leave any traces of spilled water, and carried it back to the school where we dumped it into a large, ceramic-spouted jug.

After completing eighth grade at Buffalo Creek School, I transitioned to the local public high school. My sisters and I were expected to go to high school but not necessarily the boys. For them it was a toss-up, depending on how much help Dad needed on the farm that year. Dad said it was important that the girls get a high school education so we would have a better chance of making a living if something happened to our husbands, whereas the boys could be self-employed without a high school diploma. The year Dad decided John should quit school after ninth grade to help on the farm, I was distraught, knowing John wanted to continue his schooling. I called Parke and asked him to please talk to Dad. When Dad picked up the phone and I heard him say, "Ack, my. Did she really?" I knew it was Parke on the other end. John was allowed to go back to school that year.

I was not prepared for public high school. Being surrounded by swarms of people, venturing from class to class with an armload of books, and having to do homework was a strange new world. The first few days I found myself in a dense mental fog, feeling out of touch with reality and completely clueless about how to do Algebra I in spite of Sue's patient efforts at showing me; positive and negative integers—what in the world were they? After a few days, the fog cleared, and I made some friends with whom I ate lunch. I was the only obviously Mennonite girl in the whole school and was grateful for these friends who didn't seem to care that I looked very different from everyone else.

When we got good grades in high school, Mom and Dad beamed with pride over our report cards. (And we got a dollar for every A on our report cards at the end of the year before we went to high school.) It seemed ironic to me that on the one hand getting good grades was important to Mom and Dad while on the other hand it wasn't a big deal to them if we did not complete high school. But they just wanted us to do our best.

Mom and Dad also saw to it that our learning extended beyond the class-room. When my brothers went small game hunting in the fall along the river, for instance, they learned how to skin the squirrels or rabbits they shot. They'd proudly hand their skinned, naked trophies over to Mom, who would carefully search each one for BBs lodged in the meat, then soak the carcasses in salt water. When satisfied that they were clean enough, she would put them in potpie or dip them in flour and fry them whole for an entrée. When she left the squirrels intact, they looked like they had been roasted on a spit. We'd hold them in our hands and eat around the bones. Though Mom was usually successful in removing the BBs, an occasional missed pellet showed up in an unpleasant crunch of teeth on metal, similar to biting into an egg shell.

From the time Elam and Parke were nine and eleven years old respectively, they went hunting for squirrels along the edge of the farm at Oley. They sometimes sneaked over into the neighbor's posted land and watched carefully for the owner. If they shot a squirrel on his land, they'd dash over to get it and hurry back home with their prize before the neighbor knew what had happened. Taking a risk in hunting added more excitement for them. Mom had no idea that the squirrel she fried for Elam and Parke one day was ill gotten.

At age ten, Pete went small game hunting on the farm by himself, where pheasants, squirrels, rabbits, and ducks were fair game. He shot five Ringneck pheasants by the time he was eleven years old, an impressive feat since those birds hid so carefully they could usually only be seen when they were startled and rose straight up from the ground at great speed. They were not an easy target.

We all got involved in a hunting adventure one fall when Fred talked Dad into taking Mom and the nine children still at home along with them to Colorado on an elk hunting trip. Fred's plan was for Mom and us kids—everyone from Sue on down to Mim—to stay in Denver with Mom's sister, Aunt Mary, a nurse, while he and Dad and Uncle Leon went to the mountains to hunt. Dad agreed. We left in a caravan of Uncle Leon's large, blue station wagon filled with Mom and the kids, and Dad's pickup with a makeshift wooden camper on the bed. We drove straight through from Pennsylvania to Colorado, with drivers taking shifts. We stopped only to make meals using our camp stove at roadside rests.

Winter

At the season's change, Mom took her cue from the first killing frost to replace our cool summer sheets with the warm flannel sheets. Snuggling down into the comfort of soft, fuzzy flannel, I reassured myself, "Okay, Old Man Winter, bring it on. I'm ready for you now." One night, Sue and I—sharing a bed—got in each other's space of warmth, producing an argument that quickly spiraled into a pinching fight. After Sue had pinched me one too many times, I barked at her, "Sue, stop pinching me. I want to have fair skin." Sue retorted, "Well, I do too!"

Old Man Winter defied our attempts to stay warm in our cold, drafty house, especially upstairs where there was no heat. During the coldest nights, my bedroom got cold enough to freeze a glass of water sitting on the inside window-sill, and I dreaded getting out of bed in the mornings. With traces of our breath in the air, my sisters and I flung back the covers, grabbed our clothes, tucked them under our arms, and hurried downstairs to spread them out on one of the space heaters, just long enough to get them warm, except for when we left them too long and they scorched. (My white sweater was one of those, and I never could get the orange mark to come out.)

For about two weeks one winter, the warm downstairs turned into an infirmary of makeshift beds when eight of us—from Esther on down to Elvin, the baby— got the old-fashioned German measles. This was before the vaccine for measles became routine, and all eight of us got sick at the same time. When we were our sickest, we hardly cared what was going on around us, and the days all blended together. When we began feeling better, yet were still quarantined in our shared misery, we began to feel restless. So when the box of goodies from Uncle Leon and Aunt Ida arrived one day, it seemed to drop straight out of heaven. We ripped the box open on the kitchen table and pulled out love and caring in the form of treats and special projects for each of us. Mine was a bluebird to paint, sitting on a perch. Someone else got a Baltimore oriole. Others got paint-by-number sets.

Sick or not, leaving the warmth of the downstairs stove on winter mornings was hard until we finally got a furnace in the basement. At that point, we got rid of our space heaters, and by the time Mim and Tina were little girls, each room downstairs had a small, square register on the floor through which warm air blew if the furnace fan was on. Mim prayed this would be so every time she came darting down the stairs in the morning, her feet barely touching the steps in her desperate rush to check the kitchen register—hot air or no hot air? When Mim and Tina packed their school lunches, they complained about how cold they were and fought over who would stand on the register to pack their lunches. Dad would say to them, "Well, if you would just dress warmer and put on long johns like I do, you wouldn't be so cold." They'd look at him, horrified that he would even suggest this, but for a minute the unthinkable took their mind off being cold, as Dad had probably intended it would.

It was not uncommon to find two or three of us standing in a huddle on one of the registers, seeking warm air to blow up on our legs. This could happen any time, but it was especially the case those mornings or evenings that we were not actively putting off body heat. We'd stand with our arms around one another, pulling tightly together over the small area. The warmth was comforting, and knowing we were in this together was also comforting as we quietly conversed together.

The steady warmth of the old cookstove in the kitchen was especially inviting, and when there was work that could be done sitting down, we'd pull our chairs up as close to it as possible. One of those tasks was shelling field corn by hand from ears Mom had dried out in the oven. Our fingers got sore from prying the hard kernels off the cob, but that was not reason enough for us to stop before the last kernel.

The job was less torturous when we thought about what was to come. After Mom took the shelled corn to the mill to be ground into cornmeal, she mixed it with water, boiled it until it thickened into mush, then poured it into cake pans to cool. Next morning for breakfast we could count on delicious, crispy fried mush with soft-boiled eggs or tomato sauce.

Fortunately, we had plenty of such food stored in the house for the winter months, because when blizzards blew in, huge drifts snowed us in. There was no way we could get out our lane until the county's V-plow came and dug us out.

But being snowed in was exhilarating. Time stood still, school and church were canceled, and everyone stayed inside as much as possible. One year, the V-plow couldn't get through the barricade of snow that completely filled in the space between the five-foot banks flanking the corner of the driveway in front of the house. Not knowing how long we would be really snowed in was worrisome until a larger county plow opened up the canyon of snow.

While we waited for our lane to be plowed, our trusty Ford tractor came to the rescue. This same tractor that plowed the fields in the spring and pulled wagon-loads of hay in the summer and loads of tomatoes in the fall now took us through the fields to the end of the lane when we had to get out. If the kerosene for our space heaters was getting low, Dad would throw a fifty-five-gallon barrel on the back of the tractor and drive it to New Columbia a few miles away to fill it.

Regardless of the winter temperatures, life on the farm kept moving along. In the barn, the smell of fresh sawdust picked up from the local sawmill, dumped onto the barn floor, then thrown into cow stalls filled our olfactory senses. One cold winter day when I was about four, Parke took me with him on one of these trips to get a load and asked if I would like an ice cream cone. I replied, "If you can make it warm." It didn't make sense to me to eat something that would make me even colder.

Each January we butchered several pigs. This became a major production, with all of us gathering together to make sausage, chitlins, pork chops, and roasts. Dad's specialty was making scrapple in the huge, steaming kettle over the fire, into which was dumped the ground cooked liver, heart, and brain along with buckwheat flour and other ingredients. Stirring until the mixture thickened, Dad took special pride in his scrapple if it was mostly free of lumps when it was finally poured into bread pans. Mom took the pig stomach home and carefully scalded and scraped it, getting it ready to fill with stuffing to bake. Dad hung slabs of meat in the smokehouse to be made into bacon after carefully seasoning and preparing them.

Sometimes winter seemed to drag on forever. The butchering in January broke it up a bit as did the creek freezing over at school, when we had longer recesses for skating and sliding on the ice. When my classmates began arriving at school with ice skates slung over their shoulders, it was a bittersweet time for me. More time outside was great, yet I felt disappointed that I didn't have a pair of ice skates like everyone else. They were a luxury we couldn't afford. Seeing my plight, one of my classmates offered to bring me an extra pair she had. Every morning I watched eagerly as she stepped out of her car, but day after day she forgot, almost as if the skates were an afterthought. Finally, one day she brought them. What she hadn't told me was that they were hockey skates and much too large for me, but that didn't stop me from trying them out. I learned that positioning my feet sideways kept them from wobbling so much in the cavity of the too-large skates. Somewhere along the way, I got an honest-to-goodness pair of figure skates—a tightly fitting, white pair with shiny silver blades and teeth at the tips.

Not only did the creek at school freeze solid, but sometimes when it was unusually cold, the river froze from side to side as one continuous block. As spring approached, the ice loosened from the banks with a thunderous cracking sound up one side and down the other, later floating down the river in huge chunks. The year we had record-breaking low temperatures, the river froze a couple feet thick and took longer than usual to break up. When it did, huge walls of ice remained, which meant the ice chunks could hardly move because the river was so full. This, in turn, caused large slabs of ice to pile up along the banks of the river and spill out onto the land in some places. Remnants of melting ice remained long after warmer weather came.

Winter's harshness was offset somewhat for my brothers by trapping and hunting. Parke and Elam set muskrat traps along the creek in Oley and sold the hides. One winter they trapped a total of thirty-seven muskrats. After scouting where muskrats hung out, Pete set traps along the river. One year he used one of Mom's canners to store roadkill for bait that he cut up and put in the freezer— a practical idea I suppose, but a startling surprise when I opened the lid of the canner one day to check its contents. I screamed, horrified to find a dead cat inside.

One cold, winter morning, I went hunting with Dad and the boys. I had happened to mention one day as hunting season approached that I might like to go too. Before I knew what was happening, at the insistence of my brothers

I had a hunting license in hand and a rifle to target shoot. Since there was no backing out, I conceded, and at the crack of dawn found myself silently climbing a snow-covered mountain with the male members of my family. It didn't take long for my feet to get cold. My black, dressy looking boots with the side zipper were hardly a match for the temperature that day. Embarrassed at being so unprepared, I decided to not say anything about my freezing feet. My boots didn't have the tread needed for the steeper parts, and when I began to slip and slide, John, a few steps ahead of me, quietly extended his hand behind him and pulled me to the top, not making mention of my inadequate boots.

The day became a feat of endurance with my numb feet. I was more focused on how I was going to survive than I was on shooting a deer. When a nice buck appeared in front of me several yards away, I couldn't shoot. Dad asked me why I hadn't taken a shot, and I told him I wasn't sure where he was in the brush behind the buck. He had seen the deer too and was waiting for me to take the first shot at it. Lucky for that buck, my cold feet saved the day for him as he went crashing through the brush to safety. I never again said I wanted to go hunting. And the male members of my family didn't ask me.

Christmas

Christmas time was a pivotal point of the year, when excitement mounted and anticipation was palpable. The air was so cold that my breath hung heavy in cloud formation, and so dense I could walk through it and see it dissipate around me. But the Christmas season brought warmth.

We always made Christmas sugar cookies in various shapes—animals, angels, stars, trees—and decorated them with sprinkles, raisins, and silver balls. We carefully chose which one to eat as if certain figures tasted better than others.

Cookies were also for giving. When Parke and Elam were small boys, Mom insisted they take cookies to Harry Brumbach, an old, dirty, heavy-whiskered, tobacco-chewing hermit who wore a big black hat and coat and mumbled as he walked by. Harry lived about a quarter mile away. Parke and Elam were afraid of him and would hide when he walked on the road in front of the house. And now they were being made to take him cookies. Tiptoeing up to his door, they knocked timidly. From inside they heard a gruff, "Who's there?" Together they chorused, "We have cookies for you." When Harry the hermit not only invited them to come in but also thanked them when they entered, they stood flabbergasted for a second, then turned and walked back out the door. The experience took away any fear Parke and Elam had of him.

Though we made Christmas trees in cookie form, we didn't have an actual Christmas tree in our house, because they were "worldly." Instead, we brought our "tree" in branch by branch as we cut off evergreen sprigs and laid them on mantles with tall, red candles rising up out of them for Christmas decorations. Sometimes we added shiny-colored ball ornaments among the branches.

The long-awaited Sears Christmas catalog, a thin book filled with images of things we longed for, brought its own decorative touch to the season. It was almost as if dreaming over the bikes, red wagons, binoculars, dolls, and play food was as good as having them. I knew I would never dare ask for the expensive things, but just in case, I'd mark the pages of especially coveted items, circling the items themselves. Then I'd put the open catalog in obvious places where Mom would have to move it and hopefully see what I had marked.

Though we wouldn't have had much to look forward to if Christmas had just been about getting gifts, we eagerly anticipated the one gift that we would each receive. In the weeks before Christmas day, Mom and Dad would talk quietly in Dutch—in the front seat of the car, while they were standing in the corner of the kitchen, or wherever they happened to be—so we couldn't understand what they were saying. Convinced they were discussing gifts for us, we strained to hear. They seemed strangely at ease with each other, and it felt good to see them communicating with each other in this way.

When Christmas eve arrived, Dad went Christmas caroling with the church while Mom stayed home with us. We could hear her shuffling around in the attic where she had hidden our gifts, as we lay in bed giggling under the covers, hardly able to contain our eagerness. A bunch of us would sleep in the same bed so we wouldn't sleep as soundly and would wake up easier at midnight—the time we were allowed to go downstairs to see our presents. Mim and Tina were so keyed up one Christmas evening that they sang song after song, trying their best to stay awake. As we "slept," Mom would set a plate down at each person's spot around the table, then place that person's gift on their plate. Usually she set an orange on each plate, too, and sometimes a hard-candy animal sucker.

When we awoke, we'd scurry down the stairs, run out to the kitchen, and flip on the switch, unwrapping the whole magical scene with light. I'd stand still for a moment, enraptured by the gift-filled table. They were simple gifts, not wrapped.

We'd run first of all to our own plate to see what we got, then make our way around the table ooohing and ahhhing over everyone else's gifts—a wallet, a pocket knife, a doll … We all felt the joy of each person's gift. Occasionally Dad would come down with a pleased scowl on his face, telling us we were making too much noise playing with our toys and that we should go back to bed. Mom and Dad both seemed to get joy from giving to us. They could tell by the looks on our faces that we were delighted with our gifts even though they were small.

For the rest of Christmas day, activity on the farm came to a standstill. Dad would sit in his chair reading or falling asleep as *Handel's Messiah* filled the airwaves around us. A local radio station played this music every Christmas, and we always listened to it. Dad was fond of these Christmases when we could just stay home; he referred to them as "good old-fashioned Christmas days."

Other things at Christmas were also predictable, such as Dad asking the day before Christmas, "Say, what can I get for Mom for Christmas?"; luxuries like the caramel-walnut candy Barb made; or a bowl of walnuts or mixed nuts sitting around for us to crack. We could also predict when we turned sixteen that our gift would be a wristwatch, and that when the girls were about to grow out of playing with dolls, we would get a keepsake—an older-looking doll, complete with an outfit and actual hair. This would be our last doll.

Not expected, however, was the little, blue, metal table and two chairs with thin black legs and arms near my place at the table one Christmas morning. Some other gifts, too, came as a surprise, such as Elam's wind-up Cletrac bulldozer and Tim's red-hose, toy fire truck with all the bells and whistles. And on rare occasions, when the recipient was older, a bike appeared, sitting on the floor next to their plate.

One year, Edith and I both got a copy of the coloring book *The Night Before Christmas*, with Santa Claus in a red, velvet suit on the cover. I rubbed my fingers over the velvet so much that it eventually wore off. Though *The Night Before Christmas* seemed strangely out of place with the meaning of Christmas emphasized in our home, Edith and I both memorized it from cover to cover.

Rites of Passage

Doing things for the first time was a real confidence booster, whether it was using a sewing machine, baking, driving, hunting, or embroidering. A rite of passage for the girls was embroidering a first quilt block, sewing a first dress, or baking a first cake. For the boys, it was hunting. (See pages 92–94 for a description of the boys' hunting rite of passage at age twelve.)

Mom made learning how to crochet optional but not learning how to embroider. Ideally, I would have completed thirty-two, twelve-inch squares of embroidered blocks of muslin fabric—enough to make a quilt. Mom supplied us each with a round, metal, canister-like container in which she put several blocks of plain fabric, a needle, and several skeins of embroidery thread. I could choose what I embroidered on each block. Mom showed us how to make small stitches, and when our little fingers made them much bigger than hers, she did not make mention of it, especially if she could see we were doing our best. My first completed block of embroidery was a hardly recognizable bird on a nest—bird and nest all blending into one mass of brown threads, with a few red threads for a beak. No matter. In my opinion, it was beautiful and a real accomplishment. When we had idle moments, Mom would check on our quilt-block project saying, "Now, keep at it." Embroidering our own quilt was not so much about having a quilt as it was about learning something new and completing a project.

As the years went by and I had still not completed all my blocks of embroidery, I begged Mom to allow me to tube paint the remaining designs rather than embroider them. I had seen Barb do some tube painting and thought it looked rather cool. Mom finally conceded, and I tube painted the blocks just to get them done, not being very particular about which design I chose. After completing the blocks, I stuck them away in a drawer somewhere, and when I pulled them out several years later to inspect them, the painted blocks seemed quite inferior to the hand-sewn ones. I eventually threw them away and never did complete my quilt.

I did, however, completely finish my first dress at about age twelve. I made it from a piece of plaid turquoise, blue, and green fabric Mom dug out of one of her dresser drawers where she kept odds and ends of fabric. That is also where she pulled out the first pattern I ever used. Mom assured me the dress pattern was supposed to be close to the right size for me. But how was I to know for sure since the thin sheets of paper did not have any markings on them whatsoever? So I cut out my dress, sewed it on the treadle sewing machine, and tried it on as it came together. The sleeves were much too tight and somewhat misshapen, but who cared? I had made my first dress, and the compliments I got made me feel confident I could actually make another one. I did sew many more dresses, improving on the first one as I continued to learn from store-bought patterns.

There was less guesswork when I made my first cake from scratch. I was eight or nine years old and had found the recipe for a yellow cake in the *Mennonite Community Cookbook*. Someone showed me where the ingredients were and explained the difference between baking powder and baking soda, but that was all the help I received. I mixed the cake, poured it into round cake pans, and slid it into the oven myself. I had watched my older sisters bake cakes before, so I felt confident in my first attempt. Mom told me not to open the oven door too often to peek in, because the heat would escape and the cake might flop, causing a big sunken dip in the middle. Even if a cake did flop, Mom would proudly announce who had baked it as she set it in the middle of the table as if it were a smashing success. And everyone ate it as if it were.

Routine Things

Food, clothing, personal care, newborn babies, birthdays—these were the routine things of life for us.

FOOD

Mealtimes and food preparation provided a steady rhythm for our days. We knew we could count on sitting down together as a family three times a day—breakfast, dinner, and supper as we called our meals. We could not, however, predict what might happen around the table. Who could have guessed, for instance, that Edith, just four years old at the time, would break a moment of silence with guests around the table by requesting in a clear, plaintive voice, "Please pass the worm medicine." We were all being treated for a case of pinworms, and the pills were usually passed around the table at mealtime. They were not to be passed around during this particular meal, however. The stifled snickers around the table helped relieve the embarrassment about our pinworm predicament being so unexpectedly revealed to our guests.

Our menus, on the other hand, were usually quite predictable. Potatoes of some sort—fried, mashed, baked, or cooked—were standard fare for dinner or supper. About thirty minutes before it was time to eat, Mom would stand at the kitchen sink quietly peeling potatoes, and, almost as part of the potato-peeling ritual, we'd ask her for a raw piece of potato to eat, which she would quietly cut off and hand to us without saying anything. When the potatoes were mashed and it was time to eat, if Dad and the boys still hadn't come in, Mom would walk over to the kitchen window, look out the lane and say, "I wish they would come now."

Mom saw to it that we had plenty of baked goods on hand. She did not have a set baking day, but she baked often—bread, dinner rolls, cinnamon rolls, her infamous buttermilk cookies, and pies. Lots of them. When she made pie crusts, she let us use the scraps of leftover dough to make our own little cinnamon rolls. We'd roll the dough flat, spread butter on it, sprinkle it with sugar and cinnamon, roll it up, and bake it in the oven. I could hardly wait until mine cooled down enough to eat. After a series of quick test nibbles, it was finally ready.

When Mom made dinner rolls and pulled them out of the oven, the smell of freshly baked bread would waft throughout the house. As soon as it hit us, we'd drop what we were doing and follow our noses straight to the table in the kitchen where we knew we'd find a small plate with a stick of butter. Opening our hands for the warm, just-out-of-the-oven rolls Mom handed us, we'd slather them with butter and devour them in an instant.

Potatoes, pies, meat from the freezer, fresh vegetables from the garden, fruit from roadside markets—all these were common foods on our table. Rarely did we have luxury foods such as chips, pretzels, or store-bought ice cream. So, on those few and far between occasions when Dad toted large cans of pretzels and potato chips or a couple of boxes of ice cream into the house, we declared a feast day.

For us, it was ordinary to eat out-of-the-ordinary foods such as pig stomach stuffed full of diced potatoes, carrots, and sausage after butchering day, or snapping turtle soup. On those occasions when we had turtle soup, we ate it with fascination. Maybe it was because of the "risky" adventure involved in the feat of catching one, or maybe it held appeal because we knew it was such unusual fare for others.

Each snapping turtle had its own story. The one weighing sixteen pounds that Pete got from the river came with payback. One day when he and Dale went gigging for carp, he spied the turtle sticking its head out of the mud and tried to capture it, but it got away. Unable to let go of the prospect of turtle soup, Pete took Mim and Tina in the canoe with him the next day to look for the turtle. Spying it on the shore, he paddled in, captured it, and set it down in the canoe. Before they were barely six feet from shore, the turtle started clawing its way over the bottom of the canoe in the direction of Mim and Tina, who instantly freaked out, screaming and almost jumping overboard. Pete leapt out of the canoe, pulled it to shore, and rearranged seating before rowing home with dinner. Now *that* was soup laced with adventure.

You'd have thought the younger boys were deprived of food considering the things they ate; anyone for crow, dead fish, frog legs, bird eggs, or moldy pancakes? When Mom was gone one day, Pete, Elvin, and Dale realized it was an opportune time to cook a crow just to see what it tasted like. It didn't take long to find out that cooked crow is bitter. The boys' first bite was their last.

Another day, Pete and Elvin found a fish in the stream and cooked and ate it. There's no telling what it tasted like; when Mom asked them how they caught the fish, they answered, "Oh, we found it floating on top." Thinking bird eggs were perhaps more acceptable, they found some and asked Mom to fry them. When I try to imagine her face as she scooped the tiny, fried eggs out of the pan onto the boys' waiting plates, I see a slight, amused smile.

Pete also did some quiet food-foraging by himself, unbeknownst to the rest of us, in the swampy area of one of the fields. Night after night, he silently searched with a light for the eyes of bullfrogs shining back at him. He must have become skilled at harpooning them given that he cooked thirty pairs of frog legs and offered them as an appetizer at the Cabin one year. Apparently he'd been stashing them away in a corner of the freezer till an opportune time.

Pete was one to try his hand at almost anything. One spring, he tapped some maple trees on our property and painstakingly collected the runoff liquid until he had enough to boil down into maple syrup. When that day finally came, he put his liquid gold on the stove, walked away to do something else while it boiled, and promptly forgot all about it. The instant he remembered, he ran to the house and peered into the kettle. There he saw his precious maple syrup, now hardened in the bottom. Remorsefully, he carried kettle and rock-hard syrup to the washhouse where he poured hot water with detergent on it. Only months later, long after the maple syrup had dissolved, could he bring himself to clean it up.

Tim got the prize for earliest food ventures, beginning already as a toddler. He wasn't deprived of food, but you may have thought so if you'd seen him sitting on the ground eating moldy pancakes from the dogfood dish outside. We were more careful the next time we put food out for the dogs when he was on the loose.

CLOTHING

Mom's approach to clothing was similar to her approach to food—practical and thrifty. It did not matter if our clothing was in style or not; we wore it until it was worn out. This was true for the oldest children on down to the youngest. When Parke and Elam were little boys, they wore out-of-date suspendered knickers to school with brown stockings and rubber mason jar rings for garters. The knickers were handed down from Mom's younger brother Floyd, who was just a little older than the boys. Parke and Elam, though they liked Uncle Floyd a lot, despised his knickers. They were the only boys in school wearing knickers, and they wished that if they had to wear them, they could at least wear them with belts instead of suspenders.

When I was little, I had to wear a pair of hand-me-down, white leather high-top shoes, the only shoes I had, with scuff marks on the sides and top, showing gray where the white had worn off. I thought nothing of wearing them until we went to the Philadelphia Zoo when I was about four years old. In one of those frozen-in- time moments, a little girl walking a few feet away stopped in her tracks, pointed at my shoes, and said, "Mommy, look—she has baby shoes on!" I felt ashamed and embarrassed at the same time. "Baby shoes." I was wearing baby shoes! I felt oddly singled out and realized probably for the first time that our family was different from many. In my family, shoes did not come and go with a single owner; they were passed down from one child to the next as each child grew out of them.

The shiny, new, black patent leather shoes Mom ordered for me from the Sears catalog soon after this canceled any shame the scuffed, white high-top shoes held. The day the box came in the mail, my joy could scarcely be contained. I wished it was Sunday right then so I could wear them. But I didn't have to wait until Sunday to show them off, because a few men from the New Tribes Mission organization who had set up a dental clinic in New Columbia spent the evening with us. The minute I heard them at the door, I ran to get my shoes. Knowing the men would be shown to the family room to have a seat, I quickly put on my new shoes and hid behind the door. When Danny, who was especially kind, sat down on the settee next to the door, I stuck my shoe out so he could see. When he noticed it, he looked behind the door and chuckled at me. I ventured out, embarrassed that I had been found out, yet feeling gratified at the same time that I had just shown off my new shoes.

Since clothing could be handed down umpteen times before it finally wore out, getting a new dress to wear for the first time did not happen very often. So when relatives or friends gave us some of their hand-me-down dresses, especially if they were "frilly"—meaning they had a few ruffles or a little lace—they seemed brand-new to us. Too much lace was frowned upon as appearing "too fancy," but when Barb got her new sewing machine from her restaurant tips and sewed Edith and me new dresses from bright yellow fabric, with special brown stitching on the collar and sleeve edges, that was as good as lace. When we wore these dresses with their brown sashes to church for the first time, we felt like we were putting on a fashion show.

Esther, however, did not have the good fortune of having a new dress made for her. She had a total of three dresses to wear during her first year in public high school. One was made from thin nylon with a large, orange-ish brown pattern. Since she had to wear the same dress twice in one week, she traded off sweaters with Ada to change her outfits a bit. Esther hated being the only Mennonite in public school, where the way she dressed set her apart. Working in the fields was a much happier place, so it was easy for her to quit school at the end of her freshman year.

One piece of new fabric we'd rather have done without was the bolt of yellow flannel Mom bought to make me and my sisters winter slips and bloomers. Unlike our flannel sheets, the underwear Mom made from this soft fabric was anything but comforting. No matter that they were intended to keep me warm (and truth be told, probably to keep me modestly covered); in my twelve-year-old heart I despised them, seeing them as ugly and unfashionable. I didn't have the heart to tell Mom my true feelings, though, and I didn't believe it would make a difference anyway. Clothing was meant to be practical. The most I could do was try to keep my friends from catching a glimpse of the yellow flannel under my clothes at school or at sleepovers, dreading what they might think of me if they saw it. With resistant resignation, I wore the underwear, realizing I had no other choice if I was to have any at all.

The brown stockings were yet another matter. There were plenty of them floating around in our dresser drawers, and if we wore anything with our shoes, it had to be these. They were especially annoying when we had to wear them with garters, which left red circles on our legs. But they were better than the red, rubber mason jar rings we had to use when there were no garters to be found.

Wearing these stockings in the winter with long underwear was a challenge. We tried our best to first wrap the long underwear tightly around our legs so that when we finally succeeded in pulling our brown stockings up around them, the awkward bumps wouldn't show through quite as much. While the bumps made it obvious I was wearing long underwear, at least no one knew I was wearing the kind with the slit in the back when all the other pairs were taken.

Socks with dresses in the summer were not allowed since socks were considered "worldly," so I dreamed of wearing white socks—like many little girls I saw—with my new, black patent leather shoes. And a little lace on them would have been just fine too. Then finally one day an older sister bought me my very first pair of white knee socks, and from then on, I happily forgot all about the despised brown stockings and looked less longingly at the socks other little girls were wearing.

Socks notwithstanding, Mom also had a strong aversion to us wearing red clothing. To her it was the sign of a harlot. I, however, happened to like the color red. So when Mom knitted each of the girls a vest and it came my turn, she took me to the store to let me pick out some yarn. Immediately I picked up a red skein. Mom would not relent—definitely not red. And I refused to give in. So we had a quiet standoff right there in the store—Mom standing in one spot and me circling the yarn bin hoping she'd change her mind. She didn't. I came to the realization that if I wanted a vest at all, I'd better pick a different color. I chose turquoise.

PERSONAL CARE

Some of our routines became automatic and required little from us. When Mom combed our hair in the morning at the small kitchen washbowl with its dirty bar of soap and the old tin comb and brush holder (she used the same comb and brush for all of us), she would say without fail as she started braiding, "Now, look down toward the river." We were expected to keep looking that direction until she was finished so our braids would be straight. At the end, she would put a final touch of hair tonic or light coating of Vaseline on top to keep the "strubbles" down. If we had to go somewhere in the evening and our hair was "strubbly," she would say, "Now brush your strubbles back before we go."

Other routines took a little more effort to carry out. Before our bathroom was installed, on Saturday evenings we'd put a large galvanized tub behind the stove in the living room and fill it with warm water to prepare our weekly bath. After pulling the blinds, we took baths by turns, using the same water each time. Being the first to take one's bath was preferable because with each additional bather, the water became increasingly milky from the soap. After we added a small bathroom with a half bathtub at the end of the hallway upstairs, we put the galvanized tub away. Since we didn't know what we were missing by not having a full-size bathtub, the half-size one in the corner of the bathroom was absolutely wonderful. We only knew what it was like to have one bathroom between us, so we didn't even think about wishing for another one; we just had to take turns using it. If one of us was in desperate need and someone else was in the bathroom, it was okay for the person in need to knock loudly on the door, saying, "Who's in there? Will you soon be out?" We were expected to be patient and wait our turn, but we could always try to hurry the person inside. Sometimes it worked, and sometimes it didn't. My patience was severely tried when I was the one waiting and someone butted in ahead of me.

MEDICAL CARE

Personal care was something we could control; sickness was not. In spite of Mom and Dad's best efforts to provide safe food and water for us, three of us got hepatitis, usually contracted when you eat or drink something that has the virus in it, which then infects the liver and causes it to get inflamed. Given the lack of knowledge and medical tests available for hepatitis, we can't be sure what type, but it was most likely type A. This is the least risky type of hepatitis, because it almost always gets better on its own and doesn't lead to long-term inflammation of the liver. About twenty percent of people who get hepatitis A, however, get sick enough that they need to go to the hospital. This was true for Sue and Tim, who each spent about a week in the hospital with hepatitis. Elam was the fortunate one who somehow managed to avoid hospitalization.

Elam's hepatitis hit when he was fifteen years old, attending Delaware Mennonite School and boarding with a dairy farmer in exchange for helping to milk the cows. One day while Elam was taking a math test he passed out and fell from the seat of his desk onto the floor, scaring his teacher, Leroy Pellman, and the other students. Because Elam was jaundiced, his teacher told him he needed to stay home and rest, so that's what he did. He soon recovered and went back to school and milking cows. Elam suspected that his jaundice was most likely caused by hepatitis, but our understanding of the disease at that time was quite limited, and if we got better without seeing a doctor, that was considered to be good. Only after Elam went to medical school was his inkling confirmed about having had hepatitis.

Mom was the one who noticed both Sue's skin and the whites of her eyes becoming more yellow. She called it the "yellow jaundice" and got her medical book off the shelf to check the cause. It was then that she realized Sue's symptoms matched up with hepatitis and took her to the doctor, who admitted her to the hospital.

Tim was twelve years old and hadn't been feeling well for several days, with severe nausea. Elam, who had come home from medical school on winter break, noticed that Tim was jaundiced, so he checked him out. When he examined Tim's stomach, he found an enlarged liver. This raised a red flag for Elam, and he sent Tim to the hospital to be admitted. Tim wasn't happy about having to spend Christmas in the hospital, especially when he got the painful gamma globulin shot to build up antibodies to the virus. But he eventually found it within himself to forgive Elam for intervening on his behalf.

Several years later, Elam's careful attention was the reason Tim's case of toxoplasmosis was also discovered. Tim, who was in his late teens by then, was quite fatigued, had frequent headaches, and very swollen lymph nodes. Mom made an appointment with the family doctor, who checked Tim out and did blood work, but nothing showed up. Meanwhile, Tim continued to work on his car in Dad's shop, though his eyes hurt enough that he ended up smearing grease on them from rubbing them. When Elam found out about these symptoms, he suggested Tim be tested for toxoplasmosis. So Dad took Tim to the hospital. But before Tim could be taken into a back room to have his blood tested, he threw up all over the hospital waiting room, losing a hearty helping of the rice pudding he was especially fond of that I had made for supper that evening. He remembers how kindly Dad treated him during this ordeal.

The test results came back positive for the disease, and Tim was put on steroids and a sulfa drug for treatment. The steroid kicked Tim into overdrive, and he worked all night in the shop, not able to sleep. It seemed that he had a compromised immune system since his symptoms were more severe than most with the disease. Monthly returns to the doctor for blood work showed a slow recovery, and Tim had persistent flare-ups of swollen glands. He also dealt with chronic fatigue. He was plagued with low energy and feeling sick with stomach bugs for several years following his bout with toxoplasmosis until he gradually outgrew it.

BIRTHS OF BABIES

Given how large our family was, the need for such medical care was relatively rare. Calling the doctor for a new baby about to be born was more routine, it seemed, than for other medical assistance—a new baby arrived about every year and a half to two years. Exactly when the next new baby would appear, however, wasn't always apparent to us, because Mom's pregnancies were not very noticeable, even in the third trimester; her already thick abdomen hid the babies well.

So when Mom told me and a few of my sisters on the cement front porch just outside the kitchen door one day that we were soon going to have a new baby brother or sister, we were surprised and ecstatic. (It never occurred to us that there were already many of us.) When Mom told Edith about a new baby coming, Edith asked, "Does Dad know?"

Mom and Dad relied on books for our sex education, so Edith's question was asked in total innocence. As for me, I never gave much thought to how people got pregnant until I was about eight years old and a girl in our neighborhood who often stayed in our home spelled out the facts of life for us. She informed us not only that her older sister had gotten pregnant but also how her sister had gotten pregnant.

When a baby was due to be born, baby clothes would mysteriously appear in the second drawer down of the chest of drawers in Mom's bedroom. We were allowed to open this drawer to examine what was inside: cloth diapers; yellow, hand-knitted "sakkies" (sweaters) with matching knitted caps; undershirts; rubber pants; a new baby rattle; belly button bands; and soft receiving blankets. Mom always said, "Put everything back like you found it."

Eleven of us were born on Mom's bed, which she always prepared ahead of time with fabric-covered pads of newspaper to catch the blood and after-birth. Dad was right there assisting the family doctor, who made a house call to deliver each baby. (The doctor's fee was $25 for everything.) To hear Mom and

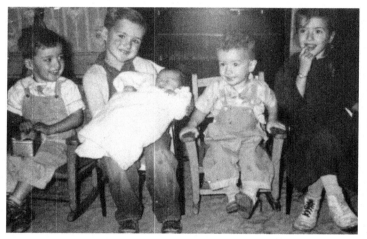

Pete, John, Elvin (baby), Tim, and Edith, who is wearing the white high-top shoes mentioned on page 132.

Dad tell about the birth of one of us children was to hear a story of something sacred and wonderful. In their words, the doctor would lay us on the bed, and Dad would clean us up and dress us in the clothes Mom had set out ahead of time. Mom refer-red to these births as "precious moments." And when someone came to our house to see the newest baby, without fail Dad would say gleefully, "It looks just like me!" with a big, proud grin on his face.

I was especially fascinated by the belly button band wrapped around the baby's waist. It was fastened with a big safety pin in front, protecting the tender area where the remainder of the umbilical cord was still attached. The cord's peculiar, unpleasing smell only got worse with time. I was excited when it turned black and shriveled and finally dropped off after about two weeks, because that was when the baby seemed "finished" to me. At that point, it could have its first bath—usually in a white, galvanized metal tub, and by the woodstove if the birth happened in the winter.

When Elvin was born during the night on October 30, 1958, Leona, who had run downstairs at the sound of a baby crying during the night, shook us awake the next morning, announcing excitedly, "You have a new baby brother!" Jumping out of bed, we heard his newborn cry and raced down the stairs to see him. As we burst through the bedroom door, the sweet smell of Baby Magic lotion enveloped us. There lay Mom on the bed, looking pale and tired with a happy, peaceful expression on her face, cradling in her arms the baby wrapped snuggly in a yellow, flannel blanket. Only a head with lots of black hair was showing.

We were told, "His name is Elvin Eugene," as we silently approached the bed with reverent awe to have a closer look. On the stand close by lay a mouth-watering giant Hershey bar Dad had bought for Mom "so she would have more milk."

Barb, on the other hand, was a realist. When she heard a baby crying during the night, she said matter-of-factly, "Sounds like another boy," rolled over, and went back to sleep, which she later said was because didn't want to wake the other children. When she was younger, during family devotions one day we read the passage about "the stork making her nest in the fir tree," and Barb asked, "Are those two big pine trees beside our house fir trees?" Dad said, "Why, yes, they are." To which Barb replied, "Well, look at the size of our family—we need to chop them down so the stork stops delivering babies."

BIRTHDAYS

With so many people in the house, our family celebrated somebody's birthday every month of the year except January and August. We could count on two things for our birthday: having a simple birthday cake with the same number of candles as our age, and getting our ears pulled the same number of times as our age.

The birthday cake, baked fresh by someone that day, was saved for supper, when most of us would be gathered around the table to witness the birthday person blowing out the candles after we sang *Happy Birthday* in a rousing manner that made the birthday person feel special, recognized, and celebrated. That was all it took—no special party inviting friends over. We were our own birthday party.

We responded in various ways to having an earlobe pulled throughout the day on our birthday. The boys were on high alert all day lest they be ambushed by other brothers intent on pulling their ears. Escaping this at all costs, they climbed out windows, snuck out at night to camp along the river, fled to the mountains, or slept in a car. Their manhood seemed linked to their success at avoiding having their ears pulled. When Pete's twelfth birthday came around, he locked himself in the bathroom, crawled out the window, stretched his toes a few feet over to the next window (which he had opened ahead of time), and somehow stepped over to it as he lowered himself into the room next door, outwitting his brothers who were waiting outside the bathroom door to pull his ears.

Not prone to this type of high drama, the girls mostly just giggled and made a show of resistance. Except for Mim. On her twelfth birthday, she avoided having her ears pulled during the day, then went into hiding that night and slept out along the river bank all by herself.

The Flood

On June 14, 1972, the interaction of a polar front and an upper trough over the Gulf of Mexico formed a tropical depression that became Tropical Storm Agnes. As the storm slowly curved northward, Agnes intensified enough to become Hurricane Agnus. A secondary low joined Agnus as a traveling companion, and together they created a furious storm moving up the east coast and making land-fall near New York City. Their claim to fame was to create one of the most costly natural disasters in Pennsylvania history as they poured rain into the Susquehanna River, which rose and spilled its banks, spreading its floodwaters out over large areas all the way from New York to Virginia, ruining houses, wrecking bridges, washing out roads, uprooting trees, and claiming the lives of many people. Four of these people, all of them swept several miles downriver, lived in our neighborhood—including Chief of Police Gordon Hufnagle, who drowned trying to save a man and his wife.

The Susquehanna River, the nation's longest, non-navigable river, was normally picturesque as it flowed past Lewisburg and the river towns of Union County. Where it passed by our house, it was wide and shallow, just right for fishing and boating. In mid-June 1972, however, it became a raging force, unstoppable as it plunged its way through our routine with destruction and chaos.

Dad saw it coming. When he awoke on June 18, the river was rising rapidly, filled with all the rain that Hurricane Agnus had deposited north of us on top of the thirteen inches we had just gotten in the previous three days. Pacing the floor and growing more uneasy by the minute, Dad wasn't reassured at all when he contacted the state police for their report and they told him it wouldn't be very serious. He didn't take their word but rather called Wolfe's General Store to see how the Pine Creek in the northern part of the watershed was doing. When he heard the amount of rainfall they'd had, he followed his better judgment and started organizing and preparing to move out. He had seen the river flood before. Our lane had a low spot where a stream flowed—the first place to flood when we had heavy rain. The farm buildings were at a considerably higher elevation, but the stream was also flooding rapidly. If we waited too long to start moving out, we'd be trapped, unable to move our belongings out the lane at all. Dad moved the beef cattle out of the barn first. We followed his lead and began working quickly to move first-floor furnishings to the second floor. We worked as hard as we could, carrying countless jars of canned goods from the basement up to the second floor. We couldn't

The epic flood of 1972 in the wake of Hurricane Agnes. It took five days before we could row around the buildings and seven before we could walk inside the house, where the water had reached eight feet high, just short of the second-story floor.

get the freezers and their full loads of frozen food moved out, however, before we had to flee to higher ground. So we tied them shut and hoped for the best.

Though Dad and the boys were working outside moving farm machinery and equipment to higher ground as fast as they could, the last load barely made it out. Elvin was moving equipment with one of the larger tractors, and as he drove past the corn shed, the pulley from the alternator and the fan were throwing water while the forage wagon he was pulling floated in the water behind the tractor.

We herded the sheep up to the second story of the barn, thinking they would be safe there.

As the water began filling in around the buildings, signaling that it was urgent we leave, the last boat, carrying Mom and Barb, crossed the flooded meadow. Mom, seeming bewildered and confused, suddenly insisted that the boat be turned around so she could rescue the chickens in the chicken house. Barb argued, "No, Mom, we can't do that—we have to leave now," and kept rowing to the other side.

From the bank of I-80, we watched our farm flood. During one of those times of keeping watch, Dad stood looking over his flooded farm and said, "Well, there goes the Lord's tenth and a new station wagon." Not bowing to defeat but expressing a hint of discouragement, he said, "Something like this hits you harder when you're not a young man anymore."

Frost had killed the first planting of all our tomatoes that year, and we had just finished the second planting—which was off to a good start—when the flood hit. We had planted most of the tomatoes near the river, so our tomato crop for that year was pretty much swept down the river. We managed to harvest one or two acres planted on higher ground, but that was it. It was too late to replant a third time.

The bank of I-80 spread out across the farm, ending close to the water where the bridge across the river began. We watched as the strong, swift current of water funneled around the bank, swirled under the bridge, then blasted full force directly into our house. Dad said if it had been a frame house instead of our sturdy brick one, he thinks it would have been swept away.

A couple of my brothers were paddling the canoe around in the floodwaters out of the way of the current next to the I-80 embankment when a news reporter who had stopped to look at our flooded farm called down to them, asking if he could join them in the canoe. He said he wanted to get up close to the house to take pictures. The boys, always up for an adventure, paddled the canoe to the bank as the reporter scrambled down to them and stepped into the canoe for the ride of his life. They paddled away from the calm waters into the swift current next to the house and almost capsized the canoe. It was only later that the reporter told them he couldn't swim. He must have felt risking his life was worth the pictures he wanted to take.

We continued to keep watch from the bank of I-80 as the floodwaters slowly receded from the buildings, giving us a clearer view each day of the destruction left behind. So much mud, debris, and a huge mess. We wondered what we would find when we could finally set foot on our property again. In the meantime, we lived with my sister Barb and her husband, Richard.

After about five days, the water had receded enough that we could row the boat around the buildings. A stop at the upstairs barn revealed the stark reality that only the sheep big enough to keep their noses up out of the water in the second story made it. Those that were too small drowned. In the chicken house, we found all the chickens dead.

After the seventh day we were able to go into the house, where we found the water level had reached eight feet on the first floor. (The ceilings were nine feet high, so the second floor narrowly escaped flooding.) We found a dead possum in the kitchen and some dead fish in the basement. The hardwood floor in the family room, newly installed, was ruined. On the ground level, Agnes had spewed several inches of mud on the floors and broken every window. The kitchen table, which we had not moved upstairs, was blocking the entrance to the front door. Wallpaper in every room downstairs hung in strips, exposing the rough, old farmhouse plaster walls. The borrowed piano we had finally been allowed to bring into our home sat plastered with mud. The tied-shut freezers lay tipped over on their sides, their contents spoiled from floodwater, adding more stench to the river mud. After another week of cleanup, we were able to move back into the house.

In the downstairs part of the barn, several inches of mud covered everything. In the upstairs, the water had risen a foot and a half, lifting the floor boards and making space for mud to settle in there as well.

Outside, Agnes had washed out a huge canyon around the foundation of the house on the bridge side by funneling a strong current against it. The force of the current had moved the tomato harvester, which weighed a couple tons, from under one bridge of I-80 to the next. Debris lay everywhere. One of the table boards, for instance, had been forced into the fence row behind the barn. Ironically, on the flip side, some of the uneven spots in our large lawn were filled in nice and smooth from flood silt, and the fields gained a new level of topsoil.

When Pete slipped away to do a little exploring as a respite from all the discombobulation of cleanup, he took a walk up along the river and came upon the tree that had been uprooted years before and had left a gaping depression in the ground on the other side of the I-80 bridges. Agnes' waters had now swirled out more dirt and enlarged the depression into a deep pit. Among the few rocks scattered in the bottom, Pete noticed that one was shaped a little weirdly. With rising excitement, he said to himself, "No way; it can't be, can it?!" To be sure, he climbed down into the pit and picked up the stone. Sure enough! It had a groove on each side and a sharp edge on the bottom. It was an honest-to-goodness Indian tomahawk. A real find.

We found out after the flood that many people were willing to come together to help us. So much help was needed, and we graciously received it. The Sunday after the flood, following the morning worship service, our pastor, John Erb, encouraged the congregation to spend the rest of that day helping us with the urgently needed, overwhelming flood cleanup. Many people came and helped. That spoke volumes of support and care to our family. We found this extension of love from family, extended family, church family, and community to be overwhelmingly wonderful.

In the months following the flood, we hated living with the ugly, forsaken-looking walls of our house. But we could do nothing with them until the moisture dried out when cold weather set in and required heat in the house. We were advised that we shouldn't do anything to the walls until a "barn burner match" could be struck on them (after about a year, we were told), which would signal to us that the walls were dry enough to be painted or wallpapered.

To clean up, we ...

❋ shoveled the mud from all the floors of the house out through the broken windows, then washed the floors with water hoses and brooms.

❋ waited just several months to wallpaper or paint the walls again (not a year, because we could strike a match on the walls sooner).

❋ lifted the upstairs barn floorboards and cleaned out the mud so they would fit in place again.

❋ got the gutter cleaner going in the downstairs part of the barn and shoveled the mud on the floors into the gutters, letting them take the mud and dump it out into the still-flowing floodwaters, past the end of the gutter cleaner. The flood had brought it in, and the flood would take it away.

After the flood, we replanted the tomatoes, but they did poorly. The fields stayed wet, and it rained often. In the wet growing season, the tomatoes needed to be sprayed for blight, but when Dad and the boys attempted to spray the fields, the sprayer got stuck again and again. It was a real mess. We hardly broke even with the profit from the tomatoes. Farmers and anyone who suffered loss received government disaster grants that did not need to be paid back. Many people scrambled to make sure they had a minimum of $3,000 loss so they would qualify for a grant. We were eligible for $15,000 with our loss—a lot of cash in those days—but Mom would not sign for the grant because she didn't believe in taking money from the government. Even though our taxes had actually paid for it, she wouldn't budge.

To try to make ends meet, Dad got a job driving escort for oversized loads at the Ceco factory across from our lane, which made trusses for large buildings. Soon after he started driving, the other drivers said, "We want to make an eight-hour day of this; let's stop for a long lunch break." Dad came on home because this violated his sense of honesty. He soon stopped driving escort. Next, he began selling firewood from trees he cut down in the Pennsylvania State Forest with a permit and with the boys' help. But he didn't sell much firewood and so ended his career as a lumberjack. Somehow we survived that year of great financial difficulty.

Through it all, Dad's stoicism impressed us, as he set his jaw and just did the next thing that needed to be done after the flood. Mom was mostly quiet, appearing rather numb and going through the motions as she gradually came to terms with the stark reality of the condition the invasive floodwaters had left her house in. But the inner strength and resources that had always been a part of us were now realized in a new way as we came together with family and friends in solidarity and unity to recreate structure out of the destruction and chaos.

Conclusion

As the writer of Ecclesiastes says, "There is a time for everything, and a season for every activity under the heavens" (3:1 New International Version). My family lived this. We marked our lives by seasons—seasons of the year, seasons of growth, seasons of passage—and within the seasons were rhythms of routines and rituals of recurring events. Now, as time flows on, the seasons provide perspective about where we have been, gift us with the present, and allow us to anticipate the future.

8. Discipline

Discipline for Behavior

Esther glowed with pride as she bragged to her first-grade teacher, Anna Kauffman, "I haven't gotten a spanking for a long time." Anna boarded at our house for the school year while teaching at the little private school we attended, sharing meals with us and witnessing our family's day-to-day activities. So she could vouch for the truth of Esther's bragging and beamed approvingly down on Esther, who was sitting on her lap. But wouldn't you know, just a few days later, Esther broke her spank-free track record. We were sitting at the supper table at the end of our meal when, acting out of character, she slipped under the table, crawled over to Sue's legs dangling from the bench, and tickled one of them. Sue's reaction was a sure, swift kick—right in Esther's face. As Esther howled in pain, Dad got up from his chair and took Sue out to the back porch to discipline her. Feeling that full justice had not yet been served, Mom turned her gaze to Esther and quietly reprimanded her. "Esther, you weren't supposed to be under the table. Maybe you better go to the back porch, too." Still sniffling, Esther dragged her feet as she approached Dad and whimpered, "Mom said I should come out, too." So Dad spanked Esther next as Sue stood close by. When Esther's spanking was finished, Esther and Sue put their arms around each other and walked slowly through the back door into the living room just inside the back porch entrance. Behind the closed door, they consoled each another, partly about the spanking they had each just weathered from Dad (he always used his bare hand to spank, and it stung, even through our clothes) and partly about their embarrassment at both having wet their pants during the ordeal. As it turned out, Sue also had just recently boasted about her "spank free" track record to her teacher.

While Mom and Dad did not hesitate to spank us when necessary, their disciplinary skills were much broader than spanking; they corrected, reprimanded, directed, ordered, and coached us. This broad repertoire enabled them to use discipline not simply to punish us but also to help us become persons able to use self-control, self-discipline, and self-restraint.

When it came to expecting specific behaviors from us all the time—no talking back and no disobedience being at the top of the list—Mom and Dad were a team. You would think with so many children they would have given us breaks when it came to discipline, but no, they were as consistent as the day was long. They enforced discipline absolutely; not doing so was simply not an option, since discipline was a crucial part of making a family our size run smoothly. Without discipline, absolute bedlam would surely have reigned; with it, we functioned as a family unit, albeit within a sort of organized chaos.

Within this chaos lay unquestioned expectations. One of these was listening the first time—there was no such thing as a parent counting to three before a child obeyed. The surety of this guideline gave us a sense of security; we couldn't even begin to manipulate Mom and Dad by talking our way out of being disciplined, and we certainly didn't try to play one against the other.

It's a good thing Mom and Dad joined together in regulating us, since our daily family life provided abundant opportunities for conflict. For example, you would think going to church just twelve miles from our house would keep us from fighting on the way. But with a car packed full of kids, someone was sure to elbow someone else or hog too much room on the seat. Mom and Dad often started singing on the way, knowing we would join in and not fight as much. When we got to church, we already knew how we were to behave: we weren't allowed to whisper, especially during children's meetings at the front of the church where we were on full display; and no matter which parent we sat with, we were not allowed to get up and go to the bathroom during church—we just had to hold it (pure torture at times). After church we were expected to stay on the porch that had the tall white pillars.

Parke discovered Mom and Dad's united front the hard way when he was four years old and went to the dentist for the first time. The saga began just inside the door of the dentist's office as Parke walked in and heard his cousin—who had gone in before him—crying. That did it. By the time he was hoisted up into the dentist's chair, he was already scared to death. Clamping his teeth together, he refused to open his mouth. The dentist, a gruff Army man, did not take kindly to uncooperative children. But Parke refused to budge. Finally, in a last-ditch effort to get Parke to open up, the dentist used a hand to muzzle his nose and mouth. Unable to breathe, Parke promised a muffled "Yes," he would open his mouth. But the instant the dentist removed his hand, Parke snatched a quick gasp of air and clamped his mouth shut again as tightly as he could. Realizing the dentist meant business, he leapt off the chair and scampered out of the room; he'd had enough of this smothering dentist. Even after Dad brought Parke back into the room and tried to persuade him to open his mouth, he stubbornly refused. At a loss, Dad walked out of the room, close to tears. Not even a spanking by the dentist with a brush had broken Parke's determined resolve. Finally, Mom and Dad had had enough and left with Parke in tow. When they got home, they told Parke he needed to hand over his new, treasured Roadmaster bike he had just received for Christmas; they would keep it, they told him, until he cooperated with the dentist. "Or," they said, "we may need to sell it if you don't open your mouth at your next appointment." Parke shot back, "well, if you do, I'll just buy a new one." To which Mom and Dad responded, "Ohhhh, no you don't." One month later, Parke got his bike back. But he has been scared of the dentist ever since.

Neither Mom nor Dad allowed the older children to discipline the younger ones when they were present. They said, "Leave the disciplining to us." When one of the older ones occasionally bypassed this instruction, Dad would say to them, "Let them go. We're able to take care of this." But sometimes when Mom and Dad were gone, older siblings did take on the role of disciplinarian. On one such occasion, it took both Barb and Fred to deposit five-year-old John—his legs flailing wildly— in the cellarway after he had misbehaved. (The cellarway was behind the door that opened to the cellar steps—a location where we were often made to sit until we got it together, usually only about five minutes.) John had heard Dad's directive to the older ones, and in his young mind, Barb and Fred weren't his boss. It was dark in the cellarway, and there was no sitting for him. Though scared stiff, he took advantage of the opportunity to defy his older siblings' bossiness, cautiously feeling his way down the stairs and through three rooms infested with spider webs, until he finally reached the door to the outside. Popping through the door, John squinted as he emerged into the bright daylight and then, with triumph written all over his face, traipsed fearlessly right back into the house.

When Mom and Dad weren't tag-teaming, they each had their own way of disciplining and had different responses to certain behaviors such as passing gas, picking our noses, and squabbling with one another. For starters, they used different tones of voice to discipline us. I don't know how she did it, but Mom didn't raise her voice at us when she corrected us. I guess maybe she didn't need to, because we all knew what was coming when we directly disobeyed her. She would immediately stop what she was doing (none of this "Wait 'til your father comes home!" business), walk over to the kitchen cupboard, and reach to the top where she kept her spanking stick—a wooden spoon, yardstick, or chair rung—always something wooden. Uh oh—we were in trouble now, and there was no trying to talk our way out of it. Too late. May as well brace ourselves and hope our behind was well padded as Mom quietly led us off to the side and delivered the spanking. She didn't appear to be angry when she spanked. She was against punishing when angry.

Wooden slats at the bottoms of window blinds worked well for spankings too, especially for punishable behavior that happened outside the vicinity of the kitchen. On those occasions, it was more convenient for Mom to simply walk to the window of the room she was in and slide out the wooden slat from the blind. This usually happened when she was quilting in the family room, where most of the space was taken up by the quilt in its frame stretching across the room. It must have been Tim and Elvin who got these spankings, because one day, just to be "safe," they plotted to forever destroy the possibility of getting a wooden-slat spanking. They sneaked throughout the whole house, upstairs and downstairs, and pulled the slats from every window blind. Absconding with a total of twenty wooden slats, they felt smugly confident they had greatly reduced the odds of one ever being used on them again.

When Mom disciplined us, we usually cooperated because if we didn't, there would be more coming, especially when it came to spankings. And if we put our hands back to protect our rumps as she was spanking us, we'd soon regret it, because it did not stop Mom, and our hands just got smacked too.

We also learned how to cry the right way while getting spanked, because Mom stopped when she heard from our crying that "our will was broken." A broken-will cry was sure to bring the spanking to a halt. (To Mom, a broken will was different from a broken spirit; a broken will brought humility necessary for strong character formation, but a broken spirit brought harm to a child.) Barb also learned how to buy some time when she had a spanking coming. It worked for a while. When-ever she was about to get spanked, she would yell, "I have to go potty," and Mom would let her go. But one time Mom ignored her, and she really did have to go—and went—during the spanking. That was the end of Barb's stalling stunt.

This type of discipline is interesting, because on the one hand it might seem harsh, almost abusive, but we didn't experience it that way. Maybe because Mom assured us she was correcting us "because she loved us" and that, far from abusing us, she "really didn't want to do it." Though our heads sometimes protested, "A fine way to show someone you love them," our hearts believed her. It was important to

Mom that we be well disciplined as children in order for us to grow up and do the right thing as adults. So she stuck by her mottos: "Spare the rod and spoil the child" and "Start when they're young—nip it in the bud." Sometimes quoting her father, she would state, "Pop used to say, 'If a child is old enough to know how to use a comb for its hair, it's old enough to learn to listen.'"

I was well past the age of knowing how to comb my hair when I discovered a large booger in my nose. Just when I had worked it down almost to the end of my nostril, Mom saw what I was doing and said firmly, "Stop picking your nose." But who can resist a booger that's sitting right within easy reach? A big one at that. So I slipped behind a door, out of sight, and got it. Or I thought I was out of sight. But not from Mom's watchful eye! I don't remember what I did with my treasure, but Mom must have assumed I had eaten it, because she marched me out to the kitchen at once and told me to stick out my tongue. I did, and she sprinkled pepper on it to create a memory that would deter me from such actions in the future. I immediately reached for a drink of water, which Mom graciously allowed.

When we were younger, Mom was with us most of the time while Dad worked outside, so she was the one who did most of the disciplining in the early stages of our lives. For lesser offenses, she used a variety of punishments. For relentless whining or fussing, she made us sit in time-out in the dark cellarway, or on a stairway step, or a chair in another room, "'til you can be quiet." For talking sassily to her, eating our boogers, or producing flatulation noises with our mouths, she put pepper or soap in our mouths. If we pretended to shoot each other, she confiscated our toy guns. When we fought with one another, Mom made us kiss each other on the cheek— in other words, "kiss and make up." Though our kisses did not actually mean we were making up, the disdained "kiss of Judas" usually stopped the fighting for the moment.

Most of the time, Mom was proactive with discipline. She believed, "If you tell them how you want them to behave ahead of time, it works better." She was usually right, especially when we were older and out in public, where we were expected to be on our best behavior. When we were younger, Mom offered rewards as an incentive for good behavior. Elam, for instance, "earned" twenty-five cents as a little boy when he behaved well at the dentist. As an adult, he can still clearly see in his mind's eye the prized yellow-and-red plastic dump truck he bought with that quarter.

Mom seemed to have the ability to know what worked best to motivate or correct each of her children in a particular situation. "Each one is different," she said. She knew, for instance, what would work for Parke when he was about nine years old driving our Ford tractor recklessly around the house. Parke loved to drive the tractor because the step-up gear installed on it added a higher gear for each of the three forward gears, which meant that the tractor had six total forward gears and could go up to twenty miles per hour. He got a thrill from driving the tractor as fast as it would go and seized every opportunity he could to sit at the wheel. Flying down the narrow driveway around the buildings in high gear, he was an accident waiting to happen. His younger siblings could have been mowed over if they had been standing around the corner of a building, or he could have miscued and hit a tree close by. When he roared around a corner one day, Mom caught him and told him he couldn't drive the tractor anymore in higher than third gear. To Parke, this was the worst punishment ever.

Though Mom usually disciplined us on the spot, sometimes she did so with sophisticated subtlety, her words occasionally even taking on the form of a mere suggestion. She used the latter on Parke once when he was fifteen years old. Bitter and angry when he learned about moving to Buffalo Valley and having to leave friends and cousins, Parke had written in his diary, "Dad sold the farm today, and it makes me so blame mad." Mom read his diary and told him she thought he ought to change it in case his grandchildren ever read it.

Mom was also able to make her point without coming down hard on us. Although one of her pet peeves was when we passed gas inside the house, she simply made the culprit run around the house three times to air off. This actually turned into fun, because when the gas passer sprinted around the house, those of us inside stood at the windows and laughed as they zipped by. The runner laughed too. In her home, Mom had been taught that the bathroom was the proper place for passing gas, whereas Dad could not have cared less about location; in his home, anywhere was okay, except maybe not in church.

It was not okay with Dad, however, when we stood in the doorway to the house and held the door open. He sometimes said in a joking sort of way, "Children live in the doorway. In the summer they let the flies in, and in the winter they let the cold in." But we knew exactly how he really felt about it when we were standing there and he said in an irritated voice, "Shut the door—don't let all the flies in! Either come in or go out!"

This was classic Dad (the opposite of Mom's style), barking out orders in a loud, harsh voice when he called us out on certain behavior. Though he sometimes laughed heartily at our "ruckusing" with one another, it usually didn't take long for him to reach his limit and snap, "Now keep on until someone gets hurt!" or, "Stop while you're ahead! Next you'll be bawlin'!" or, "Simmer down!" My guess is that stress often fueled his sharp comments.

Dad's reactionary and dramatic nature arose out of his tendency to feel things deeply. On the positive side of this, his sensitivity to deep emotion made him capable of handling our behavior in a quiet and gentle way when we were out of sorts, as he seemed to understand and respect our feelings even when they appeared in the form of apparent disrespect. Like the day Dad announced the move to Buffalo Valley and Elam bolted up the stairs along with Parke, bawling and yelling, "You're crazy!" Elam never talked to Dad like that, but Dad didn't respond—he just let Elam settle down over time.

Esther also experienced Dad's forbearance when her fifteen-year-old driving skills went awry one day as she was practicing in our half-mile-long lane. Hoping to impress her school friend in the front seat beside her, she instead missed turning sharply enough in the corner in front of the house and rammed the station wagon smack into the bank, smashing the radiator. Devastated and dreading Dad's reaction, Esther went for a walk with her friend up along the river, hoping she wouldn't be around when Dad learned of her accident; she wanted to put his scolding off as long as possible. To her surprise, although Dad wasn't happy about the damage, he didn't scold her. Esther knew we couldn't afford to pay $40 for a new radiator, but Dad seemed to chalk it up as a learning experience.

Dad didn't scold Tina either as she expected him to when she earned a speeding ticket soon after getting her license. When all Dad said was, "I'll pay for it now 'til you got a job," she heaved a deep sigh of relief. He never questioned her or got on her case about going too fast. He probably assumed she would pay more attention to the speed limit from then on.

The day eleven-year-old Parke took matters into his own hands and walloped one of our potato-picking migrant workers, Dad again demonstrated his carefully calculated disciplinary approach. That day, Parke had been given the job of driving the '34 Ford truck with the cut-off cab and the improvised hoist for the dump bed. In addition to driving the truck, Parke was given the responsibility of penciling a tally mark by the name of each migrant worker as they called out their name and dumped their basket of potatoes on the truck bed. The problem began when one worker insisted on quitting early and refused to work anymore. Parke must have assumed that since he could handle driving the truck and keeping a tally of the baskets dumped, he could surely handle this situation too. Picking up a piece of pipe used to put the crankshaft on to start the truck, Parke shouted at the worker, "Oh, no you don't; there's too much work yet to do." Hitting the migrant worker across the backside, he muttered, "There, that will teach you." Dad's hired man rushed from the scene and sped in to the buildings to tell Dad there was trouble in the potato field. When Dad arrived at the tense scene, one of the other workers, unable to get the words out fast enough, tried to tell Dad what had happened. Dad asked the worker, "Did he hit you?" "No," the man replied. Dismissing him, Dad said, "Get back to work." He then scolded Parke in front of the man he had hit, and when they were alone, Dad grilled Parke. "What were you thinking?! Those workers might have knives!" Parke smirked. "Oh, I knew they didn't have knives," he said confidently. "How do you know?" Dad asked. Parke replied, "I asked them earlier if any of them had a knife so I could sharpen my pencil, and they didn't have any."

Dad's firm, non-yelling approach could sometimes be his most unsettling form of discipline. Like the day he appeared as John was giving Elvin a well-deserved kick. John had just bought a cowboy hat and boots with all the money he'd earned picking tomatoes that year when he spied Elvin wearing his new boots without permission. Elvin, glimpsing the look on his brother's face, fled, with John in hot pursuit. Unable to snag Elvin, John kept running after him. The longer he ran, the angrier he got. Finally, with steam pouring out of his ears, he managed to grab Elvin and gave him a good, hard kick. At that moment, Dad walked in, and all he needed to say was, "John, we don't kick around here!" Humiliated, John hung his head. Experiencing that kind of reprimand was even more difficult than being yelled at.

The same thing happened to Pete one day when Dad arrived at the pivotal moment in a fight revolving around popguns that Fred had bought Pete and John for Christmas. The boys had been expressly forbidden to shoot at people with their guns, and they knew that doing so guaranteed confiscation of the guns for a while. But one day, Elvin agitated Pete so relentlessly that Pete couldn't take it any more. Controlling himself by a mere thread, he grabbed the barrel of his gun and pretended to do what he really wanted to do—clobber Elvin on the head with the stock. Enter Dad, who told Pete in no uncertain terms that if he ever saw him do that again, he'd take the gun from him; guns weren't to be used that way. Pete already knew that. He also knew that he was getting away with a close one.

Though Dad mostly disciplined us with words, when he felt corporal punishment was necessary, he used it. At those times, Dad's tenderheartedness came out. One day when Elam and Parke were little boys, they misbehaved. As punishment,

Dad gave them a choice between not going in the truck with the hired man and himself to get lumber, and a spanking. Parke chose to stay home, and Elam chose the spanking. Dad cried.

Neither spanking nor talking worked, however, the day Fred stole a quarter and refused to confess. Having developed quite a problem with lying, Fred was trying to lie his way out of this too, and Dad's efforts to get him to admit his misdeed were fruitless. Parke and Elam had seen Fred take the quarters with their own two eyes, so he was busted, but he still stubbornly denied it. Finally, in desperation, Dad said, "Fred, let's get down on our knees and ask God's forgiveness. Liars go to hell." At that point, Parke and Elam, who were standing in the wings, took off. Something changed for Fred this time, and he confessed to taking the quarters, then handed them over to Dad. Even as an adult, Fred would tear up just thinking about this incident with Dad, and he credited his strong distaste of lying to this experience.

Clearly, Mom and Dad took seriously the job of disciplining, doing everything they could to nurture the development of our character through discipline. They believed deeply that it would give us the best chance of becoming persons of integrity capable of managing ourselves. They had both been disciplined when growing up, and as a result, had internalized a strong work ethic, frugality, and the ability to shun harmful things. They wanted to teach us the same thing.

Discipline of our behavior was the precursor for being trained to work. Discipline, both for behavior and work, forged character and sped the process of personal development.

Discipline of Work

Chores and responsibilities became a part of the rhythm of life for us. We did not need to be cajoled into doing our part. Maybe this was because doing chores was just expected of us. And maybe it was because we knew if we wanted to please our parents, all we had to do was work hard. Doing our chores was one way we got individual recognition from Mom and Dad, which was sometimes as rewarding as spending one-on-one time with them. They complimented us for doing a good job when we worked, which only made us want to work more and harder. Working hard was one way, in the midst of so many of us, that I knew I'd be guaranteed approval.

We did chores before school and after school every day, starting when we were very young—taking turns setting the table before meals, clearing off the table, washing and drying dishes, and loading up the little red wagon on winter mornings and evenings to bring wood from the shop to the kitchen to fill the woodbox beside the wood range.

Graduating to new, more difficult chores and responsibilities was a rite of passage for each of us. When an older sibling got married or moved away, we advanced up the chart of chores for outside work. Beginners gathered eggs, fed chickens, and nursed calves with the "tit bucket." Next, we moved up to tying cows, giving each cow a scoop of food, washing udders before milking, throwing hay bales down from the haymow, and cleaning out the rabbit pens and chicken house. Those who rose to the top of the ladder went out to the pasture in the early morning or evening with the dog to bring the cows in to be milked, then put milking machines together and helped with the milking. They also brought in our day's supply of milk from the cans in the milk-house cooler before the milk truck got there to haul away the cans. When it was Sue's job to fetch milk in the morning, she'd wait until she heard the sound of the milk truck coming in the lane. Then she'd throw off her covers, spring out of bed, grab a robe, and with a milk jug in hand, sprint to the milk house as fast as she could before the milk truck arrived on the scene.

Barb—now big enough to drive tractor at five years old—with Fred and Leona

Another job we learned was teaching calves how to go from drinking milk from a tit bucket to drinking out of a regular bucket. To graduate to this chore, one had to persuade the calf to suck on our milk-dipped fingers, then lead the sucking calf's head down into the bucket where it could figure out how to drink the milk. Sometimes a calf made a challenging job even more difficult by acting on a wild-hair notion to butt the bucket of milk over, creating a big mess and much distress for the one holding the bucket. When Esther managed at a very young age to wean a calf from the tit bucket, she gained a great sense of accomplishment.

All of these chores were part of keeping the farm running smoothly, and it was important that they be done consistently. So Mom and Dad often checked in with us at meals—a time and place where we were all present at once—about whether or not we had done our chores. One winter evening when it got dark early, we were eating supper together, and Mom asked Fred if he had fed the rabbits. "Nooooo," he admitted reluctantly after a short pause. Before he could eat, he had to get up from the table to go feed the rabbits.

Although our outside chores started with the animals, we also did chores in the fields at a young age, many of which required driving vehicles. Dad never allowed us to ride on the tractor with him when we were little. Instead, he taught us how to drive vehicles at a young age. This was because he had confidence we could do it. We must have believed it too, because we did not shrink back in fear. Instead, we climbed into the vehicle we were to drive, reached for the steering wheel, and stretched our legs down to the brake pedal or clutch. We drove each of these vehicles very slowly, of course.

Five seemed to be the age Dad felt it was right to get us started. That was Barb's age when Dad showed her how to drive the tractor to the barn from the field, instructing her to stop by turning the tractor off when she got to the buildings. Sue was also five years old when she climbed up into what we called the "big red truck," where Dad and the boys were loading hay, and followed the simple instruction to "push the clutch in or out" with her short legs. Elvin, too, was five when he learned to drive the tractor, with Dad and Fred loading tomatoes on the wagon behind it. Once, when he jerked the clutch, baskets full of tomatoes fell off the back, sending tomatoes rolling on the ground everywhere. Elvin remembers Dad and Fred yelling, not so much at him but at what had happened with the tomatoes. Ada learned to drive stick shift in the pickup truck when just a young girl while Dad tried to load hay bales on the back of it. He stood with his legs apart, bracing himself for the jerking he expected from Ada driving either too fast or too slow. Mim and Tina each drove tractors when very young also. When Tina drove for others who were loading tomatoes, someone would run up and jump on the tractor to stop it when she came to the end of the row, since her legs were too short to reach the pedals. Mim was so little she had to get off the seat and stand up to reach the pedals.

Driving was one of the fun jobs, but many other tasks had to be done as well. When Parke was seven or eight years old, he was assigned the job of helping load clay tile pipes that Dad had made, wearing kidskin gloves Dad bought him because his hands were so small. Tiring of the job, Parke faked being sick one day. His claim became less than airtight, however, when he suddenly felt better soon after Dad left. So Mom carted him right back to work. Humiliated, Parke had to face Dad back on the job site.

As Parke grew older, he got into the swing of working. When he was close to ten years old, Dad assigned him, as the oldest child, the job of cultivating seventy-five acres of potatoes. Though Parke was envious at times of Elam exploring in the creek while he was working, he wasn't willing to share the responsibility with Elam.

Parke and Elam set the precedent for the rest of us to work hard. They did their regular chores plus helped care for the cattle since Dad usually had a lot of cattle around. When Dad went deer hunting one year when we still lived at Oley, Parke and Elam—twelve and thirteen years old respectively—did the feeding for a week at least. They threw enough silage out of the silo by hand to feed over one hundred steers. They also lugged heavy bags of chopped grain down to the first floor of the barn by the end of the week, which made them feel like they had done a man's job.

Not to be outdone by her brothers, Esther at ten years old singlehandedly unloaded a wagonload of hay bales onto the elevator to be stacked into the haymow by older siblings waiting in the mow. Even though it was very hot, Esther would not stop working or give up until she had removed every last bale. When someone in the haymow rewarded her efforts by yelling, "Slow down!" Esther's motivation kicked into even higher gear as she piled the hay bales on the elevator so fast that those stacking bales had a hard time keeping up with her.

Fred and Esther were a force to be reckoned with when they worked together in the blazing sun to fill enclosed, open tractor trailer beds full of tomatoes. Pete remembers watching their clockwork as a small boy. Esther, taking pride in shocking Dad and Fred by her ability to keep up, would swing basket after basket of tomatoes from a stack on the flatbed wagon over to the trailer. Like a runner in a relay race, Fred would pick up where Esther left off and dump the tomatoes into the trailer. They worked rapidly, their fingers getting raw even though they wore gloves. Dad often told others about it saying, "Esther worked like a man!" When Pete shared his memory of this with Esther years later, she didn't remember it. But Pete does. He sees it clearly in his mind's eye and hears Dad's payment in praise of "getting it done," applauding not only Esther's work but her character as well.

Doing hard jobs like this boosted our self-esteem. When Tina was just old enough to help Dad and the boys carry heavy irrigation pipes in the tomato fields, she felt herself swell with pride both from the knowledge that she could do this demanding job and from hearing Dad's praise. And Fred, in addition to loading wagonload after wagonload of tomatoes, took pride in also shoveling many wagonloads of corn into the corncrib. It made him feel worthwhile.

Big and small, each of our jobs helped keep the farm going. Since the farm sustained our family, Mom and Dad made farm work a priority. Parke came to this realization in a stark way at sixteen years of age when blight disease hit the tomato crop, eventually wiping it out, and he had to quit school to help out. He and Dad had to make up for lost wages by getting truck driving jobs, and Parke made his first run (to New York to pick up a load of lambs) when he was seventeen. When Mom and Dad asked Parke to give three-fourths of his wages to them to help out financially, he had mixed feelings but did as requested for the sake of the family.

Although Dad and Parke's truck driving jobs helped the family financially, the driving took them away from the farm. This meant that Elam, although he had done well in school, had to quit after tenth grade so he could hold down the farm while Dad and Parke drove truck.

After ninth grade, Esther also quit school to work on the farm. She enjoyed working outdoors and one day suggested to Dad that she quit school because her help was needed. Dad was quick to take Esther up on her offer, knowing what a hard worker she was.

One year when resources were especially lean, Mom sold whole butchered chickens once a week for grocery money. This meant that every week for a period of several months, Barb and some of the others had to butcher twenty chickens in the mornings before going to school.

Though the discipline of learning to work was not always easy and sometimes required significant sacrifice, it gave us much in return. We experienced the joy of being needed and of camaraderie in working together. We learned to work whether we wanted to or not, and we experienced the satisfaction of being praised for a job well done. We learned how important our individual contributions were while at the same time we grew to love community as we became community for each other.

Thankfully, Mom and Dad modeled both the discipline of behavior and the discipline of work for us. They taught us well as we followed their example and learned from them.

9. Diversions

The black Falcon roaring out the lane in front of a cloud of dust was barely visible when Elvin or Tim were driving it. Once our run-around car, it was now transformed into a hot rod with sawed-off roof, cut-off muffler, makeshift roller bar, and missing doors—a result of Elvin and Tim's vision inspired when Dad pronounced last rites over the battered hunk of metal. Rumbling in and out of our long lane, the Falcon bounced wildly over mud-puddle dips. What were Mom and Dad thinking? I would never have let my children do that! Our neighbor lady, Mrs. Showers, hands on hips and glaring at us from her yard across the highway, probably wondered the same. One day, the boys talked me into riding out the lane with them in the Falcon. Taking me on a bonus thrill ride, they abruptly veered off the lane, straight into the field beside it, and headed toward the tall, sloping bank of I-80 that ran through our farm. Getting a running start, the driver gunned the engine to the top of the bank, then took his foot off the gas pedal and let us drift backward straight down the bank, gaining speed until suddenly the car slowed down and drifted to a stop as it reached the level ground of the field below. "Phew," I breathed out loud. When I looked up, there, wouldn't you know, stood Mrs. Showers.

Pete, Tim, and Elvin and the hats they loved to pretend with

Diversion, defined as activity that diverts the mind from tedious or serious concerns, released our family's pressure valve, holding us together by saving us from bursting apart. It began in our individual minds and joined with like-minded cohorts—rippling within the house, flowing out to our yard, spilling over into the

161

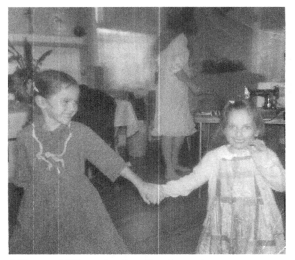

Mim and Tina, having fun from the start

river, into the barn, the borders of our farm, and up into the mountains nearby. Our whole world was our playground—a playground, if you can imagine it, with no TV and no technology, only our imaginations to create our own fun. Turning into a lighthearted outlet, our play relieved us of tension and stress and provided an escape from the cares of life.

Perhaps play is what one does when there is nothing else to do, or perhaps it is the essence of life—the preservation of a human being, the restoration of body, soul, and spirit. Intertwined throughout our daily life, play meant survival for us. We played in nature, in cardboard boxes, in the river ... there was no end to the possibilities.

Nature

Early on, my senses discovered nature as one of the best playgrounds. Summertime set things in motion, and I felt the expectation of adventure as I skipped down to the stream at the edge of the pasture in front of the house. What experience would it hold today? Would the green grass clusters that protruded up from the middle of the gently flowing water be a jungle to explore? Would I be amazed simply by the distortion of my hands beneath the flowing water? Would I collect more small rocks to finish making the dam across the stream? Or would I pack mud into a small bucket to make a castle at its edge?

I would decide when I got there. Our willow tree, which stood like a sentinel at the edge of the yard next to the former outhouse space, touched its narrow leaf tips to the ground, creating a walled chamber with bowed branches. I could enter this private chamber and carry out any plan I chose. I could be a bride waiting to meet my bridegroom. Or just sit on the ground, eating crackers and sipping my glass of water. Either way, it was my little domain.

Bushes, butterflies, Queen Anne's Lace, and dandelion puffs surrounded my domain. The flowers of the Mock Orange bush beside the swing set sported yellowish-orange on the edge of their wide-open pointed petals, inviting me to sink my nose all the way in and breathe in their heavenly, sweet, orange scent. Just a few steps away stood the Bridal Wreath bush, every small branch and twig covered with clusters of small, pristine white flowers. I could make one sweep of pinched fingertips along any of its twigs or branches and a mass of swirling whiteness would fall like snow to the ground.

The butterflies fluttering in blue, yellow, orange, black, and brown clusters in the sheep pen behind the barn and milk house gave me a feast for my eyes. Dodging thistles, I'd chase them with bare feet, or wait patiently until one alighted upon something. Then I'd sneak up quietly to it, making a quick lunge to capture it in the cave of my hands. Its flapping wings would tickle my palms as I dashed to the house before it could escape. There I'd crack open the bottom of my cupped hands over a jar lid of alcohol for the butterfly to flutter into. When it was finally still, I'd open my palms, spellbound by the beauty of its colors and design right there on my hands.

Queen Ann's lace growing on the bank in front of our house also held wonder for me. When the tightly closed clusters of flowers at the top of its stalks began loosening, slowly but surely they formed a cup-shaped bird's nest. I kept my eye on them, waiting for what was to happen next, as bit by bit they opened up into a lovely, lacey doily.

The white puffs at the end of dandelion stalks decking out our lawn were all that was left of the yellow flowers before them. All it took was one great huff of air and the white fluffiness at the end of the stem exploded marvelously into the air. Magic, pure magic, I thought happily.

And that king in a violet! I discovered if I picked a violet's petals off one by one, a king would appear, sitting on his throne, washing his feet in a tub. Amazing, for sure!

There were sights and there were sounds. After lots of practice, I learned how to stretch a narrow grass blade tightly between my thumbs and blow hard on it to make an amazing trumpet-like sound. Maybe it wasn't as wonderful as a symphony, but the music it made was mystical to me.

Though I didn't dare taste it, a mud pie in an aluminum pie tin with a few purple violets stuck in the middle looked for all the world like a delectable, chocolate dessert that I longingly wished was real. The earth stored the pie's simple ingredients on the ground by the drain behind the milk house.

All these things that summertime gifted to me filled my soul with delight as I opened each one.

Summer also brought the gift of lying under the stars at night. When we spread blankets on the lawn in the back yard to sleep on, we didn't mind the clumps of grass jutting up under us as we gazed in wonder at the ceiling of stars above us. The star show was worth any downside of sleeping out in the open. We could fall asleep with the sublime warmth of grass beneath and a magnificent canopy of stars overhead and wake up the next morning to dew covering our blankets and the grass around us. When this happened, we grabbed our blankets and scurried across the cool, wet grass to the back door in our bare feet. If we didn't want morning dew on our blankets, we could throw one over the wash line before we went to sleep, weight it down at the edges with rocks, and have a perfect A-shape to crawl into. But it wasn't the same as sleeping under the stars.

As I grew older, I discovered more of nature's playground in the great outdoors beyond the farm. On many a lazy Sunday afternoon, someone would announce a hike. At first, Dad initiated these hikes. One Sunday afternoon, he took some of us up the White Deer power-line trail in the Blue Mountain range. When we got to the top, he pointed out in the distance where the two branches of the Susquehanna River joined around Northumberland. This joining created the river that flowed by our house.

Later, it was my brothers who summoned an upcoming hike. I was right there, eager to accept the invitation to be out in the fresh air with my fellow adventurers, gung ho about accepting the challenge of climbing to one of the ridges they pointed out in the distance. Nothing compared to the feeling of being fully alive, of exhilarating triumph, when I got to the top. I felt secure in these mountains, knowing that to my brothers, who spoke of the ridges and hollows, the mountains were as familiar as the backs of their hands.

Pete led one of the mountain hikes that culminated on a grassy slope at the top of a mountain. Looking closely we could see, almost buried in grass and moss, the remains of equally spaced logs—the only remaining evidence that a logging train had also once traveled this mountaintop. These railroad ties, hewn from trees on this very same mountain, were eroded pine logs whose weather-whittled knots stuck out through the soil a few inches here and there. One particular log with multiple knots rising above the ground caught my attention. When I began to unearth it from the mossy soil, I discovered it was a work of art calling to me. Yielding slowly to my pulling and prying, the embedded log finally broke free of the ground like a piece of long-buried treasure. I stood there amazed, trying to take in its absolute beauty and came to the realization I could not leave it behind. It was heavy, but I was determined to carry it out of there. As I struggled to heave it up onto my right shoulder, Pete, who was a few inches shorter than me at the time and three children younger, snatched up the log from my shoulder as he said, "Here, let me carry that." I watched him, my heart bursting with pride as he made his way down the mountain shouldering that heavy log—a log that I've kept ever since. I've hung clothes on it and plants from it and now have it as a decorative piece above my doorway. Each time I leave the house, I am reminded of hiking in the mountains, love for a brother, and the beauty of nature.

Pete and Fred opened the way for us to enjoy nature's beauty even at night. On summer evenings, one or the other of them would occasionally call out, "Who wants to go spot deer?" and my siblings and I, instantly euphoric, would scramble to the car and pile in while Pete or Fred stood by grinning. We'd set out eagerly to find an open field along a back road, and when we came to a place that looked like there could be deer grazing in the dark, the driver would stop the car and plug the spotlight into the cigarette lighter. With bated breath, I would wait for the light to sweep over the field, eventually bringing into its circle the outline of deer with eyes shining brightly at us like two piercing lanterns. Seeing this brought a surreal feeling every bit as exciting as going to see a movie—if we had been allowed to go to the movies, that is.

Elam learned on his own how to find treasure in the earth itself. In the spring, when the fields were freshly plowed and disced, he would set out to walk the length of a field over the dark-brown, river-bottom soil, with eyes glued to the ground, searching for partially exposed Indian arrowheads. He had a good eye for finding the hand-sharpened stones, and after a rain on freshly upturned sod, the search was especially rewarding since the ground was more likely to be washed away around the artifacts. Over the many springs that Elam walked the fields, he found several hundred arrowheads that he collected in long, white socks that bulged out on the sides in sharp, jutting shapes.

When I held one of these arrowheads in my hand and rubbed my fingers over the rough surface that an Indian had carved, my imagination came alive with stories and folktales of Indians who had once lived where we were now living. I could envision our fields with Indian tribes shooting arrows at other tribes across the river and hunting for wildlife. According to local folklore, the tribe on the other side of the river left a visible dark spot on the shore where they did their cooking. I looked hard for the spot and could almost imagine I detected it, but never for sure.

Imaginations, Innovations

We didn't have TVs, iPods, iPads, computers, or tablets. But we had our imaginations, and we had each other. "Hey, let's … !" was an invitation to do something together: to tell stories at night in our beds, to go on a fantasy ride on two old jalopies, to slide stocking-footed across the kitchen floor and down the stair banister, to play paper dolls, to deck ourselves out with jelly beans, to build tunnels in the haymow, to raid our neighbors' junk pile.

The invitation often came as we lay in darkness—two to a bed on three double beds in one room—settling into the night, snug in our blankets. Someone would start a story, and that's all it took for creative ideas to begin flowing in a wonderful way from one mind to the next as we took turns adding to the story. Sometimes one of us took off on a creative streak and told an entire story, taking the rest of us along on a ride of fantasy. When it was a wild, crazy story and we all burst into a boisterous cackle, Dad's booming voice would call out to us from the bedroom across the hall, "Alright girls, time to settle down now!"

Our imaginations got a lot of mileage outdoors as well, especially when the invitation was to jump on the two old jalopies parked side by side at the edge of the orchard. The jalopies were once upon a time used to haul bags of potatoes and baskets of tomatoes, and now sat rusting away in the snow, wind, and rain. Sue and I would sit in the drivers' seats across from each other, steering the stationary vehicles wherever we fancied. Their wooden beds were rotted, tires were flattened, and steering wheels were cracked and sticky, leaving a smell of old rubber on our hands, but we didn't care. Away we'd go on a fantasy trip to faraway places.

Though we didn't have many actual toys, we didn't feel poor. We were rich in ideas, and when we put them all together, "Hey, let's …" could mean so many different things: running through the family room into the kitchen to slide across the linoleum kitchen floor in our socks (is it any wonder Mom had so many to darn? Even so, she didn't put a stop to our fun), or clamoring as we chased each other around and around the long kitchen table—the chased person yanking chairs out from the table into the path of the chaser to slow him or her down.

When someone would start to set up cardboard boxes on the kitchen floor beside the table, we would all come racing into the family room to line up. One by one we would tear into the kitchen, jump over the boxes, run around the table and back into the family room to get lined up to do it all over again. Lots of pandemonium, lots of laughter—now this was sheer joy. And we didn't even need a theme park. So what made this simple activity so enjoyable?

I think it had a lot to do with having fun together. Sliding together down the long stairway banister, for instance, was always more fun than sliding by oneself, especially when two or three of us slid down close together, bumping into one another as we came to a sudden stop at the post at the bottom. No wonder the banister became wobbly. It's incomprehensible that Mom didn't make us stop doing this.

How Mom and Dad tolerated all this commotion, I will never know. They appeared to build up a resistance to it and even enjoy it at times. Maybe it was a choice between this or becoming a nervous wreck themselves, for how was one to stop this bunch of rambunctious kids from making such a racket, without using sheer force?

In a calmer vein of creativity, when a new Sears catalog would come in the mail, we'd take turns claiming it, eagerly waiting for the next season's catalog to arrive so we could finally cut out our "family." (Mom strictly forbade us to use a current catalog to make cutouts, but we could at least look in it to claim our imaginary family ahead of time.) Our cutouts were flimsy compared to real paper dolls, but that didn't matter too much because I could choose the woman I wanted to be, the husband I wanted to have, and the children I wanted to parent. The families that Sue and Edith created visited with my family. I never played with real paper dolls until Aunt Ida bought me some. Hers came in a yellow folder with a picture of a smiling baby on the cover, and pockets inside the book where the cutouts could be stored. These were wonderful, but so were the Sears catalog cutouts.

Sears cutouts were just one of the ways my sisters and I could become who we wanted to be. We could also become a woman of our choosing by using jelly beans to wear real makeup. We discovered this when someone dropped off a huge bag of red, blue, yellow, white, green, and orange jelly beans. With only a few licks of a blue or green jelly bean, we had instant eye shadow, though very dark and sticky. And a lick or two of a red jelly bean gave us instant bright-red rouge or lipstick, which tasted very sweet when we licked our lips. When I looked in the mirror, I saw the image of Jezebel looking back at me—which was startling. But just for a little while, I had fun feeling "worldly" with my sisters. We must have had easy access to the jelly beans, because the next time we went to the dentist we had lots of cavities.

Our imaginations took us seamlessly from applying jelly bean makeup in the home to engineering haymow tunnels in the barn. With a bit of arranging and rearranging, together we maneuvered the hay bales into long tunnels with a couple different levels. At some places, we left open spaces for patches of light to shine through the top, but otherwise the tunnel was dark, so braving the whole passageway by ourselves was a daring venture. Crawling through the tunnel with a few others was definitely more reassuring.

Just beyond the fence of one of our fields sat a junk pile in the corner of our neighbor's property, lying out of sight for them but not for us. When we'd see our neighbors back their pickup truck to their junk pile and unload stuff, we could hardly wait until they were finished. We were amazed at how they could throw away almost "perfectly good" things, when we wasted nothing. After their truck finally pulled far enough away for us not to be seen, we'd go skipping to the pile to search for treasures that would go perfectly in our huts on top of the riverbank or even be added to our stash of toys. It would have felt scary to venture to the junk pile by ourselves, but not when we went together.

Though we usually had fun together, sometimes we enjoyed doing something just by ourselves. Fred was especially good at envisioning and carrying out ideas by himself in ways that challenged the rest of us. At twelve years old, he dug a deep, 5' x 6" x 5' x 5" hole near the river in a corner just outside the yard, simply because he could. When he began digging, he was hoping to make an underground house. One Sunday morning, he stood at the edge of his hole, eyeing the shovel lying close by, knowing he couldn't dig because that would be working. To follow his urge to dig while at the same time obeying the no-work-on-Sunday mandate, he slowly picked up the shovel, scooped up a bit of dirt one time, then stopped. Elam, a witness of what had happened, reproved Fred, laughing. To this day, Fred has no clue what inspired him to eventually heave shovel after shovel of dirt up out of that hole. Maybe it was the pure joy of digging or the satisfaction of accomplishing a difficult task. Or maybe it was when Dad showed a visitor the deep crater and said, "Why, I'd pity him if I'd have made him work that hard," and what Fred heard Dad really say was, "This doesn't make sense to me, but I'm proud of him for working so work hard at it." I have a hunch it was a combination of all these, because when Fred finished carving out the hole, the idea of the house vanished into thin air.

When winter came, the cavernous hole filled with snow. One day Dad was standing at the kitchen window watching as two surveyors staked out territory for I-80 soon to come. Suddenly, he burst out laughing, and we all came racing to see what was so funny. One of the surveyors had all but disappeared, waist deep in the snow-covered hole, while the other surveyor standing by laughed along with Dad. Hopefully the man in the hole was amused as well.

Games, Ordinary Play

In addition to our unique anything-goes, free-form imaginative play, we entertained ourselves with things the average kid might enjoy doing: fighting water battles; competing in a game of carrom; and playing in the barn, in the yard, on the sidewalks, and on the swing set.

On any given winter evening when someone said, "Hey, let's play carrom," someone else would go get the carrom board, two shooting sticks, and the plastic bag of game pieces, while still another person would drag out the folding table and set it up in the middle of the family room, which we called the "everyday room." We played carrom so much that eventually the nets at the corners of the board developed holes that the carrom pieces escaped through. We took carrom playing seriously but didn't hold anything against the winner.

Many winter evenings we scampered on the snow- and ice-covered path to the barn in the dark. When we opened the wooden barn door, the cows lying in their stalls heard the creaky hinges and greeted us with soft moos, slowly munching on hay, their warm breath rising. The smell of hay and fresh manure filled our olfactory senses as we played Mother May I? and Red Light, Green Light. We decided who was "it" by standing in a circle with our hands toward the middle while someone led "One potato, two potato" or "Eenie meenie miney mo" to rule out one by one those who were not "it."

In summertime, we made the yard and sidewalks our playground, playing hide-and-seek, tag, or Red Light, Green Light until it got too dark to see anymore. We also jumped our way through Hopscotch on the sidewalk that doubled as our jump-rope platform. We made our own jump rope by braiding bailer twine together, trying to keep it from curving awkwardly in various places as we braided. We jumped, one or two of us at a time, to the rhythm of little ditties that we recited together as two other siblings swung the ends of the rope for us.

The summer Barb bought us a swing set from tip money she had earned at JJ Newberry's restaurant in Lewisburg, it was as if we had died and gone to heaven. I watched spellbound as the large yellow and green pieces of the swing set were unloaded from the truck that hauled them to our house. When the wonderful, bright-green and yellow swing set with a sliding board and wooden glider swing was set up beside the old, rusty, red-and-blue heavy cast iron one that had just two swings and a ladder, it seemed like virtually a whole playground in comparison.

We loved swinging peacefully through the air, but as the writer of Ecclesiastes states, there is a time for everything. Some days practically begged for breaking the peace with the commotion of a spontaneous water battle, usually begun when someone playfully spritzed water on someone else. Payback was a little bit of water thrown from the bottom of a glass, countered with half a glass of water. It was then that Mom would point us to the door to finish the battle outside, and it's a good thing she did, because by this time the battlers usually each had a full glass in hand, often followed by a bucket. It was only after we were dripping from head to toe that we would set our buckets down and declare a truce.

One particular water battle between Mim and Elvin ended unexpectedly with a puddle rather than with buckets of water. Mim was working in the kitchen minding her own business when in through the door popped Elvin, who, unprovoked, threw water at her. Mim followed on his heels in hot pursuit with a big plastic cup—FULL. Elvin flew back into the house to replenish his water supply. On and on the battle continued with no declared winner. Then Elvin upped the ante.

Spying a basket of tomatoes on the porch with some rotten ones, he grabbed a few, and the next time Mim came out the kitchen door with ammunition in hand, he hurled one at her and fled. Well, if you've grown up on a tomato farm, you know that one rotten tomato deserves another. Not about to let Elvin get the better of her, Mim, dripping with rotten tomato juice, grabbed one herself and pursued him, her jaw set with determination. She had a hard time getting close to Elvin, however, because outside he could stay under cover better. After she chased him round and round the shop, out to the barn, past the garden, past the shop again, through the corncrib, she stopped, panting, realizing if she was ever to get him back, she needed to return inside the house to throw him off. "He's running toward the cornfield, so I'll just go in the house, look out the window to see where he went into the cornfield, and run up to the bathroom, where the window will be a perfect, rotten-tomato launching pad. Then I'll lie in wait to see if he comes sneaking by below," she told herself. Mim darted into the house and plastered her face against the kitchen window to try to catch sight of Elvin. By this time, it was getting dark. As her eyes searched to make sense of what she was seeing, she was jolted by the realization that she was staring straight into Elvin's eyes! (His face was pressed against the glass on the other side of the window so he could try to see what she was up to.) Mim screamed, jumped a couple inches off the floor, knocked the curtain down, and fell on her knees, scrambling as fast as she could away from the window. It was then that she realized she had to go to the bathroom—bad—and managed to stand upright to make a run for it. But she didn't make it. As she stood in her puddle of pee at the bottom of the steps, she thought, "Okay, no one saw this. I could keep it a secret forever. Naa, I'm not going to keep it a secret. It will give everyone such a good laugh." Sure enough, whoops of laughter swept up any embarrassment Mim may have felt.

Horseplay, Jokes, Playful Spirits

Sometimes we'd opt for a more premeditated kind of fun by playing tricks on each other. When Elam came home from college, he gathered a rapt audience of siblings, who were glad to have him home and wanting his attention. Taking advantage of the moment, he grabbed a marble and pretended to pop it in his mouth and swallow it. We stared, mouths hanging open in disbelief as he pressed on his throat, contorted his face, then rubbed his throat hard—starting below his chin and moving all the way to the bottom of his neck—pretending to swallow the marble with extreme difficulty. Finally, he opened his clasped hand to show us the marble resting quietly right there in his palm. We had hardly been able to bring ourselves to believe he had actually swallowed it, but we giggled, relieved, just the same.

For friends who were visiting, we'd try the classic Airplane game, where we'd blindfold someone and ask them to stand on a bench while two people, one on each end of the bench, lifted it a few inches off the ground, then instructed the person to jump off. Believing the distance from bench to floor was higher than it was, the person usually only jumped after considerable hesitation. Upon landing, they would rip off their blindfold, usually surprised to find that the bench had only risen a couple inches off the ground. "Dentist" was another blindfold trick, where we'd tell the person to open their mouth and bend their head back "so the dentist can look in your mouth." Then we'd ask if they wanted a gold or silver filling. If the answer was "gold," someone would sprinkle salt on their tongue, and if "silver," we would sprinkle pepper. After a great deal of spitting and sputtering, the "patient" would be offered a glass of water while onlookers and participants chuckled.

What was it about tricking someone that was so satisfying? We duped friends both in person and over the phone. To the unsuspecting person who would answer the phone, we'd say, "Is your refrigerator running?" When the person on the other end answered "Yes," we'd say, "Well, you better go catch it," then gleefully hang up. Or we'd call a friend and ask, "Do you live on Route 15?" When the friend answered, "Yes," we'd advise, "Well, you better get off. There's a truck coming!" It's a good thing caller ID did not exist back then.

A practical joke that Dale and Mim played on Tina one day turned sour. It began innocently, with Dale and Mim playing on the balcony. Venturing into the closet at the end of the balcony, Dale came upon a pile of bags containing clothes that people had donated to us. After a bit, he emerged from the closet with pantyhose over his whole head—causing a weirdly contorted face—and wearing a big, brown, furry coat he had pulled out of one of the bags. An idea sparked. Mim and Dale went into conspiracy mode, making a plan to lure Tina out to the balcony. As Mim headed to corral Tina, Dale disappeared back into the closet. When Tina sauntered out on the balcony, totally unaware of Dale lurking in the closet, Mim innocently moseyed back into the house, locking the door behind her. Dale took this as his cue to begin scratching the inside of the closet door. Instantly frantic, Tina knocked on the house door, calling out, "Mim, let me in!" Not able to let well enough alone, Dale opened the closet door a crack and thrust out one of his furry shoulders. Turning desperate, Tina banged on the door, practically screaming, "Mim, let me in!" Seeing Tina's panic, Dale took mercy on her and threw the closet door open in order to identify himself quickly. Seeing what looked like something straight out of a horror movie, however, Tina virtually climbed the door, flailing against it and crying loudly in terror. Grasping the seriousness of Tina's altered state of being, Mim sprang to the door and unlocked it, yelling, "It's Dale! It's Dale!" Tina came flying through the door and vaulted onto the bed across the room, where she lay sobbing uncontrollably. Now ashamed of what they had done, it took a long time for Dale and Mim to console her. It's no small wonder that Tina doesn't have PTSD from this dreadful experience.

Chastened but not totally subdued by the experience, Mim also took a turn one day at disguising herself—this time, however, managing to inflict only shock rather than terror. The idea spawned when Mim happened upon a short, brown wig in a bin at the Salvation Army Thrift Store. Twirling the wig on her finger as she stood by the bin, possibilities began to swirl in her mind. "Oooooh ... I could have some fun with this!" she realized. When she got home and tried on the wig, she thought, "Okay, my eyes ... I need something to cover them. Mirror sunglasses would do the trick. ... And hey, I could wear that big, fur coat Dale used to scare Tina!" Testing out her impersonation on our brothers, she strolled up to where they were working.

When they didn't immediately recognize her, her mind jumped into second gear; she could hardly contain her elation about her next step—disguising herself to Dad.

Using our missing collie as her entrance line, Mim seized her opportunity one day when the family was gathered around the table for lunch. Decked out in fur coat, wig, and sunglasses, she knocked loudly on the kitchen door. Dad opened the door and greeted "the woman" kindly, while those who knew about Mim's scheme laughed quietly in the background. To avoid the embarrassment of his children laughing at this strange lady, Dad stepped out on the porch to talk to her, closing the door behind him. The "lady," in a high-pitched, tearful voice with British accent, inquired in a whiny voice, "Are you missing a collie dog?" "Ye-e-e-s," Dad replied. "You are? Oh no! I hope it's not the one I just ran over!" she shrieked, raising the pitch of her voice a few notches. Dad tried to console her gently. "It's okay. Say, where did you say you hit the dog?" "I'm so sorry!" she sobbed loudly. (Mim wondered for a second what would happen if she were to put her head on Dad's shoulder and cry even harder, but she caught herself. "No, I can't do that to him.") "I'll buy you another dog. I'll do anything!" she implored desperately. Dad responded kindly, with just a tinge of impatience now. "Na, that won't be necessary." "Where did you say you hit it?" Dad asked a second time. "Up there," the lady gestured toward I-80. When Dad turned his head to see where she was pointing, Mim jerked off her sunglasses, When he looked back, there was his own daughter, smiling broadly in front of him. "You crazy thing, you!" Dad grinned. And from those of us listening just around the corner, a collective cackle exploded.

Dad was such a good sport about things like this. Our big sisters' skin was considerably easier to get under. Take the day that Leona was mowing lawn and Sue ran circles around her, smiling as she chanted over and over again, "Hutney Giddy"—a phrase she had made up. Leona begged her to please stop. But the more annoyed Leona became, the more fun Sue had, as she just repeated "Hutney Giddy" louder and increased the speed of her encircling. Finally, in out-rage and desperation, Leona stopped the mower dead in its tracks. Glaring at Sue, she yelled at the top of her lungs, "I wish you'd never been born!" Sue, I think, was too shocked to continue.

Poor Barb was also subjected to our intentional irritations. When we would bug her with our loud cavorting and she'd shout, "You children get on my nerves!" we didn't quiet down one iota. Instead, one of us would pipe up and smartly retort, "Oh good, let's take a ride on Barb's nerves!"

When we weren't getting on each other's nerves, we were playing jokes on each other. In our family, the unspoken rule was "Never miss an opportunity!" And sisters' dates were golden opportunities. When Esther started dating Glenn, she fixed delectable desserts for him and asked us to serve them while she and Glenn played games in the living room. One Sunday evening, Esther wanted just plain, vanilla ice cream for a snack. Boring. "Wait a minute. Didn't Dad just buy oysters? Let's do it—let's hide an oyster in Glenn's ice cream!" we conspired. And that's just what we did. But hands down, Glenn was a gentleman to the max. Without saying a word, he quietly just let the oyster slide down his throat. We never did get the immediate feedback we were waiting for. That was because Esther never knew about the oyster until much later when Glenn was comfortable telling her about it.

There were other unexpected appearances during a sister's date, thanks to the stovepipe hole in the ceiling above the living room. John, Pete, Tim, Elvin, and Dale slept in the bedroom directly above the living room. A round, yellow piece of tin with carpet over the top hid the stovepipe hole in their floor. But it didn't cover up the knowledge of the hole in the boys' minds. One evening when Edith and Merle were having a date and the boys were lying in bed overhead, a wonderful idea popped into Elvin's brain. In one leap, he catapulted out of bed, and in the next minute, Edith and Merle saw a head appear through the ceiling above them. John couldn't resist. He sprang out of bed, grabbed Elvin's legs, and lifted them in the air, holding Elvin right there until good and ready to let him down. Not long after that, the circle of tin was nailed to the floor.

Other unexpected happenings during older sisters' dates were not so subtle. There was nothing quiet, for example, about a basketful of tin cans spilling down the stairs. The living room door, opening away from the hallway, created a perfect setup for such a practical joke. All that was needed was a long rope, a basket, and tin cans from the junk barrel. Step one, fill basket with tin cans; step two, tie long rope to basket; step three, quietly tie other end of rope to doorknob; step four, quietly carry basket of cans to top of stairs; step five, stay awake until boyfriend opens door to leave when the clock strikes twelve; step six, listen for the loud cadence of tin hitting tin tumbling down eighteen steps. (Maybe we were trying to test the boyfriend's ability and/or willingness to be in our family, or maybe we just wanted the enjoyment of the joke. Either way, a sister with a young man in her company was a perfect target, since she didn't dare overreact in the presence of someone she wanted to impress.) We giggled under the covers when we finally heard the outpouring of cans, trying to imagine the startled looks on the faces of our sister and her boyfriend. But we were "sound asleep" with innocent, angelic-looking faces the instant we heard her come upstairs. The culprit could not be proven the next morning because we all had the same smug, satisfied look on our faces.

Perhaps it was a similar enjoyment of surprised reactions that inspired Pete to venture into territory not expected of the average student, a reserved one at that, but then Pete never was average. One day, in his own quiet way, he randomly took a mouse to school in a salt shaker. There's no telling where the mouse finally ended up on its visit to school, but one of the places it took up residence was the hair of one of Pete's classmates. This student had very long hair, and upon seeing the mouse, implored Pete to put it on his hair. Obliging him, Pete cautiously opened the lid, placed the salt shaker upside down on top of the boy's head, and let the mouse crawl out. Strangely, instead of making its escape in one flying leap, the mouse crawled under the boy's long locks of hair, where it peeked out, surprising and alarming other students.

Fitting right in, Siobohn and Kenyatta were quick to make their own waves. They were about three and four years old respectively when Mom asked Dad to check on them as they played in the kiddie pool beside the house. Looking out the window, Dad discovered they were not, in fact, in the pool. Opening the door to investigate further, he spotted them immediately, hard to miss as they danced free-spiritedly on the roof of the car—naked as jaybirds, their discarded swimsuits lying in a heap by the side of the pool.

The River

Ahhh, the river … what would we ever have done without the river offering us its flowing water, tree-lined banks, grapevine swing, islands, and water fowl? It was in the river that we found refuge, relaxation, and renewal for body, soul, and spirit. The river, our place of diversion, had a life of its own.

I was introduced to the river at an early age. I vividly remember standing barefoot as a three-year-old on smooth, muddy, slippery stones at the edge of the river in a light-colored, short-sleeved cotton dress, and a braid on each side of my head. I was waiting my turn for a motorboat ride. The vast river in front of me mesmerized me as I watched little bits of debris floating in the current while my siblings swam nearby. Finally, I heard the distant sound of the motor as Elam approached to take me for my ride. Sitting securely in the back of the boat with him, my eyes took in the white, V-shaped wake behind the boat as we sliced through the water, a distinct smell of gas rising from the puttering motor.

Rivers couldn't exist without banks to contain them. The banks holding our river had two levels—a bottom level and a top level. (Instead of a smooth slope down to the river from top to bottom, there was a drop-off in the middle of the bank where swift, swirling floodwater had carved out the soil). A pathway on the top had been created by wildlife. Deer, perhaps? Raccoons? Foxes? Who knew? Regardless of how the path had emerged, it spurred our imaginations. Ada, Esther, Sue, Edith, and I each created a "hut" for ourselves along the path. Every hut had a unique, personal feel, furnished with confiscated treasures from our neighbors' junk pile and castaways from our own house. It was important to keep leaves and sticks swept off the path, using an old broom, since we traveled the path to visit one another in our huts.

My hut was at the beginning of the path. I built it square-shaped, five logs high, from small, fallen trees along the bank, which I dragged to the base of a very large oak tree. It was there I began building my "log cabin." My building was interrupted, however, when some boys from New Columbia asked my parents if they could camp on the riverbank for several days. My parents consented but then would not allow us to go to our huts as long as the boys were there. We waited impatiently for them to leave, and when they finally did, we hurried to the riverbank—past the barn, under the first electric fence enclosing the cows, dancing around mounds of cow piles, under the second electric fence, and sprinting as fast as we could to our huts. Bursting through the trees to my cabin, I stopped short, and my "Ahhhh, there it is" became a wail of anguish instead. For there, in the middle of where my hut had once stood, was a pile of charred logs, the very ones I had used to build my cabin. The boys had claimed them as fuel for their campfire. I could not conceive of anyone doing this. How was it possible to be so thoughtless and uncaring? This was my first up-close, rude awakening to the reality that some in this world look out only for their own interests, not caring about how others feel.

With heavy heart, I made my way to our grapevine swing. Three inches in diameter, the swing hung from the top of a very large tree way back in the corner of the field behind the barn. Grabbing the vine, I made a running jump, held on for dear life, and sailed through the air, leaving my cares on the bank for that brief moment of exhilaration.

We loved that grapevine swing and were also proud of it. Who else could boast of such a thing on their property? Swinging on the vine was a wonderful way to entertain our friends who came to our house on Sunday afternoons after church.

Beyond the bank and the grapevine swing, the river invited us into its waters—to swim, canoe, go for boat rides, or watch birds. It was like a welcome friend in the summer, rewarding us for getting chores done, providing an opportunity to build confidence in our rowing skills (Elam prided himself on being one of the best rowers), and allowing the bird-watchers among us the chance to add new birds to their lists.

Edith and Pete, both avid birdwatchers, thought nothing of getting up at 5:00 a.m. to go on birdwatching hikes, pushing out onto the river with the canoe and paddling upriver in the darkness. Mom wanted very badly to go with them, and did go one morning, braving her tendency to get sick while on water. Not long after being on the water, she began throwing up. After the second time, she asked Edith and Pete to paddle her in to the shore. Disappointed, she walked back to the house, her birdwatching experience abruptly ended.

Another morning, Edith and Pete came back from their birdwatching ecstatic. They had seen whistling swans—a rare variety of migrating swans. Later in the day, someone else spied them too and made the local news. But Edith and Pete had the glowing satisfaction of knowing they had seen the swans first.

Not only did Pete go birdwatching on the river, he also went frog hunting in a culvert carved out by the big flood. He wanted to share this experience with Mim and Tina since he often took them places to teach them about the outdoors. Mim and Tina found the frog-hunting experience to be rather gross but went along in spite of this because they liked spending time with Pete.

Frogs and ducks—my brothers hunted them both, although they did not often hunt ducks in duck season even though we lived along the river. The exception was when Elvin and a friend went duck hunting, camouflaged by branches in the canoe they hoisted over themselves, with Dad's double-barreled 16 gauge shotgun at hand. When Elvin spotted some ducks flying overhead, he grabbed the shotgun, stood up to shoot at the ducks, and lost his balance. As the canoe pitched to the side, Elvin lost his grip on Dad's shotgun and watched helplessly as it plummeted into the river. He couldn't get the gun out of his mind, so next spring when the water was lower, he climbed into the boat and rowed back to the area where he had lost the gun. Peering intently into the water, he saw it. There it was, lying on the bottom of the river on some rocks—Dad's shotgun. He leapt out of the boat, plunged his arm down through the water, grabbed the gun, and raised it up dripping wet, as if it were a trophy. When Elvin took the gun home, he proudly returned it to Dad after he tried it out and found that, unbelievably, it still worked.

This double-barrel shotgun never was intended to be an unused trophy. After years of riding in the corn picker and the pickup truck, or being knocked around in the coat corner of the kitchen where it congregated along with other shotguns during small game season, it had accumulated a generous collection of nicks and scrapes. But somehow it retained a certain grace and class. When Dad and Mom had an auction for their farm equipment and other nonessentials, the gun surfaced again, its wooden stock blackened and wobbly, its barrels covered in a thick coat of rust, looking perfectly horrible, this time in the hands of the auctioneer. Elvin paid a high price for the gun, and to this day has kept it as a trophy.

For Fred, boats and canoes were just fine, but he couldn't dismiss his dream of making a raft to float on the river. When I looked at his collection of barrels and boards to make the raft, I wondered how in the world it would ever stay afloat. After trial and error in the construction of his barrel raft, he settled instead for large inner tubes with 1" x 6" boards tied to them. Fred found the inner-tube raft worked well when he floated down the river for several miles with a friend. He later made memories with his own children by doing the same thing with them.

Rafts were for floating downstream, so it didn't work to take Fred's raft upstream to the island in the middle of the river about one-quarter mile away. But with great effort, we were able to reach the island by boat, giving us a workout exercise that required putting our whole body into it as we leaned forward with oars in the air, dipped them into the water, and pulled back with all our strength. When we finally heard the grating sound of small rocks around the island scraping against the bottom of the boat, we knew we had arrived. These rocks were slippery and slimy, so we had to step on them cautiously as we crawled out of the boat, waded into the water, and pulled the front of the boat through the shallow water and over the small rocks to secure it. When we'd make our first trip of the summer to the island, debris that had caught in the short bushes from the last time the river had risen would be clearly visible. As high water came, it covered the island completely. But we always knew it would still be there waiting for us when the water receded.

When the island reappeared, we sometimes brought our friends there for an overnight outing. These sleepovers required two trips to the island to transport all our friends plus all our gear—sleeping bags, pillows, eggs, bread, frying pans, and matches for making breakfast over a small fire. At night, small rocks poked us through our sleeping bags, but when we rowed back to the house next morning, tired and disheveled with traces of mud on us, we had the satisfaction of knowing we had provided a unique experience for our friends.

Another island lay farther up the river, with a large, carved-out, park-like bank we had to scramble up to get onto the island. A small channel separated it from the shore close by. Though we did not go to this island often since it was farther away and not as familiar as the one in the middle of the river, it still holds special memories. Before Sue got married, Ada, Edith, and I piled into the row-boat to go camping on this island. There was a sacredness to our time as we lifted and carried big rocks to a designated spot to make a campfire, then spread out our sleeping bags and talked into the night. It was truly a diversion that united us at the core of our beings.

Risks, Adventures

Some of our diversions fell more into the risk-taking and high-adventure categories. Tim and Elvin, for example, had a history of adventure in our family cars. When I emailed them for more details about the black Falcon hot rod, their back-and-forth storytelling grew to include their experiences in the white 1966 Plymouth Fury with a V8 motor we had inherited from Aunt Mary.

Elvin: *Yes, what a car and what an experience! This car also made a few un-announced trips thorough New Columbia, quick in and quick out. … It would get nice air when hitting the RR tracks in New Columbia at a high rate of speed!*

Tim: *Remember the Plymouth that we would do donuts with in the parking area next to the corncrib? Do you remember how we would enjoy making it backfire? We would turn the ignition off and then back on, causing it to backfire. We loved to do this around a crowd. Unfortunately sometimes this blew apart the muffler. I remember Dad saying, "I just can't understand why I can't keep mufflers on this car.*

Elvin: *I forgot about the repeated backfiring events! We certainly scared the c### out of a lot of people! That car brought us a lot of good memories!*

Parke also got a thrill from driving at high speeds, only his particular thing was driving tractors fast. Once, at about thirteen years of age, when he was driving the old Massey Ferguson tractor (which could really move) and Elam was driving the other tractor on the road next to the field, Parke felt a race coming up. Putting the Massey Ferguson in high gear, he flew out across the field, trying to outrun Elam. As he hit the edge of road—hard—where there was a little ditch, one back wheel went airborne, lifting off the ground at least a foot. To Parke, this was high diversion. To Elam, it was not. Mom and Dad would not have viewed it as that either and probably were not told about it, or Parke would have lost his driving rights on the spot.

Some of the risks we took were in high places. These were usually things we just did without asking permission. As young boys, Pete and Elvin crawled onto the ledge under the bridge, across the river to catch pigeons to sell, while Tim paddled the canoe right beneath them. When Pete and Elvin caught a pigeon, they would lock its wings and drop it to the water below where Tim would rescue it. Sometimes Pete and Elvin went the whole way across the river under the bridge. They even crawled across the X braces on the bridge to reach the pigeons in the center. Their compelling drive to trade pigeons for cash replaced any fear with courage.

Climbing all the way to the top of the silo using the ladder on the outside of it was another risk we took without asking permission. The funny thing is that when something like this became known to Mom and Dad, they did not scold us, though they may not have allowed us to do it if we had asked first. Knowing them, they probably figured the fact that we had managed to accomplish such things with no harm done was reason to let things be. With slight smiles of pride, they seemed, actually, to rather enjoy hearing about our feats.

But Mom and Dad were not happy with Mim when they found out about the time she dared Tina to creep precariously across the beam high up off the barn floor. It happened when Mim had her school friends at our house to spend the night. Their plan was to sleep in the upstairs part of the barn. Tina wanted to be included in the worst kind of way, but Mim wouldn't say whether she could be or not, even though Tina begged earnestly. Finally, to get Tina off her back, Mim said, "Well ... I guess you may if you walk across that rafter up there," pointing to the beam spanning the barn from one side to the other, convinced Tina would be too scared to do it and would finally leave her alone. But she greatly underestimated her sister's courage, because, wouldn't you know, Tina promptly climbed the ladder leading to the rafter and carefully swung her legs up on it, slowly feeling her way across the entire length. Guess what—she got to sleep with Mim and her friends that night.

Risk-taking sometimes involved doing the forbidden. When Pete, Tim, Elvin, and Dale stood in a row next to the railing on the balcony, the fun of seeing who could pee the farthest was worth the chance of being spotted and reprimanded. And when Elvin really had to go and someone else was in our one-and-only bathroom—which, as you can imagine, happened frequently—he simply raised the bedroom window and relieved himself through the two-foot opening. That worked well in the summer; in the winter, however, it was too cold to open the window, so what was he to do? The solution was simple—pee on the window sill inside and let it work its way under the window to the outside wall. His plan worked well till Mom noticed the paint blistering on the window sill.

Some of the adventures we took were not just any old adventures. At the same time that they provided diversion, they also prompted concern. Fred, John, Pete, Tim, and Elvin all took road-trip adventures to faraway places. Fred, for instance, hitchhiked all the way to Red Lake, Ontario, to surprise his fiancée, Rhoda, where she was teaching vacation Bible school. When I watched Fred make his cardboard signs with names of cities in reflective lettering tape, I felt better about him leaving because it appeared he had it all under control, well planned out. Upon his return home, he had many stories to tell, including the one about the newly married couple who rode in the back seat making out while he drove their car.

John then followed suit, figuring that if Fred could hitchhike to Red Lake, he could too. But he wisely learned from Fred's experience and did it in a way that put him less at the mercy of others. John and a friend caught a ride to the Canadian border with another friend who drove. He and his friend hitchhiked to Red Lake from there, arriving just in time to help the Northern Lights Gospel Mission with some building projects before returning home with someone who was driving back to Pennsylvania.

On Pete's hitchhiking adventure to Alaska to retrieve his Suzuki motorbike, he took a slightly different route than one would expect. First, he left from Fred and Rhoda's house in Minnesota and thumbed rides to Seattle, Washington, from a drunken man, a smoke jumper, a sex-ed preacher, and an adulterer traveling to his new lover. Relieved at finally being on his own, he then flew from Seattle to Kodiak, Alaska, (it was cheaper to fly from Seattle than from home), where he finally retrieved his well-traveled, keepsake bike.

Pete's first venture to Alaska (on his Suzuki 125 bike before he hitchhiked there) is a whole other story—one for the record. The long and short of it is that he couldn't resist the spirit of adventure calling him. As he drove out our long lane, Dad watched him go. Pete was fighting back tears, but there was no turning back. The detailed diary he kept as he traveled gives a snapshot of some of his high adventure along the way: shooting a seventy-five-pound black bear in Minnesota, then tying it in a sitting position just behind him to ride along as a backrest on his small bike (he dropped the bear off at Fred's house); driving through heavy rain and snow in the Canadian Rockies; sleeping under the stars anywhere he decided to camp for the night; driving on eleven hundred miles of dirt and gravel road; panning for gold in Anchorage; getting pulled over by the police in Saskatchewan, who saw the Pennsylvania license plate and thought the bike was stolen (upon hearing where Pete was going, the police shook their heads and chortled in amused disbelief as he drove away.); finally arriving at his destination after riding 6,360 miles; and salmon fishing and working in a salmon cannery for the summer.

Others in the family took infamous rides as well. The six-hundred-mile bicycle ride to Maine to see Esther and Glenn that Elvin took at fourteen years old and Tim at fifteen and a half, along with two friends (the oldest one eighteen,) turned out to be a feat of survival, a tale to be told. It took five and a half days, accomplished with very little planning, including no figuring out ahead of time where they would stay at night. Taking only sleeping bags and a few essentials tied to an installed rack on their five-speed and ten-speed bikes, they simply up and left one day and headed out, sleeping at places they thought looked safe. Soon after they started, Elvin cut off his bell bottom jeans with his pocketknife when they kept catching in his bike chain. In the process, he cut his upper arm, and in the absence of a first aid kit, they wrapped his arm in a tourniquet and were on their way. (Elvin has a scar on his arm to this day to remind him of the adventure.) Between this on day one and a passing car going down over an embankment on day two after swerving to avoid hitting an oncoming car, they must have second-guessed themselves about the wisdom of starting out on a trip like this.

When the boys got into Vermont, they encountered a thirteen-mile-long continuous upgrade. By the time they reached the top of the hill, they were so thirsty that they stopped by a roadside ditch and drank water from it that tasted like sewage. It's a wonder they didn't get sicker than they did from drinking it. Then they rode down the hill at breakneck speed without helmets, flying by cars at about sixty-five miles per hour.

On day three, Elvin had a close call when a seventy-year-old lady whose husband was teaching her how to drive, sideswiped his bike, leaving a scratch along the entire length of their car. The impact knocked the tape off of Elvin's handle bars and threw him into the ditch beside the road. It was far too close for comfort. The lady slammed on her brakes, tires squealing to a stop, and apologized profusely. Fortunately, Elvin was fairly unscathed except for his disgruntled feelings, which he didn't mind sharing with the lady. Later that day, someone deliberately tried to run them off the road.

On the fourth night, when they were looking for a place to sleep, someone directed them to a state representative's barn. One sweep of the man's eyes over this motley crew was all it took for him to suspiciously point them in the direction of a local preacher. The preacher must have thought they looked safe enough, because he put them up in his camper for the night and fed them a hearty breakfast the next morning—a real godsend, since by this time they were out of money. (They had only brought about $40 between them, and it ran out after buying bread, ice cream, and soda to share.) An extra bonus to the preacher's kindness was finally being able to bathe when they went swimming in the creek nearby.

The fifth night was uneventful, and on the sixth day, the boys finally arrived at their destination. When they were ready to return, they got a ride back home, where Tim promptly put his bike in the barn and didn't touch it again for a long time. With the experience dimming in the rear view mirror, however, he is now able to enjoy a local bike ride without reliving the stress. In hindsight, he can brag about surviving the dreadful trip though he would never attempt something like it again.

Where did we get our adventuresome spirit? Perhaps from the same gene that enticed Dad to go to Slate Run and find the land for the Cabin, later pulling up stakes and moving to the farm along the river.

Conclusion

When we gather together now, we laugh when we recall our varied experiences of diversion. "Remember when … ?" And our laughter around these shared experiences unites us, joining spirit with spirit.

10. Pets and Other Animals

One night I waited until it was almost dark to do my chore of feeding the chickens—not a good idea considering our hostile sheep buck was lurking in the shadows. Knowing he hung around outside the chicken house at night standing guard over his ewes and lambs, I was on high alert, aware that I was in his territory now. After I fed the chickens, I walked backward toward the house, trying to keep an eye out for the sheep buck so as not to be taken off guard by his tactic of appearing behind us out of nowhere and ramming his head into the backs of our legs. Darkness provided the perfect cover for him to remain unseen by intruders who dared enter his domain. Uneasy, I strained to see through the dim light, my eyes focusing on the front of the chicken house. Suddenly, I saw him around the corner, barreling toward me out of the shadows, head bent in an all-out charge. I stood frozen, my heart beating wildly as he got closer and closer. There was no fleeing now. Any second I would feel the strong thud of his head. As he came within inches, I snapped into fight mode. Raising my empty metal bucket high, I let out a roar of anger and terror as I swung it down fast and hard, the metal clonking his head with a resounding clang. Shaking his head furiously, the sheep buck turned and moseyed back into the shadows where the other sheep quietly waited for their defender. I stood shivering, relieved that I had turned this bully on his heels just in the nick of time.

The sheep buck was just one of the many animals we had on the farm—tame and wild, birds in cages and in the sky. What would we have done without them? They intertwined and connected to almost everything we did: soft, furry, baby bunnies found in burrows in the ground; mooing black-and-white Holstein cows hanging out in the barn; wild crows we had tamed. And they gave to us in many ways: cows gave us milk; chickens gave us eggs; calves, pullets, and sheep gave us earnings; rabbits, dogs, cats, goats, and horses gave us comfort and companionship; wild animals gave us a challenge; birds gave us wonderment and enjoyment.

Mom and Dad made sure we each had our own animals. They never said it out loud, but it was important to them that we learn responsibility by taking care of our animals, that we gain the satisfaction of earning money from them, and that

Back row, l-r: Barb, Fred, Ada, a guest from the Fresh Air program, Leona (tall one in back), Esther, Sue, Rose. Front row, l-r: Edith (always cried when her picture was taken), Pete, and John.

we receive individual recognition through them. They showed their support for us as animal owners by buying food for our animals as if they were buying groceries for us. I never had to worry about my animals having food. I give Mom and Dad credit for the sense of self-worth and boost of self-confidence I received from being entrusted with the care of my own sheep and calf.

Our connection with animals began with Mom and Dad's own strong connections with them. Dad treated his dairy herd as if they were his "girls" and our dogs that herded them as his friends. Mom found equilibrium between animals and birds and her household chores, taking advantage of opportunities to escape to the barn or chicken house to check on how everything was doing. We did not always know when she made these inspections, but the fact that she could tell us what was going on with all the calves, chickens, sheep, and rabbits gave it away. She called to our attention any animal that needed food or water.

While it was important in general to Mom that we have animals, it was especially important to her that each of us have our own sheep. Dad, on the other hand, complained that sheep were a nuisance; they were given free rein of the farm, and, in addition to them often being in his way, he didn't appreciate the droppings they left everywhere. But Mom found joy in watching the sheep graze peacefully as their lambs frolicked around them. She also got satisfaction out of knowing that when the lambs grew big enough to have lambs of their own to be sold, they would provide earnings for us. And the wool they gave us added to the stash of cash.

Sheep also taught us lessons. I was impressed by how our flock of sheep stuck together. When they'd bolt pell-mell out the small doorway of the sheep pen, I had better not be standing in their way if I didn't want to be knocked aside as they blindly followed their leader's cue to go outside. I didn't consider them to be bullies when this happened (except for the sheep buck); they were just doing what came naturally.

When lambs were born on cool, spring days, Mom kept a close eye on them to make sure their mother had enough milk or that she wasn't rejecting her offspring. If either became apparent, Mom would scoop the lambs up in her arms and bring them inside. Little lambs with nappy wool and wrinkled skin were put in a large, galvanized metal tub with a bit of straw in the bottom, next to our warm kitchen range. If I woke up in the morning to the plaintive "baaing" of a newborn lamb, I knew there would a bottle of warm milk waiting for us to feed it. Offering the bottle to a hungry lamb was very gratifying. As its little tail wiggled rapidly, the lamb would guzzle the bottle down, milk dribbling from the nipple onto the hairs around its mouth. When the lambs grew and were put outside, they pursued us around the yard, butting their heads against us as we ran laughing, demanding we feed them another bottle. Ironically, the same lambs that Mom rescued became an irritation to her later when they inevitably followed us up onto the porch and deposited their droppings.

Each of us received our own lamb to raise when we were about ten years old. Esther named her lamb Mary. Mary was one of the lambs that needed to be bottle fed, and because Esther took care of her, the lamb formed a strong attachment to her. One morning, Esther woke up to a hand shaking her and a voice saying, "Get up—you've got to come feed Mary. She's hungry, but she won't take the bottle from any of us." With bottle in hand, Esther went out to the front porch and called for Mary. Hearing Esther's voice, Mary hurtled from the barn as fast as her legs could carry her, grabbed the nipple, and drank the milk right down. Esther glowed with importance, knowing she was the only one— out of so many children—able to feed her lamb.

Soon after the lambs were born each spring, it was time for sheep shearing. This usually happened after a few reminders from Mom. (Dad despised doing this job, so he waited for a rainy day when he and the boys couldn't work in the fields.) The task required Dad to wrestle the sheep to a sitting position with the boys helping, then shearing the sheep while they wiggled and thrashed, making it impossible not to nick their tender skin with the clipper no matter how careful. After the smelly, greasy wool was bundled up in burlap bags and sold, each of us received our share of wool earnings from our sheep. The pride I felt from this money was worth much more than the wool itself.

While Mom saw to it that we each got a sheep, Dad made sure that at age twelve we each got a calf, which we could raise or sell as we wished. A new calf being born, especially if the calf was to become our own, was a marvelous thing to witness. To watch this slimy, sopping-wet creature emerge, see it stand on its wobbly legs, and observe the mother cow (who knew exactly what to do) clean her newborn off, was an amazing experience.

Instead of receiving a calf, Parke and Elam were each given a cow when they were nine and ten years old, which they had to milk by hand. They got as much mileage as possible out of the unpleasant task by squirting milk into the open mouths of eager cats that stood nearby, or at one another. When Dad found out, he put a stop to it. How were we to have any milk for our own use if the boys kept this up?

Dad housed his herd of Holstein cows in the barn all winter. Their body heat and warm, puffing breaths as they chewed on sweet-smelling hay provided a comfortable enough temperature in the barn for us to play games on the cement slab between their stalls. The combination of hay and fresh manure filled the air with an oddly non-offensive, pleasant smell. When the cows were released in spring to go outside after being cooped up, they were quite entertaining to watch, running clumsily and kicking up their heels like young heifers rather than mature cows. Their footloose shenanigans the first day outside after winter always meant their milk production would be lower for the evening milking.

At milking time, our collie dogs joined us in managing the cows. When they heard Dad's footsteps on the house stairs in the morning, they were off the porch, across the meadow, under the electric fence, and out in the pasture herding up the cows before Dad could snap his fingers. This pleased Dad. They were off in a flash again to corral the cows into the barn for the evening milking at Dad's command to "Go get 'em." The dogs knew what to do not only with the cows but also with the strong, thick-necked, horned bull that lived in a corner in the back of the barn. We were relieved that the gate to his pen was secure when he angrily pummeled it with his mammoth head for no apparent reason, rattling the chains that fastened it. The dogs could be sound asleep on the cool, cement porch— with wet spots where their noses had been but the instant they heard the rattling, they would be up in a flash, making a mad dash straight into the bull's pen, barking him back into a corner where he stood shaking his head at them. I was always glad the dogs were not intimidated by the bull. They made me feel safe.

The dogs were peacemakers for the cats as well. They were quick to break up the many cat fights that took place, running and barking lustily at the yowling felines, who would scatter in two directions. My brothers some-times imitated the sounds of a cat fight, just for the fun of seeing the dogs go crazy trying to find the cat skirmish.

Rose spending time with Lassie

Our collies also provided puppies to sell. When Elam began selling the pups, he painted a large collie dog on a sign that he mounted at the end of our driveway—"Registered Collies for Sale. No Sunday Sales." Having litters of collie puppies was bittersweet. It meant income for the owner of the mother dog. But for the younger ones of us who grew attached to the cute, playful puppies, it meant saying sad goodbyes when they turned six weeks old. I grew especially fond of one particular puppy, desperately hoping no one would want to buy it. The day it sold, I sobbed brokenheartedly into my pillow as my older sisters tried to console me.

Later, a puppy from one of our litters—just several weeks old—developed paralysis of its hind quarters, and as my family discussed what to do with it, they came to the conclusion that putting it down was the most sensible option. As a ten-year-old hearing their conversation, I couldn't conceive of putting the puppy down, so I paid it a visit and examined it myself. Horrified to discover maggots crawling around in the crevice between its thigh and stomach, I cleaned the area out while the puppy looked up at me with happy, grateful brown eyes. A bond developed between us as I continued to care for the puppy and do physical therapy on its hind quarters. In about a week, it was able to stand up on wobbly legs. I don't remember what happened after this, but in a sound state of being, the puppy surely found a good home and brought happiness to someone else, while I had the satisfaction of knowing I had made a difference in its life.

Toby was Parke's large, tri-color, male collie used for stud service. He had a loud, deep-throated bark and warning growl that made us feel protected. When Parke

got married and moved to Atlanta, Georgia, for two years in voluntary service, Toby continued to stand guard for us. After Parke moved back, he took Toby with him to live on a farm about ten miles away. Three times Toby left that farm and found his way back to our farm to pick up where he had left off with his patrol duty. After the third time,

Barb, guest from the New York Fresh Air program, Leona, and Fred, with three of our collies and a beagle

he was allowed to stay put with us. The last trek had taken him longer than the others, and we knew that in spite of dogged determination, he probably would not survive a fourth attempt. Each time Toby came back, we whooped and hollered at the sight of him trotting in the lane, and we ran to meet him. We petted him for a long time while he wagged his tail, "smiling" as only a dog can, telling us he was happy to see us and was pleased with himself as well. Toby was a hero to us. The day he died, we buried him in the middle of one of our fields under a cherry tree that stood as a sentinel to his life.

Cats on our farm also received their due respect. Always outside, they kept the mice and rat population down in the barn. Mom had certain favorite cats that she held in high esteem. "Now that one is a good mouser," she would say admiringly after seeing the cat more than once with a mouse hanging from its mouth. Not only did the cats catch rodents, they were also companionable, brushing their furry hair against my legs while I hung wash on the clothesline.

When milking time approached, the cats would find their way to the milk house, hanging around in anticipation of a bowl of fresh, warm milk. But one young cat got more than it bargained for. The milking machines had to be disassembled after each use, washed, hung up, and reassembled just before the next milking. One day, the young cat crawled into one of the empty canisters before the top was put on, unseen by whoever assembled the machines that day. The milking machine with its suction hose was attached to the cow like normal, only with a cat inside this time. When Esther took the lid off the machine, the cat popped its head up with suctioned eyes bulging out eerily. Dripping with milk, it leaped out before she could dump the contents into the waiting bucket to be carried to the milk house. What unbelievable fortitude! Now this was a cat to be admired.

Many of these cats eventually had kittens, whose miraculous births I sometimes got to behold. Our black cat with the white socks, for instance, didn't seem to mind my watching her give birth to a litter of six kittens on a burlap bag beside the furnace in the basement. Taking in the whole sacred scene, I became aware of the incredible wonder of life.

When our multicolored female cat had kittens, I didn't see her give birth, but the matted-down hair around her nipples clued me in that she was nursing kittens, and I went in search of them. One day I saw her disappear into the upper part of the barn, so I spied on her through the crack in the door, watching as she climbed up into the haymow—a perfect place to give birth to a litter of kittens. There they lay, all in a black, white, orange, and striped-gray heap. But the next day when I went to visit them, they were gone. I tried my best to track the mobile kittens, and about two weeks later I finally found them stumbling around behind a hay bale in the downstairs part of the barn. I knew the mother cat was doing her job of keeping her small kittens from being disturbed, which in my eyes made her a very attentive mother. Still, I wanted to get to know the kittens, and finally, when they were able to wander from behind the hay bale, I could pick them up and hold them. (I had been told not to handle them when they were younger as this could "cause them to get sore eyes.")

We also loved the white bunnies with pink eyes that Mom bought us. Besides teaching us the responsibility of feeding them and cleaning out their cages, they were simply something to enjoy as we stroked their soft fur and watched them nibble on the orange carrots we fed them through their wire cage. At six years old, I couldn't help but cry when mine died; I was sure it had not gone to heaven since it wasn't a Mennonite.

Each spring, Mom also bought us chicks. Unlike the bunnies, however, which were just for our pleasure, the chicks would provide income for us. They arrived in a low, cardboard box with holes in the sides and sections inside so they would not smother one another if the box was tilted. When Mom lifted the lid for the first time and I laid eyes on the chicks, my heart skipped a beat. There they were—a mass of yellow fluffiness, vulnerable and helpless. I felt protective of them, sort of like a mother hen myself as I laid my hands gently on their softness. Lifting them carefully one by one, I placed them under the red heat lamp in the brooder house. Seeing them all huddle together gave me a warm, cozy feeling. Over time, as they sprouted white wing and tail feathers, the pleasure we received from these puffs of sunshine became a growing awareness that they would eventually translate into money. Each year, one of us—moving down the line from oldest to youngest—was given a little flock of chicks to raise and then to sell when they became marketable as pullets.

At Easter, Mom occasionally bought us blue and pink artificially colored chicks, which we kept in a box in the house until they were ready to join the others outside. I hoped my chick would stay blue forever, only to be disappointed when it grew white wing and tail feathers, eventually blending in with all the other pullets so that I could no longer tell it apart from them.

Once the chicks matured, they were more for function than enjoyment. Most of our chickens were confined to the chicken house where we could gather their eggs. We always dreaded finding a chicken still sitting on her eggs when it was time to collect them. I would muster up all the courage I could, take a deep breath, and reach under the hen or try to force her off the eggs if necessary. But chickens who sat on their eggs with a mother hen attitude intended to hatch them and loudly protested, "How dare you?!" as I apologetically seized the eggs. I considered myself fortunate if I could get away with no peck marks on my hands.

Guineas likewise played a purposeful role, with a voracious appetite for bugs in the garden and around the farm. Mom liked having them because of this and because of the pleasant "buckwheat" sound they made, although the pleasantness would disintegrate into a downright annoying racket of high-pitched cackling when something startled them. Mom would go in pursuit of newly hatched baby guineas carefully hidden away in tall grass, knowing the guinea hen would not think twice about dragging its chicks through wet grass and tall weeds and would simply leave behind those that were unable to keep up. With rake in hand, Mom prepared for the fierce fight the hen would put up about having her chicks taken. The mother guinea's behavior seemed odd to me because she seemed oblivious to the well-being of her chicks until Mom tried to intervene for them, at which point the hen became a fighting ball of fury. One time a guinea hen escaped from under Mom's restraining rake by flopping her arm with vicious claws, leaving deep, bleeding scratches. But Mom took the attack in stride, viewing it worth the trade-off of rescuing the little guineas and bringing them into the safety of the brooder house with the other chicks.

As if sheep, calves, cats, bunnies, and chickens were not enough to provide personal ownership for us, Mom went out of her way to make arrangements with a pony dealer several miles away to board ponies in exchange for us training them. Her idea was that the ponies would not only provide us enjoyment but would also help us learn discipline as we trained them to ride and be comfortable around children.

She began by buying us a small bridle and saddle and making sure we learned how to use them, though I preferred to ride bareback. We were more successful with training some ponies than others, depending on their personality. After I made several unsuccessful attempts to ride a particularly rambunctious one, I tied it to the metal clothesline pole with a very short rope, figuring that would lead to its eventual surrender. But the pony would have none of it and bucked all over the place, making it impossible for me to get close to it. Seeing my plight, Dad came to my rescue and firmly took charge of the pony. Thanks, Dad.

The ponies I helped train for the dealer were okay, but what I really wanted was a horse. After working with a few, I came to the conclusion that ponies were more temperamental than horses and not as personable, or so it seemed. This was especially true of the little red Shetland pony Mom bought for us that for no good reason suddenly bucked Pete off while he was riding it one day. The pony raced the half mile home while Pete walked back muttering with each step about "that stupid pony." The pony was likely saying with each gallop, "that stupid boy," as it took revenge on Pete for standing on its back to entertain us.

My wish for a horse came true one warm, balmy, summer morning when Candy, John's big black horse, had a foal a few weeks after he bought her. Candy was a big horse, so we'd had no clue she might even be pregnant. No sooner had I come downstairs that morning than John told me to come out to the back yard. There, standing beside its mother, was a little, coal-black foal. When John had gone to the barn earlier to take care of Candy, he had found the foal with her, born the night before. I stood there in shock, mouth hanging open. And when my strong, tough, "little" brother John teared up, telling me the foal was mine, I knew without a shadow of a doubt this gift came straight from his heart. The white spot in the shape of a star on the foal's face earned her the name Star. I read everything I could get my hands on about training horses and learned that the first thing a trainer needs to do is teach their horse to automatically lift the hoof of a leg that's tapped on the front so it can be checked for stones. I accomplished this but then felt clueless about how to proceed; I never did train Star well enough to ride her. So I mostly just brushed her and told her how beautiful she was and how happy I was to have her.

All these animals on the farm were assumed to be permanent residents except for the goats that came and went. They never really established citizenship with us. Their offensive smell and deviant behavior were likely to blame. Take for example the Billy goat we had for a while that we tied to a maple sapling in our front yard one day. He promptly ate the bark on one side and caused the otherwise perfect tree to grow to maturity with a strange lean. On the other hand, one good thing about the goats was that they kept the tall weeds on the riverbank trimmed.

When a fierce storm blew down the big locust tree at the top of the bank, we expected Billy, who had been tied to the fallen tree, to have perished under it. Walking out to examine the damage, what should we find but Billy standing tall and proud in the fork of the tree as only a Billy goat can. After that, we wondered if he might just have special purpose.

Mim's experience with pet goats came only after she had lost four dogs when she was between the ages of six and nine. Mim's first dog was a little terrier that a stray dog killed. She took her second small dog with her and Mom to the store one day, tied its leash under the dashboard and told it to wait, that she would soon return. After the shopping was done, she hurried back to the car ahead of Mom, eager to be with her dog. Instead of finding him under the dashboard, she found him hanging from the back of the front seat. He had tried to jump over the seat, but his rope was too short. Mim's third dog was a poodle. She didn't really have time to get attached to before it got sick and died. Not one to give up, Mim got yet another dog, but that one wandered up onto I-80 and was run over. Then it was my turn to comfort Mim, just as I had been comforted by my older sisters.

After the fourth dog died, Mim decided she'd try a baby goat instead. She found a little kid that had lost its mother, and the two of them formed a special bond. When it was not secured by its rope to a tire in the yard, the little goat scampered after Mim everywhere she went. Our collie, Brutus, befriended the little orphan goat too. They played together, dog and goat. One day, Brutus was tied next to his doghouse out of reach of the kid, who wanted to get to Brutus in the worst kind of way. Pulling on its rope, the goat realized it had become strong enough to drag its tire all the way to Brutus. There they tumbled together, over and over while their ropes got tangled together tighter and tighter until the goat strangled to death. Tina went with me to John and Marilyn's house, where Mim was, to deliver the sad news and console her.

Mim and Tina then banded together and both got baby goats. The kids were thriving until one of Tim and Elvin's friends came to our house with his German shepherd on the back of his truck. While the friend was visiting with my brothers, the dog spotted the goats, jumped off the truck, and attacked them, breaking their necks. After this happened, Mim dreaded walking down our long lane from the school bus, knowing her goat would not be there to greet her. Finally, just to be safe, she got a full-grown, pregnant nanny goat, which turned out to be ornery and obnoxious. It dragged her under the electric fence one day to get to the apples in the orchard while Mim hung onto its rope for dear life. The goat disgusted Mim when she milked it, and it made a habit of putting its feet in the bucket of milk. When the nanny gave birth to twins, Mim found she didn't have the same attachment to them as to her previous baby goats. And by now, she was becoming more independent, away from home for periods of time, which meant Mom was left to take care of the goats. When Mom asked Mim if she was ready to sell them, she was and never looked back to second-guess her decision.

Mom loved not only the farm animals and fowl but also birds in general. She was especially fond of her caged house birds. Dickie, her canary, would sing from his cage in a corner of the family room, giving Mom a boost as she came down the stairs each morning to start her day. When Dickie died one Thanksgiving day, we placed him in a box and gave him an honorable burial by the Johnny house between the pear tree and the willow tree. We visited this spot frequently to pay our respects.

Next, Mom got a pair of white doves, which she also kept in a cage in the corner. She was protective of her doves and staunchly ignored frequent complaints and requests to get rid of them. My brothers got very irritated by the incessant cooing interrupting their naps on the couch nearby, and they sometimes managed to silence the doves by throwing one of their shoes at the cage. But their relief was always temporary and short-lived.

Occasionally, we'd let the doves out of the cage to fly around the house. On one such occasion, one of our dogs got into the house and attacked one of the doves, which lost most of its feathers in a narrow escape. But the feathers eventually grew back, and the dove lived on to give Mom a few more years of companionable cooing.

In addition to our farm animals, we made connections with wild animals and birds whenever possible, interacting with them and giving them a place among us. Fortunately for my siblings and me, Mom and Dad were open to this because they too liked all kinds of animals and birds.

With the same excitement that we went looking for litters of kittens, we scoped out the barn for nests of baby pigeons. When the mother pigeon landed on a rafter in the upstairs part of the barn, it was our clue that she was headed up to feed her offspring. On our conquest to locate the baby pigeons, we climbed up to the same rafter. Our concerted effort was rewarded when we found the pigeons, looking fuzzy and homely, peering up at us. They reminded us of our doves, only with shades of gray and brown instead of white.

Fred had about twenty pigeons in a pen out beside the chicken house. When a bunch of them got out of their pen one day, he remembered a story he'd read of how a boy caught some pigeons by propping a stick under the corner of an upside-down box with corn inside. In the story, the boy had tied a string to the stick, taken the other end of the string with him around a corner, waited for the pigeons to come into the box, then pulled the stick down, collapsing the box over the birds. Fred tried it, and it worked.

Birds were all around us—in the barn, in the house, around the farm, and in the fields. Spring brought the stereo song of baby starlings and sparrows around the house. We learned to identify them by their sounds; starlings were guttural in the tall pine tree just outside our bedroom window, and sparrows were high-pitched in the eaves of the attic. Sparrows were also, I found out, in the cross-section pipe of the washline pole, as I came face to face with a baby sparrow peeking out from its nest one day, looking straight at me with its beady, shiny little eyes.

The barn swallows were a bit more sophisticated than the sparrows and starlings. They flew with grace and swiftness around the farm buildings and often built nests in the barn. The baby birds I heard cheeping up in the chimney from the fireplace opening belonged to chimney swifts that built their nests there.

Sometimes we would find a baby bird that we considered respectable, such as a robin, on the ground out of its nest, and we would try to keep it alive by setting it in a box lined with a soft cloth and feeding it worms. To our disappointment, these baby birds rarely survived, but that didn't stop us from trying to save them.

When we discovered nests of baby kingfishers in the holes of dirt banks by the river, it was like unearthing great treasure. The kingfishers' unique sound and head formation were unlike any of the other baby birds around, giving them a distinct charm. Much to Edith's delight, she discovered that when she tried to imitate the parents by making tongue-rolling sounds like a Spanish "rrrrr," the little kingfishers actually stuck their heads out of the holes, expecting to be fed a worm by their parents. This gave her a gratifying, up-close-and-personal look at them.

Some of the birds we came in contact with were in fields around the farm. When we mowed the hay in early summer, we sometimes spotted a nest of pheasant eggs or baby pheasants and could rescue them just in time before the mower ran over them. We carried the exposed pheasant eggs and babies carefully into the chicken house and put them under the mother hens. A hen adopting baby pheasants as her own was a fascinating merge of wild and tame. Just as captivating were the baby pheasants that hatched, covered with brown and yellow stripes of fuzz.

Kildeer built their nests on the ground in the heifer pasture, carefully hiding them. When we'd get too close, the mother would try to distract us by flailing on the ground to fake being injured. Between the antics of the mother and the hidden nests, we were not very successful in finding the baby killdeer.

With an opposite nesting approach, crows filled the upper branches of the tall trees lining the river. In spring, the sound of baby crows from somewhere high in these trees was all it took for my brothers to embrace the challenge of climbing up to find the nest. There they would retrieve one or two baby crows, then carefully climb down, cradling the small birds in the crooks of their arms. Once the crows were inside their new home in a cardboard box beside the kitchen refrigerator, they would peer up at us with piercing, somewhat formidable dark eyes until we fed them bread cubes soaked in milk. The second we held a dripping-wet cube next to their beak, they would grab it and gobble it down with a cawing, gurgling sound. I'd try to withdraw my hand quickly after the crows grabbed the milk-soaked piece of bread, lest their beaks clamp down on my fingers. The startle effect of the crows' sudden grabs, plus the fact that the baby crows seemed to be so grateful, made feeding them strangely appealing.

The baby crows were covered with a mixture of small, shining, coal-black feathers and grayish-black fuzz. Their feathers grew rapidly, and it didn't take long for them to start flying. Growing very tame, they would come to a landing stop on our shoulders when we walked from the house to the barn and would make soft cawing sounds as if wanting to have a conversation. When we slept on the balcony, it was common to be awoken by a crow pulling back the covers and cawing in our face as if to say, "Hey you, it's time to get up." When a crow pecked at Mim's face one morning, she pulled the covers up over her head. Not to be outsmarted, the crow simply walked down the length of her body and began pecking at her toes. This same crow would peck at Pete's bedroom window in the morning to wake him up. Ever full of it, one day it came along and stole some spikes Elam and Fred were using to build a trough. When they approached the crow to get them back, it flew off teasingly with the spikes sticking out from either side of its beak.

Mom was not very happy with the crows when they pulled the clothespins off the laundry she had just hung on the line, leaving the clothes to fall on a heap on the ground. One of the crows became just plain pesky, hopping up on the wet clothes in the wash basket before they had even made it to the clothesline. When Mom plucked it up out of the basket and set it on the ground, the crow lay on its back and squalled like a spoiled child that couldn't have its way.

Though Mom wasn't a fan of this crow, just the same, she ran to try to save it the day the fox pounced on it. My brothers had captured this particular fox from its den when it was just a cub and kept it chained to a doghouse. On the crow's fateful day, the fox had carefully calculated its attack, watching as the crow pecked at the fox's food, thinking it was staying just out of reach as usual. Unbeknownst to the crow, however, the sly fox was stealthily narrowing its circumference to create a slack in the chain. When the unsuspecting crow came within reach, the fox pounced. It had finally outwitted the crow. Mom's rescue attempt was too late; by the time she snatched the crow from the fox, it was already dead. She had tried to come to its aid for the sake of my brothers, who were quite fond of it. The fox didn't earn any more brownie points with Mom when it also killed one of our chickens that had strayed too close. At that point, Mom would not have shed any tears if the fox had met its end as well.

For the rest of us, foxes in all their slyness held a compelling fascination. Enough so that when Parke and Elam were boys, they nabbed another young male fox from its den, stuffed it into a burlap bag, and lugged their trophy home. Their determination to tame it paid off when they almost had it eating out of their hands. But that never quite happened, because one fine day the cunning fox chewed a hole in the chicken house where the boys kept it, and it escaped. Dad was not pleased by the gaping opening in the side of the chicken house.

Most wild animals, like the fox, preferred to be in the wild in spite of our desire to befriend them. This was true of the deer that one day came walking up to us seemingly out of nowhere when we were planting tomatoes. It was oddly tame and stayed close until one of us had the bright idea of trying to tie a rope around its neck to keep it as a pet. The deer bolted, taking with it our hope for a new pet.

The turtles we found along the river, however, were an exception to the rule. They didn't seem to mind being confined. We liked to think we had tamed them when we could pick them up without their head, legs, and tail hastily withdrawing into their shells. Not only did they chomp down on the lettuce and carrots we gave them, they also had an appetite for noodles. We found this out during a family picnic in the back yard where the turtle was a guest with us. Someone put their plate of noodles on the ground, and the next thing we knew, there was the turtle in the middle of the plate, with noodles hanging from both sides of its mouth, happily chomping away.

One day along the river's edge, I discovered a turtle that sat motionless as I approached. Curious, I drew closer. Still no movement, but not because the turtle was tame, I soon realized. It was sitting over a hole it had dug in the dirt, intent on laying its white, oblong eggs into the hollowed-out cradle beneath. When the last egg fell into place, the turtle lost no time pushing dirt over the hole with its back legs, then scurrying away, trusting me to leave its incubating offspring undisturbed.

Some other wild animals, we knew, were also meant to stay where we found them. This was true of the tiny baby bunnies we discovered in burrows in the fields. Nestled in the pulled, soft, gray and brown fur from their mother's body, they seemed to say, "Don't touch, just admire."

When Edith found two baby possums in the pocket of their dead mother, however, she couldn't just let them be. Filled with compassion, she pulled them out and got permission to bring them into the house. She fed them milk with a tiny bottle, even after they were too big to stay in their box. They grew rapidly for about two weeks but then died after eating a tomato. Must have been too much acid for them, we speculated.

Pete was about ten years old when he encountered a groundhog on one of his exploring walks along the riverbank. The tangle of roots jutting up from a very large, fallen tree had drawn him in like a magnet. As he crawled in to check them out, his eyes fell on the groundhog snuggled down between the roots, oblivious of his presence. Pete seized the moment. With his heart beating wildly and a burst of daring bravery coursing through his veins, he slowly, quietly reached his bare hands through the mass and with one quick move grasped the groundhog. There. He got it. Mission accomplished. Just as quickly, he released it, glowing with pride and grinning from ear to ear with the satisfaction of his mastery.

The weasel that my one of my younger brothers (no one will claim ownership of the deed) caught in a trap one day was a different story. Rather than let it go after catching it, he made a harness from a rope so it couldn't slip out. Mim remembers walking close to the willow tree with the weasel and several of us sharing in the excitement. The weasel was then put in a box on top of the clothes washer in the kitchen, with a brick on top to keep the lid in place.

But one day when Mim peered into the box, the critter was gone. It had simply "weaseled" out of its chamber and was nowhere to be found. Eventually, it was spotted in the kitchen cupboard, where it had apparently taken refuge. All our attempts at cornering it were unsuccessful, and eventually it escaped from the cupboard and found its way under the washer. At this point, everyone was on high alert for a weasel sighting. One day, Mim got down on her hands and knees and peered under the washer with a flashlight. What should she see staring back at her but two shiny eyes. She sounded the alarm, and help was on its way. Someone moved the washer and opened an outside door, and the weasel escaped back into the wild, never to be heard from again.

In the rhythm of our lives, animals and birds were a normal part of things for us, individually and collectively, tame and wild—from our dogs rounding up the cows, to the baby crows we found in trees. They belonged to us, and we belonged to them as we moved within their circles and also drew them into ours. When we needed to release them, it was enough just to know they were there, sharing our world with us.

11. Accidents, Near Accidents, Risk-taking, Adventures

Twelve-year-old John watched with riveted fascination as Dad sawed through logs from cut-down trees, with sawdust flying and chunks of wood falling. It seemed easy enough, and it looked fun too. Dad had just gotten a new chain saw, and John wanted to try it out in the worst kind of way. So in his quiet, determined manner, he asked Dad repeatedly, "Can I please use the chain saw?" At first, Dad firmly said no, but finally he relented. After watching John cut off a few chunks without any problem, he reassured himself that John was indeed ready to take the chain saw in hand.

Full of confidence and convinced Dad wouldn't mind, John snatched up the chain saw one day and sauntered off to the woods to try out his woodcutting skill by himself on the log cabin he was building. The chain saw buzzed away, and all was going well until the saw cut through the log, dropped onto his left thigh, tore through his jeans, and cut a five-inch-long gash about a half-inch deep into his leg. John stared in disbelief at the blood oozing from his thigh. Laying the chainsaw down beside the log, he stole quietly into the house, went upstairs to get a new pair of pants, snuck back out to the Johnny house, changed pants, and threw the ripped ones down the hole to bury the evidence. Scared and ashamed, he did not tell anyone about his chain saw accident—the day it happened, at least. The next day, he told Pete but swore him to secrecy. Trying to take care of the wound himself, he first poured peroxide into it as he gritted his teeth against the fierce stinging, then bandaged it with our family's stash of Band-aids. He continued to care for the wound undercover, telling no one. When a bullying classmate in his shop class whacked his leg with a board—unknowingly right where the gash was—John didn't flinch. It began bleeding, but since this was the last period of the day, he just got on the bus and went home. After a few days of quietly raiding the cupboard for Band-aids and hoping no one would notice the dwindling supply, John soon ran out and had to ask Mom for more. Suspicious, she asked him why he needed so many. Since the wound was a month old by then, he figured it was safe to finally confess. Besides, Elam (who by then was a doctor) was home, visiting from Belize, and John wanted him to take a look at the wound because he was concerned it wasn't healing fast enough. It is truly amazing his injury did not become badly infected. Now as an adult, John has several times used needle and thread to stitch up wounds on his hands. For someone else, the wounds would have required sutures by a doctor, but who needs a doctor when one has inherited the gutsiness and fortitude of great-great-grand-father David Mast?

Considering the wide array of things we were exposed to without close supervision, it's nothing short of a miracle there were no fatalities in our family as I was growing up. Especially since the more people in a group together at one time, the more possibility for accidents, injuries, close encounters, and risk-taking. And when those same individuals are given almost unlimited freedom to explore and take risks, the likelihood of major injuries increases exponentially. We had farm equipment accidents, injuries from household appliances, electrical shocks, burns and explosions, injuries to bare feet, serious falls on ice, near suffocation in straw, near drowning, escaping-by-the-skin-of-our-teeth train accidents, close-call tractor and plane accidents, and serious car accidents. Mom and Dad were aware of some of the things that happened to us but not all of them. They could not be everywhere at once, and I guess they figured we would look out for one another. We did, although sometimes we also created our own danger through risk-taking as we threw caution to the wind and fed off of each other's dares.

Farm Equipment

A farm can be a dangerous place. On a daily basis we were exposed to hazardous farm equipment with highly unsophisticated safety features. It was almost as if incidents involving farm equipment were an expected part of our life even while they were to be taken seriously.

I guess you could say we had free rein of the farm, wandering and exploring at will. This meant young and old alike had access to farm equipment. Elvin, for instance, as a two-year toddler was spotted only after he had climbed almost to the top of the long, inclined grain elevator. Instantly a verbal alarm went out. Somebody, quickly! Get up there and rescue that boy! Retrieving him took no time at all.

We were probably most exposed to tractors and tomato wagons. In the fall when we loaded tomatoes, all able-bodied people were needed. It was a team effort. Someone drove tractor while one or two others on either side of the wagon dumped baskets of tomatoes into it. When the wagon was nearly overflowing, another empty one was hitched behind it to be filled. One day Dale, about twelve years old at the time, was hitching the second wagon onto the first one while one of our younger nieces drove tractor. Thinking he had finished, she began to pull ahead. With no time to escape, Dale was knocked to the ground as the wagon wheel ran over him. Fortunately, the second wagon wasn't full of tomatoes, but Dale's sore chest and tire tread marks bore witness to the incident for a long time after this. Now that was a close one!

Another tomato-loading incident happened in the summer of 1970 when John and Fred were dumping tomatoes into the wagon, one of them on each side. Out of nowhere, John let out a roar. Rushing over to him, Fred found John holding his foot in distress. The wagon had run over it. Fortunately, even with the weight of the wagon, there was no permanent damage. Just a sore foot.

Our feet got entangled with farm equipment on more than one occasion. When Leona was just a little girl watching Dad grade potatoes, her shoe somehow got caught in the grader chain. Scooping her up away from the chain, Dad hot-footed it down the barn hill, burst through the kitchen door, and sat Leona on a chair. As quickly and gently as he could, he wiggled her squashed shoe off her foot, expecting the worst. Heaving a sigh of relief, all he found was a red, bruised-looking foot. Coaxing Leona to stand, he had her put weight on the foot. Thankfully, it was fine.

Then there was the time Sue got her foot stuck in the hay elevator. About ten years old, she was heaving hay bales onto the elevator to be carried up to the haymow. There the bales would be stacked by those waiting in the mow. When Sue's foot got stuck in the elevator's moving links, she struggled helplessly to free it. What else could she do but ride the elevator all the way up, with her foot trapped by its metal links. When she got to the top, the elevator thrust her off. Fortunately she was wearing saddle shoes that tore apart at the side stitching, allowing her to free fall into the haymow. It could have been much worse.

My own foot incident happened the day I was running beside the cultipacker, barefoot and carefree-as-a-butterfly in the freshly loosened, brown soil. Parke was driving the tractor, and I was scampering beside it. Getting too close to the heavy cultipacker, I screamed as it ran over my foot. Parke jumped off the tractor, scooped me up, and carried me, whimpering, to the settee in the family room. My foot throbbed with pain as I lay there in my purple nylon dress—and no wonder—

considering the long, deep-red indentation on the top of it. It's a good thing the soil under the cultipacker was loose when the sharp, heavy edge of the disc pressed down into the dirt.

Driving tractors was equally precarious with or without farm equipment behind. Elam and Parke spent a lot of time on tractors considering how young they were. Elam was about ten years old when he was driving a big, borrowed John Deere G tractor with a hand clutch to help Dad fill silo. As he was bringing the tractor in from the field and had finally gotten it in gear, it began picking up speed. Frantically, Elam tried to stop it but couldn't. He wasn't used to the hand clutch, and it was too tight for him to pull. The tractor roared up to the lane at the end of the field where there was a steep bank going up from it. Wide-eyed, Elam drove the speeding tractor in circles in the field below the bank until he was able to bring it to a standstill. If there had been no field lane, he probably would have gone up over the bank and flipped over backwards. According to Elam, when he and Parke were little, they had more close calls with tractors than anyone realized. This was especially true for Parke, who, even as a boy, was always in a hurry when driving tractor, wanting to keep things moving.

Accidents also happened within proximity of the house. Dad sheepishly told us the story of the time he got his pants ripped off when he was digging potatoes. The potato digger, pulled behind the Oliver Cletrac, was powered with an unshielded power take-off shaft. Dad was very careful around power take-offs, but this time he managed to get too close. As he made a stop and jumped off the Cletrac, the spinning shaft grabbed and wrapped his pants, stripping them from him in a few seconds. There he was, naked as a jaybird, shocked and somewhat dazed. Startled, he suddenly realized he was on full display, indecently exposed to a mixed crowd of potato pickers, some of them women from Laurelton State Village. I can only imagine there were some nervous snickers among the potato pickers as they tried to pretend they had not seen Dad. Quickly crouching behind the Cletrac, Dad yelled for the hired man to get him some clothes. Who knows what Mom thought as the man knocked on the house door, urgently requesting a pair of pants and underwear for Dad. Dad was fortunate not to be seriously injured or killed, since power take-offs are not known to be kind to anyone coming in contact with them. Safety regulations today require them to be covered.

Household Appliances and Fences

Outside was the danger of farm equipment. Inside was the hazard of household appliances, especially when we were learning on the job. Such was the case with Elam as he watched Mom wash clothes with the wringer washing machine when he was four or five years old. Since the rotation device in the tub circled quickly forward then backward, Mom gave Elam fair warning about not getting too close to the wringer that was feeding washed clothes into the adjacent tub of rinse water. Then she went into the house, telling him she would be right back. Intently, Elam watched the

Barb and Leona making sure the diapers get through the wringer washer without wrapping around the roller

two revolving rollers, trying his best to resist the desire to stick his fingers in just to see what would happen. The longer he watched, however, the more irresistible the rollers became. Grabbing a handkerchief from the water in the rinse tub, Elam fed it into the wringer, watching it wrap around the top roller because it was too small to go through easily by itself. After a moment's enjoyment, he panicked, realizing the lone handkerchief would provide evidence of his misdeed. Desperately, he tried to pull it out, as the rollers grabbed first his fingers, then his hand, and then his arm. Mom heard him hollering and dashed from the house to quickly release the tension in the wringer. By the time she got to him, Elam's arm was swallowed up to the elbow, and it hurt. It wasn't called a wringer washer for nothing. Not one to let a teachable moment slip by, Mom said to Elam, "Now see, this is what happens when you get too close." Elam somberly shook his head slowly up and down.

Like Elam, I too got my fingers too close to objects that tempted and taunted. For me, it was an old treadle sewing machine that I learned to sew on. Connected to the machine was a wrought-iron, square-shaped foot mechanism that I pressed on with both feet—hard—first to the front, then to the back to get the sewing mechanism going. It was certainly safer than learning on a speedier electric sewing machine. That is, until I got my left hand too close to the needle, which didn't stop but went straight through the right side of my first finger. I was too embarrassed to cry out, and I struggled by myself to pull my finger out of the needle—thread and all. When it was finally free, I squeezed my finger tightly, partly because it hurt so much and partly because I wanted to quickly put on a Band-aid before anyone noticed the blood on it.

Barb's finger injury happened one evening as she was getting ready to mix formula for two puppies she was bottle feeding. Using her left hand to lower the beaters into the mixer—the kind that had the two beaters fastened together—she accidentally bumped her right hand against the switch on the back of the mixer. As I sat cutting figures from the Sears catalog at the kitchen table, I heard the mixer turn on ... then stop abruptly like something got stuck in the beaters. Just the spatula, I thought. But then I heard Barb cry out, and I looked up to see the unthinkable. The beaters, spinning rapidly, had grabbed Barb's left hand and sucked it in. Seeing the same horrible image, Mom rushed to her side and pulled the beaters out of the mixer with Barb's hand stuck in between, fingers bleeding profusely. Dad, who was sitting in the next room, took one look and bolted for the wire cutters. I couldn't believe how brave Barb was through the whole ordeal. Afterward, I walked over to the mangled beaters lying on the counter and stared. Wow, that had to hurt! It's a wonder she didn't need stitches.

Fingers in a wringer washer, fingers in beaters, and next was my finger with a U-shaped burn on it. "How did the burn happen?" you might ask. Well, there was a lamp in my bedroom without a plug at the end of its long cord, and at six years old, I decided I could fix this situation as well as anybody. There—that big, metal hairpin lying on the dresser next to the outlet should work just fine, I thought. I wanted light, the lamp didn't have a plug, and here was a hairpin—a simple solution and rather smart of me. Naive about how electricity worked, I confidently threaded the hairpin through the end of the cloth-covered cord and proceeded to push it into the outlet. Wham! A sudden, explosive bolt of electricity sizzled my finger, and I jerked the hairpin from the outlet. I stared at the brown, burnt shape of a U branded on its tip, too shocked to cry. Maybe this wasn't such a bright idea after all, I realized. Instead of the lamp lighting up, my finger glowed with the pain of the electric burn. "I can't show this to anybody," I thought. "I don't want to hear what a bad idea this was. I'll just deal with the pain myself." So I did.

Sue also suffered electrical burns—bad ones—both on her fingers and her hands. It happened when one of our older brothers shot a crow that dropped and lay dead in the field behind the orchard, sparking Sue, Esther, and Ada's curiosity. Wanting to see the crow, they set out in the direction of the field. To get there, they had to cross the orchard, which meant they had to first grapple with the electric fence wire around the orchard. This was no ordinary fence, however. It was a weed chopper, with an especially powerful voltage. The cows had determinedly broken through the previous fence multiple times, so Dad had installed this stronger one. The girls ducked under the fence. All, that is, except Sue. Before Ada and Esther could stop her, Sue grabbed hold of the wire to lift it over her head. As if that were not bad enough, the fence was not working correctly. Instead of its shock being intermittent, the strong electrical current remained constant. Sue could not release her grip on the fence as the current surged through her small body. As she screamed, Esther and Ada wrapped their arms around Sue, trying to pull her off, but they got shocked too. Dad heard their cries for help and instantly knew what was happening. He bolted out to the milk house and flipped off the shocker switch. When Sue was finally able to let go of the fence, there were bad burns on her fingers and palms.

It didn't take long for Dad to uninstall the fence and put the original one back. He wasn't taking a chance on this happening again. What was the inconvenience of cows breaking out of their pen compared to his little girls' safety?

Burns and Explosions

Fred also took a turn at acquiring burns. His were blister burns on the bottom of his feet when he was just a little guy and didn't realize what his older brothers were doing. Elam and Parke, young boys themselves, had decided to try out their engineering skills and build a fireplace in the back yard. When it was finally finished, they put it to the test, building a fire in it to roast hotdogs for a family picnic. Discovering that the steel plate on top of the leaping flames in the fireplace got in the way of roasting the hotdogs, they flipped it off onto the ground. Enter barefoot Fred, who stepped straight down onto the hot, steel plate. Crying out in pain, he instantly sprang off of it. Elam and Parke ran to his aid and saw, there on the bottom of both his feet, big blisters already forming. It was an accident, they knew, but they couldn't help feeling a little responsible. It was a lesson learned about where not to put the hot steel plate, especially with little people walking around in bare feet.

Like the hairpin burn on my finger, Leona's burns were also a result of taking matters into her own hands. Her burns, however, were severe and proportionally greater than mine. She got them the summer she decided she'd had enough of a burn-resistant pile of brush. Every year we hosted an "open air singing" for our church next to the river, and every year we flew into a flurry of trimming, mowing, and weeding the week before as if our yard and flower beds were being showcased. One year Leona took a lot of ownership in whipping the outside into shape. The pile of accumulated brush along the edge of the yard was an eyesore and had to go. In spite of Leona's best efforts, however, the bush refused to catch fire. So Leona grabbed a gas can and thought to herself as she poured gasoline on the dry brush, "This will do it." But the instant she lit a match to throw onto the brush pile, a huge fireball erupted from the gas fumes, enveloping her in its intense, licking flames. Leona fled the scene, but not before the skin on her bare forearms had been exposed to the searing flames. I saw her running toward the house with a pained, terrified expression. There on her arms were huge blisters from second-degree burns. The look of held-back misery on her face as her arms were being tended told me she was enduring burns ten times worse than the one on the tip of my finger.

The explosions didn't stop with Leona's accident. One day, Parke and Elam—just little tykes at the time—were at Dad's feet as he performed his usual ritual of emptying out the contents of his shirt pocket into the wood fire in the kitchen cookstove. No sooner had he done this than he had the terrifying realization that a small bag of dynamite caps was in the trash that had just left his hands. He frantically snatched Parke and Elam up in his arms and escaped from the kitchen just as the top of the stove blasted up against the kitchen ceiling. Large sparks showered out over the kitchen floor linoleum, leaving whopping burn marks before they could be stomped out. Dad's chest could barely contain his pounding heart as he trembled at the thought of the tragedy narrowly averted.

Head to Toe Injuries

Our injuries were not seasonal. They happened anytime, anywhere.

For some of us, ice skating in winter turned out to be a bit perilous. When Buffalo Creek, just outside our school, would freeze over, we would frequently be granted longer recesses for skating and sliding on the ice. If we begged just enough, our teacher might allow us to hike to a wider place in the creek about a quarter of a mile upstream. On one such day when we indeed got permission to go, we draped our skates over our shoulders and trudged along on a tractor lane at the edge of a field to our destination. The last thing I remember, I was happily skating with my friends. But I never saw the stick jutting up through the frozen creek, and I fell hard, cracking my head on the ice. The next thing I remember, I was being helped to walk back to school, one friend under each of my limp arms slung over their shoulders. I saw only darkness but could hear their voices urging me to keep walking. I drifted back into shadowy awareness in the school next to the warm stove, with Mom standing there. Admitted to the hospital for three days with a concussion, I continued to drift in and out of consciousness—hearing Mom talk to the doctor but unable to see her—until the third day. When I finally opened my eyes, I saw the sunshine box my classmates had put together for me sitting on the tray beside me. They had put small, wrapped gifts into it, intending that I open one each day as I began the long recovery at home.

My accident didn't stop us, though, from the thrill of gliding across the ice. Anytime an ice skating was announced, we excitedly got ready to go meet other youth from our area for an evening of skating at someone's pond. A stack of old tires burning at the edge of whichever pond we went to would cast a semi-eerie glow across the ice, giving just enough light to skate by. The burning tires also provided warmth for cold hands and feet. Inevitably, as the evening wore on, a skater weaving in and out across the ice would call out, "Hey, let's play crack the whip.'" This was the cue for skaters to form a line and hold hands, with a strong person at the beginning and a brave soul at the end. The line of skaters would start out across the ice, gaining momentum until at just the right moment the strong person would stop suddenly, dig his skates into the ice, and make a sweeping arch, pulling the arm of the person next to him with both hands while the person at the other end of the line flew across the ice. One time, Edith volunteered to be at the end. Being quite petite, she gained an added burst of speed as she sailed across the pond. When she could hold on no longer, she fell, clunking her head on the ice with a resounding thud. Her severe concussion required an extended stay at Geisinger Medical Center.

Between the whole lot of us, we sustained injuries from head to toe. At the beginning of summer, when we were finally allowed to go barefoot, we kicked off our shoes, stripped off our socks, and ran out the kitchen door and down over the cool, concrete porch steps. At first I walked slowly and cautiously over gravel in the driveway, the bottoms of my feet tender, but as my feet gradually toughened, I barely felt the stones anymore. It was then that I threw caution to the wind and hardly noticed the long, thick, rusty nails that had come loose on the ends of the boards around the square sandbox. Until I stepped on one, that is. Even the puncture wound on the bottom of my foot looked rusty around the edges, which sounded the alarm bell for Mom. Rusty nails always sounded the alarm bell for her. She would stop what she was doing, check to see if our tetanus shot was up to date, and if not, drive us straight to the doctor. It was serious business. We'd pour peroxide on the wound, smear stinky salve on top of it, and gauze-wrap the foot several times, protecting the wound from dirt. The thick and laborious wrapping also served as an exclamation mark to the seriousness of injury. No ordinary Band-aid for a nail wound.

Usually, we seemed to have an instinctual awareness of the debris lying around the farm and were able to avoid it. But Pete didn't spot the jagged piece of glass sticking up from the ground one day as he walked through the tall grass that was hiding it. The glass inflicted a deep, long gash on the bottom of his foot that required stitches and special care. For a long time Pete could only walk on the heel of his foot and felt crippled until the wound healed.

If You Had Not Been There

So many of our accidents could have been life-threatening if another one of us had not been there. We looked out for one another, and it was good we did. Without that kind of mutual care, there's no telling what could have happened.

Edith and John, for instance, were in the upstairs barn playing on the hay bales in the mow one day when they looked down at a deep pile of lose straw just below one end of the stack. Giving in to the urge to jump, John leapt into the straw. But when he landed, he kept sinking. Farther and farther into the straw until only the top of his head was showing. Leaping into action, Edith reached down from the hay bales, grabbed John's hair, and by some strange force of strength, pulled him out. (Hmmm … Is this why John is bald today?)

And if it had not been for Elam when the creek flooded at Oley, who knows what would have happened to Barb. After a heavy rain, the creek below the barn often overflowed, spreading out across the meadow like a big river. A driveway with a bridge crossed the creek, and Dad would drive heavy equipment over it. After the creek had overflowed one day, Elam went down to it and waded out as far as he could, splashing around with careless abandon, having a good old time. When his eyes landed on the bridge, he stopped splashing and pondered it—an adventure waiting to happen, he thought to himself. So he began to cross the bridge, hoping to get to the other side. But then he discovered that the water was getting deeper on the lower side. Not one to give up easily, however, he managed to get himself over to a fence running through the stream beside the bridge, gingerly side-stepping his way on it across the water. He had no clue Barb was quietly following him, until he heard her scream. Whirling around, he saw Barb hanging onto the fence rail for dear life, muddy water swirling swiftly around her. She had lost her footing on the fence and as she was falling into the waters had grabbed a rail. Elam lost no time making his way back across the fence yelling, "Barb, hold on!" as he watched her head bob up and down and occasionally go under water. When he reached her, he seized her arm, pulled her out of the water, and helped her back across the fence. Her coat was found downstream several days later. Thankfully Barb was not.

Trains, Planes, and Cars

The close calls we had with things surrounding us in our day-to-day living would have been enough in themselves, but we also had wrecks and near wrecks in trains, planes, and cars.

For starters, simply having a train track at the end of our lane multiplied the risk of train accidents. Compounding the issue was the fact that the trains by our lane passed by infrequently enough that it was easy to assume one was not coming "this time" even as we made a casual, automatic quick check. This assumption was in full operation one winter morning when Dad and some of the younger boys headed out in the pickup truck. With the truck's side windows iced over, blocking a clear visual out the window, Dad didn't see the train right beside him as he crossed the track. The blast of the train horn practically at his head and the feel of the rumble just behind him after he had barely crossed the tracks jolted him into the awareness that he had come within a hair's breadth of being in a train wreck. That night he tossed and turned in bed, trying to block mental images of the tragedy that could have been. But every time he closed his eyes, he heard the train's horn and felt the tremble. Over and over. Sleep just wouldn't come that night.

This wasn't the only close cataclysmic collision with a train. When Sue drove for the first time after recovering from a car accident that she and Esther had been in, she was the designated driver to "haul the school children." This meant driving sixteen miles one way, twice a day, to the private school we attended—once to drop us off in the morning and later to pick us up. The five younger boys were the school children with Sue that day as she approached the track near the school. There was no posted railroad crossing sign there and tall weeds had grown up around the track. Just as they were crossing, Sue saw a big shadow looming on her left. Instinctively she stomped on the gas pedal. If she had not reacted so quickly, there is little doubt that she and the five children would have been hit by the train. There was not even time for the engineer to blow the horn. As the train barreled on by, Sue pulled off to the side of the road, her knees shaking, and cried. The five boys were too frightened to say a word, until John, who was sitting in the passenger's side, reached across the seat, patted Sue's knee, and said comfortingly, "Sue, it didn't hit us." Sue continued to cry, trembling, until she was finally able to regain her composure.

Barb was by herself when she was driving Richard's lime-green Ford sedan on loan to her while her own car was in the repair shop. It was Wednesday, and she was en route to evening prayer meeting to return the sedan when the car stalled— on the tracks—just as she was crossing over, getting ready to turn out onto the highway. Heaving against the front of the car with all her might, she tried pushing it back off the track, impelled by the dreadful thought swirling inside her head. "What if a train comes?" The car wouldn't budge. She checked the length of the track once more to make sure no train was coming. Then, as if in a bad dream beginning to play out, she saw a bright light approaching in the distance. Running down Route 15, she frantically waved, trying to get someone—anyone—to stop and help. But the drivers passing by just ignored the "crazy woman" wildly waving her arms. Finally, a man driving a truck stopped. Barb ran toward him yelling at the top of her voice, "My car is on the tracks, and a train is coming!" The man ran with Barb up the road to the railroad track. Barb jumped into the car, making one last attempt to start it while the train rapidly bore down. The engineer laid on the horn, and the man yelled, "Lady, get out of the car!" Barb jumped back out of the car, ran to the front where the man was pushing, and with one big rush of adrenaline, they edged the car off the tracks just in the nick of time. It rolled down the incline that led up to the tracks, just three seconds before the train passed by—Barb on one side of the track and the man on the other. Barb buried her face in her hands and cried inconsolably while the man patted her on the back, trying to comfort her. Not knowing how to thank him, Barb ran back to the car, grabbed her purse, reached into her wallet, and pulled out some dollar bills. She knew she could never repay him for what he had done, but it was the only way she could think how to express her heartfelt appreciation. He dazedly accepted the money … until the next day when he came to our house to give it back.

Plane Wreck Averted

There were trains and then there were planes. And the five boys had narrow escapes with both. When Fred and Rhoda went to the bush country in Northern Ontario as newlyweds to do voluntary service with Northern Light Gospel Mission, Mom and Dad, John, Pete, Tim, Elvin, and Dale went to visit them. It took two trips in the small, two-engine plane from the Red Lake mission headquarters to fly them all into the bush. When they flew back out, Mom and Dad were in the first flight and the boys in the second. As Mom and Dad stood on the dock watching the boys' plane in the distance, they became puzzled as it began its descent far away from the water where it was to land. Inside the plane, Tim heard the pilot radio in to headquarters, "We're going down." He watched through the window as the tops of trees came rapidly closer, and just when he thought the plane would hit them, it suddenly leveled out. The pilot shifted nervously in his seat, saying something about this plane being different from the one he usually flew. The plane, as it turns out, had ice on its wings. At the last minute, the pilot had discovered the plane had a de-icer, and when he turned it on, he was able to regain control of the aircraft. In my mind's eye, I can see the five boys crawling out of their seats onto the dock, and Mom and Dad hugging them gratefully as they stepped onto solid ground.

Cars

The day Mom watched the family car drifting down the road with Dale, Mim, and Tina in it, she must have felt just as helpless as she had watching the plane dropping out of the sky with her boys inside. Mom had stopped at Sones Department Store in Vicksburg that day as she frequently did, on the way home from school to buy fabric and, I suspect, to let her mind slip into neutral as she browsed. We always had to take turns going into any store with Mom, no more than two at a time. This time it was Elvin and Tim's turn to go inside while Mim, Tina, and Dale stayed in the car.

Barely inside the store, Mom heard the terrified screams of children outside and stopped dead in her tracks. Wait—she knew those voices! They were her children. Dashing out of the store, she saw the car rolling slowly down the middle of the highway, farther and farther, with her three children inside screaming while she stood rooted in the empty spot where the car had been parked. Mom knew it was useless to run after the car. All she could do was watch, her heart in her throat, and desperately hope a car would not come down over the hill to find an unmanned car in its path.

Finally, the car drifted to a stop in a dip in the road. Laying all dignity aside, Mom ran down the road and flung the door open—there were Mim, Tina, and Dale sobbing and shaking. They had gotten bored waiting for Mom and were pretending to drive. While "changing gears," they had knocked the gear shift out of park into neutral and had frozen helplessly as they coasted down the road, scared out of their wits, not knowing to push the brake pedal. Mom didn't need to scold them much.

Realizing they had already learned their lesson, she drove back to the store to pick up Tim and Elvin, who were waiting outside wondering what in the world was going on.

Years later, the drifting car scenario played itself out again, only this time with Siobohn and Kenyatta, who were about eight and nine years old, playing in the car parked on the hill leading to the upper level of the barn. They must have been messing with the gear shift and knocked the car out of gear, because the car started rolling right toward the garage and hit the dumpster just outside of it, giving everyone, including Siobohn and Kenyatta, a scare. Dad, with his fondness for both girls showing, remarked how their different personalities came out in their responses. Kenyatta, like most girls her age in a situation like that, was all upset and crying. Siobohn just said something like, "Well, I guess we need to stop playing in the car."

Any accident has at least a component of helplessness to it, but in Esther and Sue's case, they were totally powerless to prevent their car accident. It was the closest we came to losing one of us. It was August 12, 1966, and Sue was excited about going to the get-acquainted activity for upcoming seniors at Lancaster Mennonite School. She had barely finished sewing the new dress she had made from pink, flowered fabric for the occasion. After admiring how well it had turned out and checking her wavy hair in the mirror one more time, she hurried out to the car where Esther was waiting to drive her to meet her ride. It was like any other summer day. Mim was playing in the kitchen when the phone rang and Mom answered it. Then Mim saw Mom fling the phone down on the hook and say something hurriedly to Fred. Together, the two of them rushed out the door. I was hanging laundry on the washline when they came running down the sidewalk. "The girls were in an accident," they called out to me. I knew it was not a fender bender by the grim, scared looks on their faces. This can't be good, I thought, as a strange weakness took over my body. Mom and Fred tore out the lane in the '61 Ford Falcon station wagon, a big cloud of dust billowing behind them.

As Mom and Fred approached the intersection where the accident had happened, they saw a crowd of people huddled, a few leaning in on the passenger side where Sue was sitting. One of those in the huddle was a man who had been delivering gas to the little store on the corner. After taking one look at Sue's neck injury, he had rushed into the store, grabbed a pack of Kotex napkins off the shelf, and ripped it open as he rushed back. Pressing one of the pads against Sue's neck, he had held it there to slow the bleeding from her severed jugular vein. Sue's head had gone through the windshield upon impact, creating jagged pieces of glass that had cut deeply into her throat as her head snapped back through the windshield. The young man who caused the accident (and who also had recently lost his license) had stopped in front of the stop sign and without looking, pulled out directly in front of Esther and Sue, leaving them no time to brake. With no seat belts in the car, there had been nothing to stop their forward momentum.

Someone called an ambulance.

When Mom and Fred pulled up, Esther was sitting in the car with Sue's head on her shoulder, holding the pad to Sue's neck wound and applying pressure as the man had instructed her to. Esther spoke urgently to Mom and Fred through the window, "We can't wait for an ambulance. "We've got to get her to the hospital quickly. She's lost too much blood."

Following Esther's lead, Fred lifted Sue out of the car and placed her on the middle seat of the station wagon. Esther left her sister's side just long enough to let Mom get situated in the car. While Mom held Sue, Esther sat next to them and placed Sue's head on her shoulder, continuing to apply pressure with a Kotex pad to the gash on Sue's neck. When the pad became saturated, Esther quickly grabbed a new one.

When they got to the light at West Milton a mile or two down the road, the traffic light was red. Esther said, "Just keep going." Fred had barely turned his head to check for oncoming traffic when the light turned green. On the way to the hospital, they met the ambulance. (We found out later that the primary ambulance was already out on a call and they'd had to bring a backup.) The station wagon couldn't be safely driven over seventy miles per hour, but Fred kept it there. Coming up behind a slow-moving vehicle, Fred blew the horn and Esther held up something that was bloody. The driver pulled over, getting out of their way. Mom, her own chest now covered with blood from Sue's blood-drenched clothes, pled with Sue to stay awake.

As they came within sight of the hospital, Sue began to struggle, her brain now deprived of oxygen, and Mom panicked. She later described this as a death struggle. Someone at the accident site called ahead to alert the hospital they were coming. When they arrived, a nurse rushed out with a stretcher. As Fred lifted Sue out of the car and laid her on the stretcher, he looked down at her and said, "You'll be alright now?" Sue nodded her head yes. Dr. Woodcock, the on-call emergency room surgeon, just happened to be at the hospital at that exact time and was waiting in the emergency room for Sue. When he saw her as she was being wheeled through the door white as a sheet, he hesitated for just an instant, not knowing whether to call the coroner or get to work right away on her. Though he couldn't find Sue's pulse, he jumped into high gear immediately to try to save her life. Her blood-stained, pink floral dress had barely been cut off before medical staff began pumping blood back into her.

Sue's blood type, A-, was rare, and the hospital's short supply ran out quickly. An emergency call went through the hospital intercom that type A- blood was needed immediately. A cook in the cafeteria with that type of blood heard the announcement and rushed to the emergency room to donate.

After Dr. Woodcock closed off Sue's external jugular vein and she was given several units of blood, she finally stabilized. Visibly shaken, Dr. Woodcock came into the waiting room and told Mom and Dad what a miracle it was that Sue was alive. She was the closest to death, he said, of any patient he'd ever had who'd recovered. His voice quivered when he told them how deep the gash was—so deep that it had come very close to cutting her internal jugular vein. He could feel a scratch from the glass on her vertebra, and the glass had severed a nerve affecting her voice.

On any other day, Dr. Woodcock lived up to his name, as he was known for being downright cocky. He had a haughty attitude, and his expertise as an emergency room surgeon inspired a gait and posture most often seen by emperors. But now his demeanor was one of humility as he acknowledged that a Power greater than his own surgical skill was at work bringing Sue back.

The first thing Sue became aware of after waking up in her hospital bed was Dad sitting beside her holding her hand. His big, calloused hands felt warm and secure.

At first, Sue could only talk in a hoarse whisper and was not given any promise of being able to speak audibly again. After a few days, however, she croaked out some audible sounds. Eventually, she even regained her singing voice, though it had changed from alto to soprano. Sue had also suffered multiple gashes on her chin, and her right ear was sliced through. In order to stitch up her many lacerations, the doctor shaved the right side of her head. Curious about how she looked, Sue asked Mom for a mirror to examine her injuries. Mom refused because she was concerned Sue would be demoralized by what she saw. This only made Sue doubly curious— it must be pretty bad, she reasoned, if she wasn't allowed to look. But she wanted to see for herself. If Dr. Woodcock had looked at Sue's eyes when he leaned over her to examine her wounds, he would have seen her peering intently into his glasses, where she was finally able to see her reflection.

The visible scar today on the right side of Sue's throat is a constant reminder of why we value her so much.

Esther had injuries from the accident as well, which she quietly endured—injuries that could not be seen on the outside. One was a nasty nose injury from where her face had crashed into the windshield. She also had chest injuries where the steering wheel had held her back from going through the windshield. The bent wheel told its own tale of how hard her chest had hit it and why she was in so much pain. Not wanting to take attention away from Sue, however, Esther did not make a big deal out of how badly she was feeling. Instead she drew from her deep, inner well of strength. For about a week after the accident, she spent a lot of time in bed, weakened from loss of blood from her nosebleeds.

Despite Esther's efforts to recover, the injury inside her nose refused to heal because of what the doctor described as "proud flesh,"[4] which caused ongoing, profuse nosebleeds. For a while, her spirit stayed afloat as she was buoyed from visits by family and friends who stopped by. As she grew steadily weaker day by day instead of gaining strength, however, no one seemed to notice. Not even Glenn, whom Esther had just begun dating before the accident. When he brought flowers to her, he noticed the strength of her determined spirit and was struck by the fact that she did not complain at all. But even as he fell more deeply in love with her, he was not aware of how weak she had become.

Esther was so weak that she could not call loudly enough to be heard. So Mom gave her a stick to pound on the floor if she needed something when she was alone. But sometimes, no one heard even the pounding. One day when she was having an extra-heavy nosebleed, she pounded the stick on the floor, desperate for help, but no one heard. When she passed out on her bed and regained consciousness, Esther begged Mom to call the doctor. But Mom, probably because she was overwhelmed, remained steadfast that we should just continue to pray. When Esther was finally taken to the doctor for a check-up, her blood count was extremely low—about five when it should have been fourteen to fifteen. When she told Dr. Woodcock she was very lightheaded, he simply told her to walk more slowly. To stop the bleeding, he packed her nose so tightly full of gauze it could not possibly bleed any more. Today, I see Esther as an unsung hero. Barely hanging on at some points of her recovery, she persevered. I'm so glad she did.

---

[4] Swollen flesh surrounding a wound caused by formation of new connective tissue and tiny blood vessels on the surfaces of the wound—which can keep it from healing properly.

Dale's accident happened on a different continent just before he got married. He was in Grenada teaching school, having recently returned from being home for a summer in the United States, where he had become used to driving on the right side of the road again. Now back in Granada, he started out for church one Sunday morning on his motorcycle, a little behind schedule, to teach Sunday school. Coming to a turn in the road, he saw the semi in front of him swerving all over and taking up the road to get around the corner. Because the semi wasn't staying on a specific side of the road, Dale wasn't taking any cues from it. And since he had so recently returned from the States, he unconsciously slipped right back into the way he had relearned to drive while back home—in the right lane. Dale figures the semi must have disappeared from his vision while going around the corner and that's why he didn't notice that it went to the left side of the road to avoid hitting the oncoming car in the right lane—which was headed straight toward Dale. At the last minute, Dale jerked the cycle far to the right, but there wasn't enough room between the car and the bank beside him. Before he knew what was happening, he flew over the motorcycle handlebars and hit the windshield of the oncoming car with his left hand, shattering the glass and landing on the ground on the left side of the car. Sitting there taking stock of his injuries, with his upper lip bleeding and a few teeth chipped, Dale could tell by his misshapen wrist that it was broken. A passing police officer took him to the hospital, where his upper lip was sewn and a temporary splint put on his arm in the emergency room. His wrist needed surgery, but considering he hadn't been wearing a helmet, he was very fortunate his injuries weren't worse. He flew back to the United States for surgery then returned to Grenada to finish the school year.

Risk-Taking, Near Accidents

Accidents just happen, but taking a risk usually involves conscious choice. When such a choice flirts with the possibility of an accident, the risk borders on being foolhardy, but when it courageously pushes out the edges of adventure, it can be personally enhancing and confidence-building. Part of the challenge is, you don't know the outcome for sure 'til you try. The risks we took were on a continuum, with danger on one end and opportunity for growth on the other. Perhaps we were propelled in this by the same risk-taking spirit of my parents and ancestors as they charted unknown territory.

Animals were one source of temptation that pushed us out on the edges of adventure. One day when Ada was in the chicken house with Dad, a rat started running up one of the posts. Thinking to herself, "I can't let him get away," Ada, who was a young girl at the time, grabbed the rat's tail with her bare hands, causing Dad to yell, "Throw him down, or he'll bite you." She threw it down, and Dad killed it—a trophy of Ada's courage. Because Ada was the one who had grabbed the rat, she collected fifty cents bounty even though Dad had done the killing. Well worth the risk, she felt.

Elam was also courageous with animals. He knew the bite of snapping turtles was ferocious, but that didn't stop him from grabbing them by their tails and flopping them over on their backs on the creek bank just because he could. One day, he saw the head of a snapping turtle sticking out of the water at the edge of the creek. It saw him too and ducked into the water. Elam dove right in after it, as if on a deep-sea adventure. I would have just let the ugly old snapping turtle go. But that wasn't Elam's style. Where there was a conquest to be had, he plunged right in.

The same spirit of conquest was probably also behind Elam's reaction when he spied a snake one day down along the creek. No sooner did it slither under an old door lying on the ground than Elam jerked the door up, exposing the startled creature. When it high-tailed it for an adjacent hole in the ground, Elam leaped into action faster than the speed of lightning and grabbed the end of the snake's tail just before it disappeared. Who knows what he would have done with an angry snake on his hands if he had managed to pull the whole thing out. Fortunately, he wound up instead holding just the last few inches of tail that the snake left him.

Taking risks with living creatures was one thing. Taking risks with vehicles was another. But Tim and Elvin were up to the challenge. Both of them had always wanted to ride on the back of a buggy, so one evening they and one of their friends came up with a strategy for accomplishing the feat. First, they waited by the side of a road on a hill until an Old Order Mennonite came by in horse and buggy. When the buggy slowed as the horse trotted up the hill, Elvin jumped onto the back of it. Tim also made the leap successfully. As he reached down to help their friend get on, however, he lost his balance and fell off, and one of the buggy wheels ran over his leg. Instantly, Elvin jumped off and joined his fellow would-be stowaway on the ground. How was Tim to explain the long bruise on the calf of his leg? He didn't—he just kept it carefully hidden.

Tim and Elvin seemed to naturally gravitate toward peril, and the black Falcon hot rod provided another way to ride on the edge. Even its conversion into a dream hot rod was dangerous by nature. Tim and Elvin worked relentlessly at the project, beginning by cutting the roof off with a welder since there wasn't a plasma cutting torch around to do the job. Afterward, when Elvin was barely able to see for a day or two and Tim felt like he had sand in his eyes, they both knew they had gotten too much welders' flash. It took Elvin two eye surgeries later—one at thirty years old and one at thirty-five—for the damage to his eyes to be corrected.

The difficult start with the Falcon's transformation did not deter either Elvin or Tim, however. They finished the job and proceeded to get a lot of mileage out of their new hot rod. Sometimes they drove it along the railroad tracks to the country store in New Columbia about a mile and a half away. Or they took wild joy-rides through the streets of New Columbia, quick in and quick out, distressing the residents with their loud noise and crazy driving. This was after they had entered the town airborne by cranking the Falcon up on one of the streets close to the end of the railroad tracks, then hitting the slight upgrade leading up to the tracks at about seventy miles per hour before sailing across the tracks through the air. Landing on the other side of the street, they'd come to a skidding, sliding, screeching halt just before the stop sign. It's a wonder there wasn't a town cop assigned specifically to catch them. Trouble was, the black Falcon always appeared without any warning.

It was no secret to the townspeople of New Columbia who the Falcon belonged to. Young boys opened their front doors and watched enviously as Elvin and Tim rip-roared around town. One day a group of these town boys came to our house, but Elvin and Tim weren't there. So one of the boys asked Dale instead to "give me a ride I will never forget." Dale drove the boy and his friends out the lane. As Dale was turning the black Falcon around, the boy decided Dale's driving wasn't thrilling enough, so he asked to drive himself. Reluctantly, Dale consented. The boy turned left onto the road next to the railroad and spun out—too fast. The black Falcon hit some gravel on the railroad bank and began fishtailing, narrowly missing a telephone pole. At that point, the boy lost control. The Falcon shot over the railroad track on the right and landed on its wheels in the bushes on the other side. One of the boys who was standing on the back of the Falcon during the ride was still standing when it came to a stop deep in the bushes. The boys walked slowly back to New Columbia, and Dale trudged home sheepishly to ask John to come pull the hot rod out of the bushes with the tractor. Did Dad ever find out about this? I don't know. But the boys' guardian angels certainly knew. I'm guessing it cured these town boys from ever wanting a ride in the black Falcon again.

Conclusion

What is it that separates an accident from a close encounter? A split second? Quick thinking on someone's part? A prayer? Protection from a guardian angel? When a close accident happens, in the mind's eye it's almost as if the accident really happened, leaving one with an acute awareness of vulnerability. With all the close calls and accidents my family experienced, especially given the fact that we didn't have much supervision, what "could have been" is more than enough reason for me to not take life for granted.

12. Music

Burrowing deep down into my sleeping bag, I was trying to stay warm in my tent in the morning mountain air when boisterous singing suddenly startled the morning quiet awake. "On the farm in the morning many birds awake, trying each to be loudest, sweetest music make … Cherrie, cherrie, cherrie, the birds are singing in the tree; cherrie, cherrie, cherrie, it's morning on the farm." There, on the porch of the Cabin was Dad, standing straight in light-blue shirt and dark-green pants and suspenders, sending a wakeup call to his sleeping family in tents across the lawn. And he didn't stop until he had sung all three verses, including roosters, ducks, and turkeys. Dad's loud singing so early in the morning happily annoyed me. I'm sure many of the other sleepers weren't exactly thrilled to have their morning slumber interrupted either. Yet we all responded to Dad's musical call by crawling half-awake out of our sleeping bags and stumbling toward the Cabin for breakfast.

Music was our family's common language—language to express our feelings of joy, excitement, sadness, and even anger. It flowed freely through our lives, just as freely as the river flowed at the edge of our yard. It's hard for me to imagine my family without music. It was as though we inhaled and exhaled invisible notes floating through the air around us. The music surrounded us and came through us in nature, in recorded song, and in our own singing, while we were working, playing, having fun, eating, nurturing, and sharing. It engulfed us all in one huge refrain.

We heard it reverberating in the deep-throated croak of bullfrogs in the river at night. And it clanged from the large, cast-iron dinner bell on the white post close to the porch, singing out to us wherever we happened to be—the river, a field, upstairs, the basement, the barn—"It's time to eat."

Not only did the sound of the dinner bell mean it was time to come for supper, its resounding call was the prelude to singing around the table before we ate. Something happened when we sat together and sang. A sacred pathway formed, taking us straight through the cares of life.

Whether Dad had run into trouble with farming equipment breaking down that day, or Mom had needed to settle multiple disputes between us kids, or any one of us was having a bad day, making music together consoled us. Dad's full-voiced, confident bass and Mom's slurry, lilting soprano added to fledgling basses, tenors, and altos, creating four-part harmony to *Great Is Thy Faithfulness*, comforting and reassuring us no matter what had happened that day.

Just before supper, Mom would instruct someone to gather up the stack of songbooks and pass them out, one book for every two of us to share at the places where we sat around the table on the long, green benches. We took turns choosing a song for the week from the songbook. When I was born, the chosen song was *There Is Beauty All Around When There's Love at Home.*

When we sang around the table together, it was as if each of us was in our own little world yet part of the other. Singing was both an intensely personal experience and a shared experience, blending our souls together. Though we sang with abandon, nobody commented on or corrected anyone else's singing. That is, until one of our Fresh Air girls giggled as she said, "Barbara took and squealed" when Barbara, who was a young girl at the time, reached for the high notes. Barbara was so embarrassed she refused to sing for a while.

But no one refused the music after supper when it drifted from the kitchen to an adjacent room where someone would begin playing guitar, harmonica, or piano. Others would join in with singing or with another instrument for pure enjoyment or as a stress reliever. When Fred played one of his large, impressive harmonicas, particularly the multi-sided one with different keys, in our eyes he was definitely a cut above the rest of us.

Our love of making music flowed from both Mom and Dad, who each grew up in a setting where high value was placed on music. Dad spoke fondly of his mother as a "little spunky woman" who had a beautiful soprano voice. Mom talked adoringly about her father's beautiful singing. She also spoke in a whimsical manner about her uncle with the striking white hair and long beard sitting in church in the amen corner (often elderly people sat to the side of the pulpit and spoke "amens" in response to the preacher). When she described hearing his lovely tenor as a young girl and how it could be heard clearly above everyone else's singing, she seemed transported right back to that time and place. It was as if simply reminiscing about her father and her uncle singing made the world about as perfect as it could be for her.

When Mom and Dad were young adults, they were part of a group of young people who got together regularly to eat and have "singings." Not much stopped the group from meeting. In winter when they got snowed in, Dad just invited everyone to climb into his bobsled and off they went to the singing, serenaded by the ringing of the bells on the sled.

But nothing close to the sound of bells or other musical instruments was present in the church that Mom and Dad went to during this period of their lives. Their congregation was strongly influenced by Amish tradition and sang only a capella in unison (though in time the church approved four-part harmony). It was fitting that Mom and Dad, who would eventually bring into being a family of singers, sang with this group of young people the evening before their wedding after sharing a meal together with them. Dad had always said he wanted a singing family, but little did he know he would have a whole choir, complete with four-part harmony.

Dad's singing family gave him much joy. He expressed this best when yodeling exuberantly from mountaintops. His outbursts of glee, I suspect, were both about his delight in us and about the beauty of nature. One day, Dad and Fred had a race to see who could reach the top of a mountain first. Fred knew Dad had won when he heard yodeling above him. Smiling, he translated Dad's yodel as, "Fred, I'm so glad you're out here with me in this beauty." One of the reasons we begged Dad to yodel, I believe, was so we could hear the joy tumbling like a mountain stream over rocks, right out of his soul. When I heard him yodeling, I felt happy and lighthearted. Maybe because he was feeling this too.

Dad frequently obliged our requests that he sing *Oh, Those Pennsylvania Hills* or sing and yodel *Buffalo Valley, I'm Longing for You* while we planted tomatoes. We smiled as he sang on the tractor ahead of us. It was both for ourselves and for Dad that we asked him to sing and yodel, because we could tell from his expression when we asked, that he enjoyed singing with us and for us.

We could also coax Dad into singing German hymns after a meal. He would stride to the bookshelf in the living room with a twinkle in his eye, grasp the black German hymnal from the shelf, position himself again at the head of the table, and with great gusto sing the songs of his childhood. There was a reverential feel to the way Dad sang these strange-sounding German hymns.

Sometimes we requested that Dad sing the songs he had learned from elementary school. Those also sounded foreign to our ears. Some had a patriotic theme, and some were just plain fun. I was surprised he knew them and had carried them with him for all these years. But clearly he had, not only the tunes but also all the words.

Singing with others was a necessity for Dad. When John went to his first-ever men's chorus practice at Beaver Run Church with Dad, he remembers how excited

Dad was on the way. Dad rarely missed one of those practices. Of the many things that could have taken him out of the tomato field at planting or harvesting time, only prayer meetings and chorus practices did; he went even with ripe tomatoes lying on the ground everywhere. Dad put his whole heart into being a part of this chorus. I could tell this when I watched him standing in straight-backed posture during a chorus program, as if making a salute, wearing a pleasant expression and singing so heartily it was obvious that this was somehow vital for his survival.

While Dad used music to express happiness, Mom often sang to articulate deep feelings she found hard to voice. Hymns seemed to help get her through the day, the words giving her strength in the moment. Singing to babies was something different; it was clear at those times that she was feeling a stirring of deep love.

Most of the music Mom sang was serious business, except for *The Old Woman Who Lived Alone* song she taught us. It was playful, each line building in suspense until the predictable yet always startling "I Gotcha!" at the end. (This same song is now being sung to Mom's great-grandchildren, who likewise squeal with scared delight at the end.)

We also saw a more lighthearted side of Mom when she sang from her composition book, often when we were doing some tedious task together such as shelling lima beans. This book was where Mom in her youth had neatly copied ballads of all sorts—songs from a different time and place that were popular in her day. The spaces between the songs were decorated with meticulous artwork, carefully colored.

The composition book held a compelling fascination for me. On its pages, in both the artwork and the songs, I saw a side of Mom I hardly knew. Some of the songs were thought-provoking, some were just for fun, and some were about true stories. They were about Bessie, a little orphan girl freezing to death on the doorstep of a rich man who refused to let her in; a little girl dying in her mother's arms while describing her vision of heaven; a goat who ate a red shirt off his master's wife's clothesline and was tied to a railroad track, whereupon he coughed up the red shirt just in time to flag down the would-be murderous train; a young man, Floyd Collins, who died in a collapsed cave after his mother begged him not to go; and so on. Whether Mom sang the ballads to us or we eventually sang them ourselves, their message found a lodging place deep within our souls.

Mom and Dad communicated to us that singing well was important to them, and Mom worked with us to stay on key as soon as we could sing. Before Dale could walk, he held onto the side of his crib, smiling gleefully and swaying to music from the record player while we cheered and clapped for him.

When Elvin was about four years old, he sang at the top of his voice, "Sit down, I can't sit down … I just got a spanking, and I can't sit down"—his revision of *I Just Got Religion and I Can't Sit Down*, a song on a record album by Sixteen Singing Men that we frequently played. At the same age, from the corner bathroom in the hall, Elvin gave Glenn a fortissimo serenade with his rendition of *Ain't Gonna Study War No More* revised to "Ain't gonna go potty no more," as Glenn walked in the door to pick Esther up on one of their first dates. We all watched Glenn with baited breath. He just grinned, and we could breathe again and laugh.

Elvin had to change his tune when Mom drove us at a young age to sing for our elderly neighbors while they smiled and nodded their heads in approval. Did

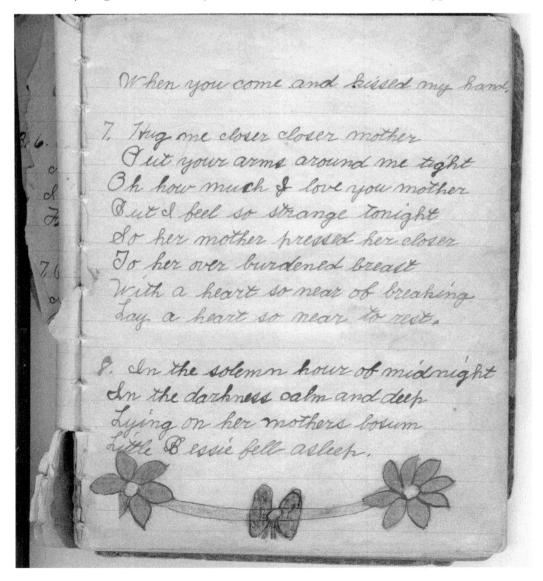

she have us sing for them to bring them cheer? Or did she want to showcase her young singing children? Probably both.

I guess you could say we were also on display the many other times our family sang for others. The first time Mom and Dad's family "choir" was asked to sing— by the Oley Church just before we moved to Buffalo Valley—I was one year old and Mom held me while the family sang two songs. Later when I stood with my family to sing in front of a group of people, I felt important, as if we were on stage being admired for our singing. As an insecure little girl lacking self-confidence, I often felt inferior to my peers (I felt they were always dressed better than I was), but when

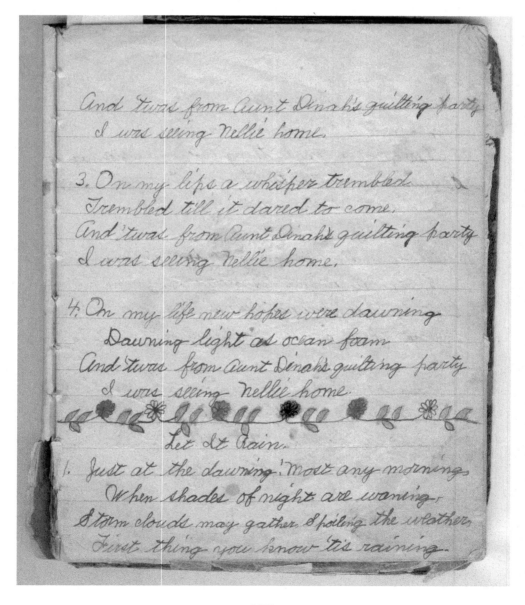

I sang with my family, I felt confident and self-assured as I thought to myself, "At least I'm doing something my friends weren't asked to do."

We started out singing as a whole family, but as we grew up, we broke off into quartets and trios to fill requests. I guess you could say that smaller groups of us singing together in public began with my younger brothers. I'm not sure how this was initiated, but when they sang at Beaver Run Church during winter Bible school, one of the songs Mom chose was *We Are a Missionary Band* (surely a reflection of Mom's desire for her children to be in mission work). Afterward, my brothers went outside with some other kids. And wouldn't you know, Elvin got in a fight with another little boy who ruffled his feathers. A little girl observing from the sidelines said tauntingly to Elvin, "Sooo, you're part of a missionary band, huh?" Her point about actions not matching words probably zinged right over Elvin's head—after all, he didn't choose the song.

Another way we shared our music with others was recording an album. I was one of a string of five girls, and we decided as young adults that we would create an album together before we all went our separate ways. Our feature song was a variation of *Bridge over Troubled Water* by Simon and Garfunkle: our version referred to Jesus as the "bridge over troubled water." Another song we recorded was *My Faith Looks Up to Thee*, which pleased Dad because it was his mother's favorite song. As we practiced for the recording, we often linked arms—a symbol of our harmony solidifying our enduring togetherness.

Singing in four-part harmony was natural for us, partly because Mom and Dad surrounded us with this kind of music in any way they could. Besides having us sing around the table at dinner, they supplied us with Mennonite Hour and Chuck Wagon Gang records with four-part harmony. (They even went so far as to mail order little rpm single song records for us to listen to.) We didn't have iPods with individual ear buds, just a turntable loud enough for everyone to hear. And there weren't many times that it wasn't turned on, usually full blast; the music was best when we could hear it from anywhere in the house while we worked or played. As soon as it stopped, someone would simply flip the huge stack of records over on the other side, ensuring continuous music. Frequently when Al Longenecker came to see Ada, the loud music got the best of him, and he would quietly amble over to the record player and turn down the volume. That would last until someone said, "Hey, what happened to the music?" and turned the volume back up.

Mom and Dad's preference for our listening ears was hymns sung a capella. When Aunt Mary gave us a few secular records, our music selection expanded.

(Aunt Mary was Mom's younger sister, whose musical tastes were a bit more worldy than Mom's.) Surprisingly, Mom and Dad conceded to the records. Maybe because they came from our aunt. One of the songs, *Oh My Darling, Clementine*, made an impression on me. I hardly dared imagine the part that went "Ruby lips above the water ..." as Clementine drowned, leaving her love. When we listened to the cowboy songs, we traveled west to prairies, cattle roundups, and watering holes. The music of The Staple Singers had us swaying and singing along with great enthusiasm. (Elam had bought their album for us at Christmas one year, not aware of the rollicking twist this group put to common hymns.) And we also grew to love the von Trapp Family Singers, J. T. Adams, the Vienna Boys' Choir, and others.

Somewhere along the way, an album of classical music came into our possession as well. We grew to appreciate this genre of music, too, putting a fun spin on Mozart's *Symphony No. 40 in G Minor* at one place where we inserted the words, "Ole Mozart's in the closet, get 'im out, get 'im out, get 'im out, get 'im out ..."

The circle of our music world rippled out even further when Barb drove us to school the days she worked at JJ Newberry's. None of our cars had a radio aerial, because Dad would always snap it off when we got a new car so we couldn't be negatively influenced by worldly music. But Barb was undeterred by this. She would stop at the end of the lane, pull out a wire clothes hanger safely hidden under the seat, and slide its looped end onto the base of the snapped-off aerial. Thus, we learned our share of worldly songs. One of these was *Teen Angel*, a tearjerker song about a high school couple getting stuck on a railroad track with a train approaching. In the song, the girl runs back to the car to get her boyfriend's high school ring that "they found clutched in her fingers tight." There was also a song about a girl being in love with a boy named "Fred." When this came on, Fred would plug his ears with his fingers, or stick his head out the window. And when *God Bless America*, popular at that time, came across the air waves, Esther would show how seriously she took loving her enemies as she countered the lyrics by conscientiously singing "God bless Russia" for the duration of the song. (This was when the "threat of communism" was at our back door and we deemed the Russians our enemies.)

We were cautious about singing any of these songs around the house. But we freely sang silly songs together when we were outside on the tomato harvester as it crawled cumbersomely through the field scooping up tomatoes. The job of picking green tomatoes out of the sea of red tomatoes riding up the conveyor belt could become rather tedious and boring. Singing silly songs helped the time go faster and made the job more enjoyable.

Music could also quiet us, releasing stress and tension. This was especially true when we traveled long distances. With several kids packed into the back of the station wagon and very little wiggle room, our restlessness would turn to bickering and then to quietly pinching one another, ending up in wild protests. When Mom and Dad strategically started singing, the squabbling usually stopped as we took their bait and joined in; we really couldn't fight and sing at the same time very well. Occasionally, we came up with our own solution for our packed-together situation, such as someone spontaneously singing *Go Tell Aunt Rodie* and progressing mournfully through all the verses until finally at the end, "The goslings are crying, the goslings are crying, the goslings are crying because their mommy's dead." It wasn't until years later that my brothers confessed that this part made them cry quietly in the back seat.

We also sang in the car on the way to church, our spirits quickening as we continued singing almost without stopping as we walked through the church doors— since the opening song of the service had often started by the time we arrived. The singing we did there stirred deep feelings in our souls. The high ceiling of the old Buffalo Church provided wonderful acoustics for the congregational four-part singing, and songs such as *Spirit of God, Descend Upon My Heart* or *Day Is Dying in the West* (in evening services as the setting sun glowed red through the window), created a profound entrance to my soul. There in that space with the four-part singing of my family and church family soaring up to the ceiling as an offering, it seemed I met God personally.

Dad's deep and unwavering resonant bass stood out above the rest. (Today when Tina hears singing groups, she wants to tell them how much better their sound would be if they had her Dad's "wonderful, beautiful" bass to help them.) When Dad chose *There Is a Fountain Filled with Blood* during a Sunday evening song service and switched to melody, his voice could still be heard above everyone else's, singing, "and sinners plunging 'neath that flood lose all their guilty stains." He sang like it meant something personal to him. And when we sang together *Will Your Anchor Hold?* I knew his would.

When I got old enough to go to the evening church service with the older kids in the run-around car, I stayed out in the car with them after we got home, where we would stretch out the music from church long after everyone else had gone into the house. We'd listen to a Wheeling WV station with folksy-sounding hymns, chatting happily into the night with the music in the background.

Music flowed easily between home and church. When the younger set of kids played church on the stairs, they each held an open songbook while Dale stood in front of them swinging his arm in a wide swath, leading the music. Not able to read, they turned random pages to a song of their choosing. Singing along with Dale was as natural as playing in the sandbox outside the kitchen window. Even when the kids weren't playing church, Dale often stood around holding a songbook in his hands, singing. He remembers Dad saying to him, "I'm glad you like to sing, Dale." Later, when Dale was ten years old, he bought his first guitar from Elvin. He's had one in his hands ever since, often along with a songbook. He clearly got an early start to being the song leader he is today.

When we moved to Buffalo Valley, Mom and Dad brought with them some old carols they had learned at the singings when they were young. These same carols have become part of the repertoire of songs we now look forward to singing every Christmas season: *Christmas Time Has Come Again*, *The Message*, *The Silver Star*, and *Glory Be to God*—carols with beautiful four-part harmony, one part often leading out at a certain place in the song while the other parts float around it. For instance, we sing the version of *Silent Night* where the bass leads out on the second verse—beginning with "silent" and then the first word of each following phrase of the verse—while the other singers echo, singing the regular version. We miss Dad's bass leading out on *Silent Night*. That was his signature. These Christmas songs have spread out into the community and are now being sung by many others beyond our family. They will surely continue to be sung by the next generation.

My family also sings together now at the Cabin. There we gather on the porch or back deck in the evening as a few guitar players beckon others to join in singing. On Sunday morning, the music takes on special meaning as we gather into a makeshift congregation facing the creek flowing below the bank, to sing *How Great Thou Art*.

Singing brought us into the world, and it has accompanied those who have left this world. As a little girl, I remember when Aunt Della, Mom's sister whom she dearly loved, died from cancer. At Aunt Della's graveside, I stood on grass carpet looking up at mom, who looked the saddest I'd ever seen her as those around the grave sang *Silently, They Pass Away* while the body was being lowered into the ground. It was such a sad-sounding song that her grieving family and friends sang.

After Dad's viewing, we were all standing around in the church sanctuary when the last visitor left, the whole family weary from the long evening of smiling and shaking the hands of those who had come to pay their respects. Then someone started spontaneously singing "606," the choral rendition of *Praise God from Whom All Blessings Flow*, a song with beautiful harmonies that is considered by many Mennonites to be the Mennonite anthem (found on page 606 in *The Mennonite*

Hymnal). We sang joyfully, tearfully, from our hearts, filling the sanctuary with four-part harmony in no time at all, arms reaching out to one another. Dad would have loved this.

After Mom died a few years later, we gathered together again in the church sanctuary late at night, emotionally exhausted after the last visitor had finally left. Almost on cue, we all burst into singing *Lift Your Glad Voices* as we stood in groups together with arms around one another's shoulders. Through tears of sadness and joy, the music instantly filled the sanctuary. Mom would have loved it.

We were sad, but how could we keep from singing? The music flowed right out of our souls, and it will continue through future generations.

PART IV
Our Life Flows On

13. The Cabin

When I woke up on Saturday morning after the first night of the Cabin weekend, it was raining hard. My heart sank. The creek water, usually "home" to the children at the Cabin family get-together, was already high and muddied, so all this new rain wouldn't help matters any. The children would surely be banned from playing in the creek, which also meant that catching minnows, crayfish, and tadpoles or going tubing or fishing was out. I was feeling their disappointment. This is what they looked forward to all year. What would they do now?

Wait ... were those happy, excited voices I just heard? A group of children sprinted joyfully across the yard, colorful inner tubes in hand—blue, yellow, florescent pink, and green—making a rainbow parade. They were heading toward a pond of rain water that had formed during the night just outside the campers where some of the children were staying. The creek had come to *them*. The older kids pulled trains of inner tubes loaded with little kids through the water. Or they held inner tubes midair as the kids dove straight through the inner circle to the water on the other side, making a big splash. Who needed the creek now? In the spirit of all that is true about the Cabin experience, these little champions of innovation were rallying together to make the best of the situation.

The children reminded me of how Dad and his friends had come together in the northern mountains of Pennsylvania near the little town of Slate Run to become the Dutch Masters Hunting Club. They started out in tents pitched in a meadow, then built the little red and white cabin with its log-railed front porch (and eventually the back deck overlooking the creek) right in the middle of a sanctuary of mountains, trees, and wildlife including deer, bear, turkey, and rattlesnakes.

I wonder what Dad was thinking when he found this piece of land. What connected him to this particular place? Was it the sheltering mountains on either side of the railroad track winding through the narrow valley? Was it Pine Creek flowing at the base of the mountain? Was it the friendly little country store close by? Or the peaceful retreat he experienced in these surroundings? Did he feel the same connection we all now feel? Whatever it was, this place drew Dad back again and again after he borrowed his father's car in 1932 for a hunting adventure in the north and found the spot where the Cabin now stands. His initial five-hour drive to this destination would become one he would make every year for the rest of his life—first as a single man, then as a married man, then as a father.

In their beginning years of marriage, Mom and Dad drove to the Cabin on a winding dirt road with no guardrail along its steep drop-off. Dad viewed the

The Cabin

precariousness of this road as an opportunity for creating a gasp-and-hold-your-breath moment by driving close to the edge to tease Mom. The first time she saw the sharp drop-off by her side of the car, she let out a shriek and Dad laughed. This ritual of fun for Dad was just the beginning of segueing from cares and responsibilities to a time of enjoying just being. Little did anyone realize then that driving this road to the Cabin would offer the same coveted treasure of simply "being" to future generations.

Dad's yearly summer trek to the Cabin with his family began with his first child. Some of our earliest memories are embedded in the Cabin experience—a vacation for everyone except Mom, who said the expedition made a lot of extra work for her. Looking forward to going motivated us in many ways. My older brothers pushed themselves hard to get the straw in and the corn cultivated because Dad told them this had to be done before we could go. Several weeks before the long-awaited departure date, Mom and Dad would start reminding us we needed to earn money to spend at the Slate Run country store. Mice, flies, rats, and pesky birds would begin disappearing around the farm with Mom's promise of paying us a bounty for each. I'd scurry around the attic, cupping my ear to hear the chirping of baby starlings or sparrows in the eaves that would earn me five cents apiece. If I caught a mouse in a trap, I doubled my stash. We must have had a lot of flies, because swatting one hundred of them earned us one penny (Though confiscation of rats and snapping turtles landed a reward of fifty cents each—big money back then—I never cared to earn fifty cents this way.) The treats I bought at the candy store with the hard-earned coins I'd stashed in my coin purse and the lightweight airplanes my brothers bought to assemble were worth every bit of effort it took to get them.

We took the hour and a half trip to the Cabin on roads paved with gold. Our excitement leading up to the trip would rise to the level of grand adventure. The year Uncle Levi's family left Oley with us we had even more excitement on the way. My siblings and cousins, totaling ten children, rode on the twelve-foot bed in the back of a truck with four-foot sides, sitting on hay bales for a total of one hundred and fifty miles. Suddenly, from the midst of us all, the wind snatched Elam's brand-new cap and blew it off his head. Everyone hollered, and Dad slammed on the brakes and ran back down the road to retrieve it.

When we set off on these trips, every mile closer made it that much harder to sit still. The right turn onto Route 44—which led to Route 414 taking us straight to the Cabin—was our cue to start bouncing off the seat. We couldn't help it; the feverish excitement in the car was electric. The Route 44 turn was our signal to cram our heads together at an open window, eagerly scanning the woods and small fields for sight of a deer. Dad would promise a Popsicle from the candy store to whoever spotted the first one. Catching a glimpse of these shy, graceful creatures on the way to the Cabin was certainly more exciting than seeing them in our own field at home, as it heightened our awareness that we were leaving behind cares and responsibilities of home to enter a world where animals were somehow admired more, respected more—as if we were their guests.

Dad would fuel the exhilaration of getting closer to the Cabin by having us count railroad tracks to be crossed on the way. There were at least six, the last one being at the Cabin itself. After crossing that one, we would turn onto the long lane beside the track and cruise past the country store, craning our necks as we held our breath in anticipation of catching sight of the red and white cabin through the trees.

The collective mounting anticipation of heading to the Cabin every summer around July fourth has now grown to include in-laws, grandchildren, great-grand-

Tubing at the Cabin

children, and great-great-grandchildren. The children begin asking their parents in early spring, "When are we going to the Cabin? How many days is it yet?"

The beautiful setting of the Cabin in nature with its offer of peace, rest, and relaxation is like a magnet pulling us back together year after year. Yet there is something else besides the setting that beckons. To us, the cabin experience has become "the Cabin," an entity all its own. It is a holding place for reinforcing tradition, strengthening relationships, laying aside differences, entering varying depths of conversation, and connecting spirit with spirit as family members with differing political views, theological leanings, and lifestyles mingle and laugh together.

Though the Cabin is not able to physically accommodate all of us now, it still contains us in our differences as we gather in the yard and pitch tents of all sizes, unfold pop-up campers, and set up motor homes. And more than just the physical structure of the building, our experience of the Cabin is the occasion of being embraced by the mountains, Pine Creek, and one another as we come together. One of my young-adult nephews said it well: "I get to see all the generations in family coming together, loving each other. I see how things have changed and how they have stayed the same in this tradition of coming together and appreciating the heritage of family."

Part of the heritage of my family is the way we value one another and give each person a place of belonging. The Cabin is a perfect setting to remind us of this, where we excitedly gather 'round for a peek at newborn babies making their first-time appearance, shout out whoops of joy and run to greet family members who have arrived from their homes far and wide, and welcome anyone who joins the family through marriage or adoption as they find connection to this place.

Children form a special bond to the Cabin, where they find acceptance even by some they hardly know. Young cousins coming to the Cabin who have never seen one another before lay shyness aside as they become acquainted. Children of varying shades of brown and white (some from other families have joined our family) play together holding hands as they scamper around; take a trek to the candy store; shout "There's an eagle!" pointing to the sky above; and play in the creek catching tadpoles and crayfish, swimming, fishing, kayaking, canoeing, throwing rocks into the water to see who can make the biggest splash, or skipping smooth stones across the creek's surface to see whose goes the farthest.

Young parents stand together at the creek's edge or sit on chairs in the creek watching their children play in the water while they talk about childrearing. The Cabin is a joining of the parents of children now and those to come with the original parents—Mom and Dad.

Individuals come together at the Cabin in many ways. They join together when space is created for heartfelt sharing while taking a walk with another person or sitting around in little groups that form spontaneously; playing a volleyball game where young kids, youth, young adults, or older adults combine to make teams; playing card games in small groups or board games at the long table in front of the window overlooking the creek; or working around the same table to cut, slice, or cube a gigantic fruit salad for Saturday lunch while breaking the monotony with varying twists of conversation and silly songs about one another. Groups also gather to hikes trails in the mountains around the Cabin; a pickup load of tubers takes off for a drop-off point upstream; a few people sit down on the porch to play instruments, where a huddle quickly forms to sing along; little groups cluster inside the Cabin, on the porch, or around a campfire late into the night, where conversations take on a life of their own as politics, theology, and world events are hashed out (if a particular conversation is not especially interesting, there is always another one to gravitate to); and a group laughing together quickly draws others who want to get in on the fun. It is in these circles that we end up laughing until our sides hurt, reminiscing about "remember when" times. Other individuals choose to quietly read books or magazines on chairs or couches opposite each other in the Cabin, comfortable with not feeling the need to converse. But on Sunday morning, we all gather together into a "congregation" in front of the pavilion on folding chairs, where a couple of guitar players lead four-part-harmony singing and the mountains on either side provide our acoustics.

The Cabin experience past has become the Cabin experience present:

❋ Little children still save money to buy candy at the store. Only now there are many more people to walk there with them—parents, grandparents, aunts, uncles, cousins.

❋ The train track—holding memories of the train horn blasting around the mountain and inspiring quick runs to lay money and hairpins to be flattened on its rails—is now a biking trail where we take long, leisurely rides.

❋ My brothers once stood on the rock ledge opposite the Cabin, with fishing line attached to the end of a stick, dangling an earthworm-baited hook in front of rock bass swimming below them. Now, little boys with fishing poles slung over their shoulders head up the creek in a canoe or stand in the water up to their waists and cast their lines with an enticing, colorful plastic worm on their hooks. Their slightly different methods yield the same results, however. Their fish are put in the sink at the pump to be washed or admired, just as many fish before theirs.

❋ When I was little, the beds at the Cabin were not just for sleeping; they were for jumping on and leaping across. Children still bounce on the beds or catapult from one bunk bed to an opposite one a few feet away; only now there are more mothers worrying about their children falling and cracking their heads.

❋ The large-scale water battles of the past—buckets of water dumped by adults from the roof of the Cabin on some unsuspecting person below—are now carried out by little children wielding water squirters of various shapes and sizes. But the glow sticks, bracelets, and necklaces adorning these children who are running and glowing in the darkness are just as much fun as a water battle.

❋ We can still count on a pancake breakfast Saturday morning. However, where once there were only a few platters with stacks of pancakes, there are now cake pans full of them, piled high. Instead of most of the family sitting around the long kitchen table at one time to eat their plates of pancakes, families now come in shifts with sleepy, tousle-haired children in tow.

Last year I asked family members young and old what the Cabin means to them. The young children were quick to say it is the candy store and the creek.

Some of the older children said it means:

❋ My family's here; it's fun. It's really joyful basically.

❋ The main thing is the creek, but I also like friends and family.

✳ It's a time to get together with all the family, cousins, and friends and have a blast with everyone around you.

To young adults, the Cabin means:

✳ A sense of my own immediate family disappears, and I become part of this larger community, under a warm, protective blanket I can both come under and come out of at will. It is where I feel the care of people. Even if conversation stays very light, it is personable and interest is expressed in me.

✳ A wonderful tradition that uses the promise of candy and fun to teach kids wonderful values of godly community.

Young parents responded with:

✳ It is the highlight of the year; the "go-to" place.

✳ An escape from normal schedules.

✳ A beautiful, peaceful, restful setting.

✳ The same but different each year.

✳ A centering place.

✳ A grounding place where I can breathe deeply without having to remind myself to breathe as my soul settles in.

✳ Differences with common ground.

✳ A physical sense of space and identity that is really unique and fabulous.

✳ Getting to re-experience it through my children—their anticipation and excitement about coming—watching them have the same simple pleasures I had growing up.

✳ A reminder of who I am at my core, feeling really familiar and grounding me, bringing me back every year.

✳ A marker, a reminder of the changes of people and places over time—now more heirloom than adventure—my childhood remembered.

✳ A reference point of people highly valued, a wealth of experience, a variety of perspectives, people richly rooted in their faith, a representation of what true Christians are—diverse with a variety of opinions being shared freely and openly—an environment where gentleness, kindness, and consideration are shown to one another.

In the eyes of some of my siblings, the Cabin is what has kept our family close together, providing an opportunity to keep track of everyone and to watch everyone's children grow. It is seen as the bedrock of connection for the Stoltzfus family—a place for keeping relationships intact, catching up with one another, having great conversations, and experiencing the richness of interacting across generations. For those who have returned home from the mission field in other countries, it is an invisible thread tying everyone together, a stable place in life where the setting and people are consistent and important no matter what changes may have happened. It is given as the reason why there is no acid stomach caused by hard feelings and conflicts when one hundred and eighty people come together.

As we got older, it was important to Dad that the entire family gather together at some point during our Cabin time so he could talk to all of us at once. During one of these "together times," Dad got unusually soft-spoken, saying to us in an imploring manner as he teared up, "The most important thing is that we love one another." This showed us how deeply his priorities lay. The next year he said the same thing. I'm guessing he could see that deeply held differences between us were inevitable in the years to come. Today, his entreaty is still with us. There have been many changes and differences, but we continue to love one another and look forward to coming together every year. Dad told us during one of these meetings that he has heard some fathers say how their children have stomped on their hearts, but he could honestly say he has never experienced that. We have not said it in so many words, but I believe that even in Dad's absence we want to make sure our actions would not cause him heartbreak.

Dad would be pleased to see how his grandchildren, great-grandchildren, and great-great-grandchildren love the Cabin today. If Mom and Dad were here, they would be sitting on its porch smiling as they watch everyone playing with the children, see how lovingly new babies are held, and hear young parents say how much they want their children to experience the Cabin. They would be pleased to know that approximately 50 percent of the children at the Cabin are there because of adoption.

Creek + nature + mountains + wildlife + family = the Cabin experience. One of my brothers summed it all up when he said, "It doesn't get much better than this."

Is it any wonder that, as a little boy, Pete kissed the Cabin before leaving to go home?

14. In Memory of Fred Stoltzfus

Killed in a logging accident on October 31, 2015

Part I: as told by Pete Stoltzfus (Fred's younger brother) with details provided by Mel Stoltzfus (Pete's son)

It was late Saturday afternoon. Our married children (except for Elaine, who we'd been with the previous weekend in Kansas) and their families were home for an early Thanksgiving. The euphoria of having all seven grandchildren and their parents in our house had worn off, and I had drifted to sleep while sitting on the couch. Sensing Eliana, my granddaughter, sidling past, I opened one eye. Sure enough, she wanted me to read her another story.

"Go get a book," I said. She went to the bookshelf and made her selection—Dr. Seuss's *Green Eggs and Ham*. (Mimi is a wonderful grandma. She's picked up over a hundred children's books at yard sales.) Eliana sat beside me, and I started reading. My grandson Peter, wanting to be part of the action, clambered up on the other side.

Soon it would be time for supper. It was Josh and April's turn to make the meal.

At 5:14 p.m., the phone rang. Mimi answered it and handed it to me. "It's for you, Pete," she said. On the other end of the line, I heard Fred's son Mast. "Uncle Pete, I'm out at Blairsville for a wedding. I won't be home for a couple of hours. Mama called and said Papa didn't come home at the normal time. Mama went over to the job to check on him."

Mast then told me that Rhoda had walked a ways back the skid trail—she knew the skid steer was somewhere back there in the woods—and had called him again. Mast had asked his mother, "Do you hear the chain saw running?"

"No," she replied.

"Don't go any farther. I'll call someone to check it out."

That's when Mast had called me. I hung up the phone, worried. "Fred didn't come out of the woods. I'm going to run over to the New Berlin Mountain to check it out," I announced, trying to hide my concern with a business-like attitude but fooling no one. Everyone was instantly on high alert.

Grabbing a headlamp, I headed for the door. "I'm going with you," Mel said. Mel, Josh, and I left in a hurry. My cell phone rang. It was Andy. "Hey, I wanted to go with you. I was getting the bow saw." Turning the mini-van around, we went back, and both Andy and Laverne jumped in. Chava, my little dog, had also jumped in somewhere in the mix. She enjoys riding along, and I enjoy her company.

We drove as fast as we safely could, sometimes talking, mostly silent. "How can we make the best use of our time?" I pondered silently. "The sun is soon ready to drop below the horizon. Fred is very dependable. Something is majorly wrong." Trying to shed a ray of hope, Mel offered, "Dad, the fact is, we don't know what happened. A similar situation happened this spring to two of my friends, and they were fine."

"But it doesn't look good," I replied. "I don't like it."

I started calculating … forty to fifty percent chance he's dead. Forty to fifty percent chance he's badly hurt. Ten to twenty percent chance something offbeat happened and he's okay. "Get control of yourself," I told myself as emotions flooded over me. "Shut that part down for now. Think rationally." Just then, Laverne spontaneously and calmly prayed aloud, echoing the silent prayers of the rest of us, and God's peace drew us together. During the prayer, Mel opened his eyes and saw a tacky little sign on the right side of the road that read, "Troubled? Cry out to God."

"Why don't you call Elvin and let him know what's happening?" Mel suggested again. I handed him my phone.

"Look for the skidder," Mast said. "He'll probably be close by."

We hustled back up the logging trail with Chava running gaily ahead. As we met a tear-stained Rhoda, Josh and Laverne each gave her a quick hug. We talked briefly and then continued on at a rapid pace. "It was so comforting to see five men come down the trail," Rhoda said later.

A light skid trail angled up the mountain. Andy and Laverne followed it. Mel, Josh, and I took the bottom road and spread out looking for both the skidder and Fred, shouting Fred's name.

"I'll whistle if I find him," Andy said.

"Whistle if you see the skidder, too," Mel responded.

Ten minutes passed, and we still weren't seeing anything. No skidder, no Fred.

That's when Josh said, "I think you better call more people."

Just as I got off the phone and we arrived at the end of the lumbered area, a shrill whistle sounded from the top. Josh and Mel ran ahead to Andy in the direction of the whistle. More shouts, and Mel hollered back, "Whaaat??"

"Hurry up!" they yelled.

Mel ran up the mountain. Spotting the skidder, he hurried to where Josh, Laverne, and Andy were clustered together. To his great relief, there was Fred, with chain saw, ax, and broken hard hat lying beside him. Andy was doing chest compressions, and Josh was holding Fred's head. Fred's lips were gray and he appeared beat-up, but his hands were still warm. His heart must have just stopped beating. Mel took over holding his head while Andy, with a few rapid blows of the ax, chopped off the top of the tree that had fallen on Fred and pulled it to the side. Josh, a nurse by profession, continued giving Fred chest compressions, trying desperately to get his heart going again. Laverne called 911, and Josh and Andy took turns doing compressions.

As Mel cradled Fred's head in his hands, he assessed the situation before him. Fred had obviously been hit very hard on the head—there was little hope. He knew Fred was gone. Still, he prayed like never before to the Creator of the universe to bring back his uncle. As Mel's heart cried out, "Fred, wake up! Wake up!" he groaned aloud, "O Father in heaven. Bring him back." Looking up, he saw through the trees a beautiful blend of orange and red color in the sky where the sun was setting. Slowly, a peace filled his heart. At the same time that he recognized God would not be answering his prayer the way he wanted, he felt the influence of this man of God along with tremendous love for him as he held his head. Dignity filled the scene even as Josh and Andy worked in vain to get Fred's heart beating.

Mel recalled his conversation with his Uncle Fred at the last pig butchering the winter before. "I just can hardly wait to get back in the woods on Monday mornings to work with my grandsons," Fred had said. "Wish I looked forward to Monday mornings like that," Mel had thought.

Leaving the scene, I went to tell Rhoda that we had found Fred. It was almost 6:00 p.m.

"There were no signs of life. They're trying to get his heart beating again," I told her.

"Just let him go," Rhoda cried. "I know he's in heaven."

The wail of sirens drifted through the air. "Someone needs to go out and show the medics where to come," I said. "Go ahead," Rhoda nodded at me. I started out.

Right then, Laverne appeared. "I'll run out and bring them in," he offered. While Laverne ran ahead, I walked out with Rhoda until we met the paramedics headed our way. At that point, Laverne and I traded places. I took the paramedics back up the trail, and Laverne accompanied Rhoda out of the woods.

It had been about thirty minutes since we'd found Fred, and his hands were cold now. The night was closing fast.

The first responders finally arrived on the scene with their equipment and put leads on Fred's chest as a precaution. As suspected, they found no heartbeat. Josh told the medics what Rhoda had said, and they stopped the chest compressions. Elvin had arrived by then, and we nephews and brothers hugged each other and cried. The night had fallen, and I couldn't deny reality any longer. My brother Fred was dead. Mel put his arm around me, and I squeezed him hard as we wept together.

The law says the coroner must come before the body is moved. The law also says the state police must investigate the scene of an accident before the body is moved. So we waited in the chill night air. Mast said he would stop at his home to get his boys before he came to the mountain.

While a loose cluster of emergency personnel talked quietly a few yards to the side, family and a few of Fred's church family stood in another circle of light by Fred's body. A light cloth had been placed over it. Where had the two preachers and a deacon from Fred's church come from? Oh yes, I had walked back in with them. One of them had lent me his light after I had lost my headlamp before it had even gotten dark. I was a numbed, dazed mess.

Into the circle of light stepped our brother Elam and a tall man in a suit coat and hat. It was Mast, still in his preacher's clothing. Mast knelt by his Papa's side and held his father's big, calloused, work-worn hands in his own. Talking to his Papa, he wept and wept as his mind slowly made the transition that the man he loved so much was no longer in the body he was touching. Elam stood by Mast's right side and placed his hand on his back. I hesitated and then stepped through the treetop to Mast's left and laid my hand on his shoulder. Mast cried, making space for his own honest mourning. An older, close family friend standing outside the inner circle surrounding Mast offered an attempt at consolation: "Rhoda said he didn't come home, but he did." This was hardly comforting, so he tried again. "Fred is in a better place." Mast looked up with tears streaming down his cheeks and responded with clarity, "But we aren't yet." Mast dropped his father's hand, stood, and hugged his uncles tightly in a strong embrace. He almost lifted me off my feet.

In time, the coroner arrived and wrote down the statistics. Name: Fred F. Stoltzfus. Address ... and so on. He expressed his condolences, and we thanked him for coming. A state policeman in plain clothes arrived and solicited the same information. Full name: Fred Floyd Stoltzfus. Wife's name: Rhoda Stoltzfus. He asked who was first on the scene, then beckoned to me. "Could we step aside and talk?"

I gave the officer my official name and address, and he asked about the timeline of events. He needed to take a few pictures, he said, even though Fred's death was obviously an accident. The officer continued to call me by name. Then he interviewed a few others. I was impressed with the professional, yet caring attitude of this representative of the Pennsylvania State Police.

They put Fred's body in a body bag and laid him on a long, plastic stretcher with molded handholds that made it easy for six men to carry him out. Two men walked in front with lights and charted our course, trying to find the way with the least amount of brush, fallen trees, and low branches. Mast was at the front corner on one side of the stretcher and Elvin on the other. Family and church family carried Fred one hundred fifty yards to a gravel access road, then east about one-half mile to the New Berlin Mountain road, finally laying the stretcher down at the edge of the woods. Long hours had passed since we had found him.

Mast returned with his mother and family and stood beside his mother, his seven sons flanking them as one man. They stood in silent homage in the night, Fred's body lying before them on the ground, covered with a long, white cloth and strapped to a board. Husband, father, and loving grandfather—the rugged, kind, and gentle man who had nourished and cherished them was no longer here in this body. His earthly work was finished. Mast got down to his youngest son's level and held him, talking gently to him. Would the five-year-old even remember his grandpa?

Was it only a year ago I told Fred, "Fred, you're getting older. Your reflexes aren't as fast as they once were. You are worth so much more as a teacher, a mentor, a grandfather, a godly counselor. Logging is so dangerous. You've had several close calls. Twelve years ago when you got hit by a branch, you aged years."

Fred had replied, "I just love working in the woods with my sons and grandsons. I want to do it as long as God gives me the ability."

And he did.

As we stood together, Mast talked about how his Papa had come to him recently and had said, "I'm not as productive as I once was. You don't need to pay me so much." Mast had replied, "Papa, I would pay you just for your influence on my sons as they work with you. You enjoy working with them, and they enjoy the privilege of working with you." Fred had recently said the same thing to me.

The next morning we were processing our grief and trauma at home with our married children and their spouses. It was Sunday, and we had church at home. Laverne led us in singing about a dozen songs, including one that he taught us—*Come Bring Your Burdens to God*.

Josh had mentioned late the previous night that it would be good for us to debrief and talk one by one about our experiences and feelings since we had all been involved at some level. Each of us would have a time to talk, uninterrupted by anyone else while we held a spoon that signaled it was our time to talk. Anyone could ask us questions to draw us out or clarify what we were feeling.

"Dad, you go first," my daughter Julie offered.

"I would just like to sit," I said. "Too numb to think."

When my turn came, I tried to talk but only sobbed. Fred had always been there; for him to be dead was unfathomable. But I had seen his blood-stained, ashen face. I had seen the tree that struck him down. I had seen my sons and son-in-law try vainly for half an hour to revive him, even though they knew it was futile.

Finally, I squeaked out a few words as my voice slowly returned. My daughter Julie prodded me. "Do you feel angry?" she asked. "Maybe a little," I said. "Just a great sadness and sense of loss. We had so many shared experiences." Mixed with the tears that wouldn't stop flowing was also joy for the man Fred had developed into, the man I knew.

Part II: by Rose Huyard

After Fred died, some of us shared our thoughts on Facebook, trying to grapple with the reality that he was really gone:

God has blessed "us" the Stoltzfus family more then we could ever imagine, with nineteen siblings and all in fairly good health and wonderful parents that prayed for all of us more then we will ever know. But when God calls one of us home it makes you think how short life is here on earth. Rejoicing to know that he is in heaven with our parents. —Tina

My brother Fred was in a logging accident today and has gone to be with Jesus. He is sitting with Jesus, and my mom and dad right now as I write this. Life is so uncertain but knowing he is in a better place does make it a little easier ... Please keep everyone in your prayers especially his wife Rhoda and his children ... (Later) I was the youngest of the family and didn't get the chance to get to know Fred in his younger years as my other siblings did. Tonight we had a time of reflecting on his life and just telling stories from his life. If you think about it over the next few weeks, pray for Rhoda and her children as they adjust to life without Fred. Rhoda has lots of decisions to make in the next few weeks that are going to be hard to make. Thanks again for your prayers and support. —Siobohn

Life is uncertain. I've had three in-laws who left this world, but today the first one of my siblings went to heaven. My seventy-year-old brother, Fred Stoltzfus, was killed in a logging accident. Please pray for his wife, Rhoda, and her children and grandchildren. —Ada

Leaving soon for PA to attend the viewing and funeral of my older brother, Fred, killed in a logging accident. Memories swirl of his escapes to the mountains or the island in the river to avoid ear pulling at birthdays, chuckling at us younger sisters pounding his chest to test how his Charley Atlas strengthening exercises were working, his life-saving decision to race me to the hospital before the ambulance arrived when I was in a car accident and bleeding to death. His passing leaves a hole in our hearts. —Sue

We head off again today. My brother Fred, age seventy, died in a logging accident on Saturday. I've been blessed with many siblings. We've had good health and though of course I knew it wasn't true, sometimes it seemed like we were immune from suffering loss of each other. Losing a sibling is a new journey. We thank God for his life and now we go to say good-bye for now. —Edith

Tonight I am thankful for ... good memories of my brother, wonderful family members with whom I can cry, sing, & share memories, my daughter who sang softly as we rode home (from the funeral) through the dark, Heaven, and Jesus who made it all possible! —Mim

Yesterday we buried my brother. We shared memories, we laughed, we sang, we cried, and we laughed and sang and cried some more ... we tried to wrap our heads and hearts around the reality that Fred is gone from our circle as we stood at the place on the mountain where a falling tree took his life while he was logging last Saturday. Gone, yet not gone. I'll miss seeing my brother's head thrown back in laughter, yet even now I hear it tumbling right out of his soul. There is something so painful about losing a sibling—and so unexpected. Singing together helped—partly because we knew Fred would have loved it, and partly because, mysteriously, a sacred pathway was created, connecting our souls and carrying us together through our grief. —Rose

After Fred's funeral, many of us gathered somberly in late afternoon at the spot on the mountain where Fred had died. First, Pete explained to us how the accident had happened. Then someone started singing *Come, Bring Your Burdens to God*,[5] a powerfully moving song that echoed the only thing we knew to do in that moment.

After we left that spot, together we ate a meal, shared memories, and sang. Many of the memories we shared came out of Fred's zest for life, his transformed life, his self-denial, his caring heart, his full and fruitful life, his delight in his younger brothers' hunting stories, his helping to shape others' character and ideals, the good brother he was, his conscientious thoughtfulness, his rugged wildness, his commitment to God, his love for God's Word and desire to live it faithfully, and the way he served God with joy.

I told about the time I went to Red Lake, Ontario, the summer after I graduated from high school, to spend some time with Fred and Rhoda, who were living in the bush country serving with Northern Light Gospel Mission. I went because Fred, who knew of my depression, wrote me a letter urging me to come spend some time with them. In his opinion, a change of scenery would be helpful. I went, and Fred was right.

Someone else talked about the time Mom looked out the kitchen window one day and saw Fred walking across the yard with John, Pete, Tim, Elvin, and Dale all following him like so many little ducklings. He hadn't seemed to mind. In fact he'd had a slight grin on his face like he rather enjoyed it.

Fred's siblings remained close to his heart wherever he was. When he was living in Red Lake and received a letter from his younger brothers, tears welled up in his eyes upon seeing who had written the letter, confirming the deep love he had for them.

Fred had a way of connecting with others from his heart, a heart with a great capacity to love and care. It wasn't always this way. Who he had been compared with who he became has made us realize the significance of his life even more profoundly and feel the pain of his loss even more keenly.

As a child, I watched apprehensively as Fred, a troubled teen, struggled fiercely. Confused, hurt, and rebellious, he suffered from the influence of poor choices about friends, and his behavior in turn brought suffering to others. Then, right before my eyes, I witnessed a dramatic change in him after he reversed the direction of his self-destructive path as a young adult. His choice to change course affected the legacy he now leaves behind, especially for his wife, Rhoda, and his children.

[5] *Come, Bring Your Burdens to God (Woza nomthwalo wakho)*. Words & melody: South African traditional, from the singing of the Mooiplaas congregation.

What happened? How was he transformed from a self-centered, troubled hurter to a God-fearing healer? How did Fred find healing and peace? He tried to face his problems honestly. He used his tough experiences not as a cloak to wrap around himself in isolation and self-protection but as a springboard to empathize with others through their struggles. With God's direction and Dad's encouragement and patience, he developed a sense of what it means to be a man of integrity.

The week before Fred's death, Pete had returned from a hunting trip in Colorado with some other brothers. Several evenings later, Fred had stopped by as was his custom when they returned from Colorado. The brothers had talked at length about where Pete had seen three white mountain goats. It was the same basin where Fred and Dad had shot their big mule deer in 1967. Miles, their tough old outfitter, later said that he worked harder to pack that meat out of that rugged area than any other game he ever packed out.

The hunt had been an incredibly wholesome bonding time for Dad and Fred. Dad had gone high up on the dangerous, steep side of the mountain. Fred had gone to the jumbled valley floor below. "What am I looking at?" Dad had asked himself, staring in the distance. "Are those elk? No! They're mule deer. Five big mulies looking at me." He'd started shooting, and the mule deer had run to the bottom only to encounter Fred. Fred had begun firing away too, and with the final volley, after the dust settled, to Fred's dismay, two big mule deer buck lay on the ground. Each hunter was allowed only one deer. "Was one of them dragging a leg?" Dad had asked when he got down. "Boy, am I glad to hear you ask that," was Fred's reply. It was the one Dad had shot from the top, though Fred's shooting felled it along with the second deer. Years later, during a revival meeting, Fred's conscience bothered him. He wrote to the Colorado Division of Wildlife and told them what had happened. They asked for more information, and he supplied it but never heard from them again. That was Fred at twenty-five, conscientious to the nth degree. He had charted his course. He had determined to be a man of integrity.

As a young father, Fred had struggled with deep depression. Rhoda had stood by him through thick and thin, and her loyalty had given him confidence. He had received professional help and developed even more of a caring heart and the ability to offer God's love and grace to others.

The legacy Fred leaves is exemplified by his wife and children, whom he loved deeply. Their love for God and their love and acts of service to others bear witness to the depth and ongoing effect of his genuineness and commitment. Fred was a beloved work in progress. As we all are.

Epilogue

The big, red brick house by the Susquehanna River now stands as a shrine to my childhood memories. On those rare occasions when I drive by it on I-80, my eyes scan the landscape below me as if trying to make a lasting imprint. The local family who lives there graciously welcomes our visits, even though they can't possibly know the flood of memories that draws us back. As we drive in the long lane of nostalgia, I see the house standing solid as it did long ago, even as I anticipate that when we arrive at the buildings some things will have changed to accommodate the needs of the farmer who now plows the fields and grows the crops. The interior, too, has changed, reflecting the decorative touch of the farmer's wife. As I leave this place, I can take only my memories, but they, at least, are etched—indelibly—within me.

In writing this book, I have often felt a deep stirring connecting me to the things that have shaped me. I have opened my arms wide to embrace my past and, at the same time, let go of it as my life in the present gives new meaning to the past.

My five beautiful children have taught me that the deepest connections are those of spirit; to be family, one does not need to be blood-related. The Adoption Creed has proven to be true for me: "Not flesh of my flesh or bone of my bone, yet still miraculously my own. Never forget for a single minute you did not grow under my heart but in it."

My family blended together in different ways. Jonathan and Katie came into my life when I married Al. Shayla, Drew, and David came later, "special delivery." Each has opened their heart to claim me as mother, even as I have opened my own heart to give each one a permanent dwelling place. Enriching my life further are my daughters- and sons-in-law Kellie, Jeremy, Jason, and Ashley.

My family of origin gave me a heart home, and now my immediate family does the same, all of us belonging to one another, each giving the other a home for our hearts to come back to as we create our own stories.

Then there are my grandchildren—Kylie, Adam, Preston, Lili, Carter, Dylan, and Tucker—priceless, awesome gifts to me, all of you. As I play with you, laugh with you, connect meaningfully with you, try to model for you how to persevere as your ancestors did through setbacks and disappointments, and just be with you, I am giving you a heart home. I hope I am teaching you to do the same with others who come after you.

I see you growing up right before my eyes, and I imagine still others as yet unborn, who will have a place in my heart as well.

And my life flows on …

Fun Songs and Ballads
Our Family Sang

There Was an Old Woman Who Lived Alone

Mom taught this song to us.

There was an old woman who lived alone, Oo-oh, Oo-oh.

And all she was made of was skin and bones, Oo-oh, Oo-oh.

One day she decided to take a walk, Oo-oh, Oo-oh.

And on her walk, she came to a church, Oo-oh, Oo-oh.

She opened the door and stepped inside, Oo-oh, Oo-oh.

And there lay a dead man on the floor, Oo-oh, Oo-oh.

The preacher said, "I GOTCHA!" *(yelled as loudly as possible)*

Go Tell Aunt Rhody

Go tell Aunt Rhody,
Go tell Aunt Rhody,
Go tell Aunt Rhody
The old gray goose is dead.

The one she was saving,
The one she was saving,
The one she was saving
To make a feather bed.

The goslings are crying,
The goslings are crying,
The goslings are crying,
Because their mother's dead.

The old gander's weeping,
The old gander's weeping,
The old gander's weeping,
Because his wife is dead.

She died in the mill pond,
She died in the mill pond,
She died in the mill pond
Standing on her head.

Go tell Aunt Rhody,
Go tell Aunt Rhody,
Go tell Aunt Rhody
The old gray goose is dead.

The Orphan Girl

Song in Mom's Composition Book

No home, no home, said the little girl
As she stood at the rich man's door
And she trembling stood on the marble step
And leaned on the polished wall.

Her hands were cold, and and her feet were bare,
And the snow had covered her head.
"Oh, give me a home," she feebly said.
"A home and a bit of bread."

"My father, alas, I never knew."
And the tears dimmed her eyes so bright.
"And my mother lies in her new-made grave.
There's an orphan here tonight."

The night was dark, and the snow fell fast,
And the rich man closed his door.
And his proud lips curled as he scornfully said,
"No home, no bread for the poor."

"I must freeze," she said as she sank on the step
And strove to wrap her feet
In her tattered dress all covered with snow.
Yes, covered with snow and sleet.

The rich man sleeps on his feather bed
And dreams of his silver and gold,
But the orphan sleeps on her bed of snow
And murmurs, "so cold, so cold."

The morning dawned, and the little girl
Still lay at the rich man's door,
But her soul had fled to a home above
Where there's room and bread for the poor.

They buried her by her mother's side
And raised a tombstone fair.
And on it carved these five short words,
"There'll be no orphans there."

Little Bessie

Song in Mom's Composition Book

Hug me closer, closer mother.
Put your arms around me tight.
I am cold and tired, mother,
And I feel so strange tonight.
Something hurts me here, dear mother
Like a stone upon my breast.
Oh I wonder, wonder mother
Why it is I cannot rest.

All the day as you were working
I was lying on my bed.
I was trying to be patient
And to think of what you said;
How the kind and blessed Jesus
Loves the lambs to watch and pray.
Oh, I wish He'd come and take me
In His arms that I might sleep.

Just before the lamps were lighted
Just before the children came
And the room was very quiet
I heard someone call my name.
All at once the window opened
In a field of lambs and sheep.
Some from out a brook drinking,
Some were lying fast asleep.

But I could not see my Savior
Though I strained my eyes to see.
Oh I wonder if he saw me,
If he speaks to such as me.
In a moment I was looking
On a world so bright and fair,
Which was full of little children,
And they seemed so happy there.

They were singing oh so sweetly,
Sweeter songs I never heard.
They were singing sweeter, mother,
Than can sing our little bird.
And while I my breath was holding,
One so sweet upon me smiled
That I knew it must be Jesus,
And he said, "Come here, my child."

"Come up here, little Bessie.
Come up here and live with me,
Where little children never suffer,
But are happier than are we."
Then I thought of all you told me
Of that bright and happy land.
I was going when you called me,
When you came and kissed my hand.

Hug me closer, closer, mother.
Put your arms around me tight.
Oh how much I love you, mother,
But I feel so strange tonight.
So her mother pressed her closer
To her overburdened breast,
With a heart so near of breaking
Lay a heart so near to rest.

In the solemn hour of midnight
In the darkness, calm and deep,
Lying on her mother's bosom
Little Bessie fell asleep.

The Billy Goat Song

Song in Mom's Composition Book

There was a man, his name was Hun.
He bought a goat away last fall.
He did not buy the goat for fun
But bought him for his little son.
One day the goat so big and fine
Found a red shirt on the clothesline.
He rolled it up in a cherry ball
And swallowed shirt, clothesline and all.
The farmer said, "You're not so sly;
This very day you'll have to die.
They took him to the railroad track
And strapped him down upon his back.
When Billy heard the whistle blow,
He thought of times long, long ago.
Tears in his eyes like showers of rain,
Coughed up the shirt and flagged the train.